LIBRARY IN A BOOK

EDUCATION REFORM

REVISED EDITION

Ian C. Friedman

Facts On File

An imprint of Infobase Publishing

Facts On File, Inc.
An imprint of Infobase Publishing
132 West 31st Street
New York NY 10001

Library of Congress Cataloging-in-Publication Data
Friedman, Ian C.
  Education reform / Ian C. Friedman. — Rev. ed.
    p. cm. — (Library in a book)
  Includes bibliographical references and index.
  ISBN 978-0-8160-8238-4
  1. Educational change—United States—History. 2. Educational change—Research—United States. 3. Education—Aims and objectives—United States. I. Title.
  LA212.F75 2011
  370.973—dc22   2010043133

Facts On File books are available at special discounts when purchased in bulk quantities for businesses, associations, institutions, or sales promotions. Please call our Special Sales Department in New York at (212) 967-8800 or (800) 322-8755.

You can find Facts On File on the World Wide Web at http://www.factsonfile.com

Excerpts included herewith have been reprinted by permission of the copyright holders; the author has made every effort to contact copyright holders. The publishers will be glad to rectify, in future editions, any errors or omissions brought to their notice.

Text design by Ron Monteleone
Composition by Hermitage Publishing Services
Cover printed by Art Print, Taylor, Pa.
Book printed and bound by Maple Press, York, Pa.
Date printed: December 2010

Printed in the United States of America

10 9 8 7 6 5 4 3 2 1

This book is printed on acid-free paper.

For Lene

CONTENTS

ACKNOWLEDGMENTS

I would like to thank my editors at Facts On File, Nicole Bowen, for taking a chance on a first-time author, and Dorothy Cummings, for her valuable guidance and support.

I am also grateful to my entire family, particularly my parents, Marcia and Leon Friedman, for always encouraging me to pursue my interests and for providing an environment in which education is respected, valued, and enjoyed. Thanks also to my brother Keith for consistently coming through with much needed technical assistance and fun conversation during the time I was writing this book.

To my wife, Darlene, my thanks for her always strong faith, encouragement, and love.

Finally, to my children, Evan, Mason, and Lily, my deep gratitude and love for their gifts of perspective, inspiration, and happiness that they bring to me every day.

PART I

OVERVIEW OF THE TOPIC

CHAPTER 1

INTRODUCTION TO EDUCATION REFORM

It seems appropriate that a book about education reform in the United States begin with a standby of American schooling—a multiple-choice question.

Analyze the quotations below and answer the question that follows.

> "The educational foundations of our society are presently being eroded by a rising tide of mediocrity that threatens our very future as a nation and a people."
>
> "Our standard for high school graduation has slipped badly. Fifty years ago a high-school diploma meant something."
>
> "Whether we like it or not, we're beginning to see that we're pitted against the world in a gigantic battle of brains and skills."

The quotations above reflect beliefs about the condition of U.S. public education commonly held in the

    A   1980s
    B   1950s
    C   early 1900s
    D   all of the above

The correct answer is D.

The first quotation is from the landmark 1983 publication *A Nation at Risk*, which served as a key catalyst for the growth of education reform activity over the past 25 years. The second quotation is from a 1958 *U.S. News and World Report* interview of education historian and author Arthur Bestor.

3

The "fifty years ago" referred to by Bestor is almost exactly the date of the third quotation, taken from Stanford education dean Ellwood Cubberley's 1909 book *Changing Conceptions of Education.*

Although more than 25 years have passed since the most recent of these quotations, each would be entirely plausible in the context of today's debate on education reform. The issue of education reform—the effort to improve the quality, methods, and purpose of elementary and secondary schooling in the United States—traces its origins to the inception of public schools, which preceded the founding of the nation by almost 150 years.

Since that time, education reform has both reflected and led social change in United States. The widely held belief that schools play a critically important role in shaping the nation's future has led to intense discussion on a variety of issues, including assimilation of immigrants, integration of African Americans, economic strength, the role of the federal government, constitutional rights of parents and children, and opportunity for individuals from lower economic backgrounds.

At present, as in the past, issues of effectiveness, fairness, and competitiveness shape the arguments over education reform. Advocates often have sharply contrasting views on such leading questions as

- Can school choice, including vouchers, charter schools, and privatization, successfully combat the cycle of poor children trapped in failing schools?
- What are the causes, outcomes, and implications of homeschooling?
- What are effective accountability measures for students and schools? Do curriculum standards and reliance on standardized assessments promote academic achievement? Are policies ending social promotion and bilingual instruction helpful and fair to students?
- Who will teach, particularly in chronically underserved areas? How can teaching become a profession that attracts, trains, and retains top candidates, especially in light of an expected teaching shortage?
- How can the culture within schools be strengthened to promote learning and safety? Are class-size reduction initiatives, zero-tolerance policies, and dress codes effective?

The background, themes, events, people, and movements that have shaped the history of education reform in the United States reveal a consistent though paradoxical tradition in which Americans maintain enormous faith in public schools while combating the nagging fear of their failure. This tradition is now at a critical juncture as the key issues of education reform evolve and assume an increasingly prominent place in U.S. politics, culture, and society.

PHILOSOPHICAL FOUNDATIONS OF U.S. EDUCATION

The roots of American notions of education reach back to ancient Greece and ancient Rome. The link between the state and support of the educational system was first described in Plato's *Republic* written around 360 B.C. The Greek philosopher's beliefs that the most intelligent were best able to lead the state and that education promotes the happiness and fulfillment of the individual by fitting him or her into his or her role in society have been espoused by education reformers of various ideological and pedagogical persuasions. Plato also expressed the belief that education could prepare individuals to function positively within society. Roman educator Quintilian extended these thoughts in the first century A.D. by emphasizing the advantages public forms of education could have, particularly on the socialization of a person. Quintilian, the tutor of the emperor's grandsons, believed that education should be concerned with a person's whole intellectual and moral nature, with the goal of producing an effective person in society. He recommended a broad literary education that included music, astronomy, geometry, and philosophy, preferably in public schools where a student could develop relationships and learn from his peers. Quintilian's views and methods helped establish a foundation for the education reformers in the United States, particularly leaders of the Progressive movement, who would follow almost 2,000 years later.

The Renaissance in Europe, which began in the 13th century and lasted more than 300 years, also had a significant impact on the development of U.S. educational thought and practice. Early in this period, Dominican monk and scholar Thomas Aquinas (1224–74) advanced reason, as well as faith, as sources of truth, helping to provide the basis for formal Roman Catholic education through curriculum that contained both theology and the liberal arts. Toward the end of the Renaissance, Dutch humanist and writer Desiderius Erasmus (ca. 1466–1536) criticized the ignorance of the clergy and the injustice of society, advancing public education as a means of equity. His calls for the systematic training of teachers, abolition of corporal punishment of students, and recognition of the value of play and the importance of understanding the student's individual needs and abilities helped provide a philosophical base for subsequent education reform in the United States, including the current debates.

Other important contributors to Western educational thought included Martin Luther (1483–1546), John Calvin (1509–64), John Locke (1632–1704), and Jean-Jacques Rousseau (1712–78). Luther advanced the resounding notion that education is necessary for the economic well-being of the state and that it should include vocational training. Luther's views influenced development of the concept of free and compulsory education as well as the concept of universal literacy, which became essential components of U.S. education. Calvin extended Luther's thought by stressing the need for elementary schools for the masses where they could learn to read the Bible and secondary schools to prepare the leaders of church and state. This helped establish a European tradition of a two-track system that was imported to the colonies and eventually spread throughout the United States.

British philosopher Locke and French philosopher Rousseau were leading advocates of education that promoted the development of reason, morality, and individual freedom. Locke's views helped establish a strong link between learning and participatory democracy, and Rousseau's beliefs—which led him to be considered by many the "father of modern child psychology"[1]—were instrumental in establishing the adaptation of instruction for children at different stages of development. Although their impact on U.S. schools has been enduring, the extent to which Locke's views of civic education and Rousseau's belief in adapted instruction should be implemented have been argued throughout U.S. education reform history.

EDUCATION IN EARLY AMERICA

The English, the predominant settlers of the North American colonies, had the greatest influence on the educational system that emerged in early America, though the cultural diversity and the presence of many different religious denominations in the colonies had a considerable impact on schooling. Colonial governments allowed individuals and religious groups to establish schools of their own. In general, colonial governments did not engage in close supervision of such schools. This early form of church-state separation came about largely due to the variety of religious denominations in the colonies, each seeking freedom of worship and each uninterested or unable to reach consensus regarding religious principles to be taught in schools founded by civil authorities.

Social and economic differences among colonial regions of British North America were also reflected in the formation of schools. In the southern colonies, religion was reverently practiced but was not the dominating force of life, as it was in New England. Therefore, the desire to have each person educated so that he or she could read the Bible was not of high importance to the wealthy English gentleman governing the southern colonies. This commonly held attitude was expressed in 1671 by Virginia governor Sir William Berkeley, who believed that every man should instruct his own children according to his means, explaining: "I thank God that there are no free schools nor printing, . . . for learning has brought disobedience and heresy, and sects into the world."[2]

Introduction to Education Reform

Some efforts at organized schooling did exist in the southern colonies, though the financial commitment to them was usually lacking. Educational opportunity was determined almost exclusively by social class, and many wealthy families sent their children to tutorial schools, essentially private institutions in which a tutor would instruct young people. Dame schools in which a woman would provide rudimentary instruction in her own home, often while carrying on household tasks, were also common throughout the colonies, including the South.

The Middle Colonies featured a striking diversity of faiths, languages, and cultures and tended to develop many different kinds of schools. This diversity prevented one particular group from imposing its will on the others and created a kind of tolerance of necessity. As a result of this, a coordinated system of public schools and state support or regulation of public schools failed to develop.

Among the Middle Colonies groups, the Quakers of Pennsylvania were the most active in education, particularly at the elementary level. Quaker schools were open to girls and the poor, and some provided education for free blacks.[3] Practical education, similar to what would later be termed vocational education, offering training in merchandising, navigation, trade, and mechanics, was emphasized at Benjamin Franklin's academy in Philadelphia, which opened in 1751.

New England was witness to the greatest and most influential educational endeavors of all the colonial regions. Education in New England during the colonial period was driven by the Puritan philosophy, a tenet of which was that man's sinful nature required activity to prevent idleness and instruction to avert evil.[4] New England had less fertile land than the rest of colonial America and consequently developed a greater emphasis on such occupations as shipbuilding, manufacturing, and trade. Because of this economic activity, it was essential to have people able to read, write, and think efficiently. The establishment of schools served the specific desires and needs of the people in this region.

In 1635, the Boston Latin School became the first public school in the British colonies. Seven years later, the first compulsory education law in the colonies was enacted with the passage of the Massachusetts Act of 1642. This law stated that parents and masters of those children apprenticed to them were responsible for their basic education and literacy. It also stated that should parents and masters not meet their educational responsibility, the government would have the right to remove the child from the home and place the child where he or she could receive adequate instruction. A half-decade later, Massachusetts again led the way in education legislation with the passage of the Massachusetts Law of 1647, also known as the Old Deluder Satan Act. Provisions of this law required the establishment of elementary schools in all towns of 50 or more families and the establishment of secondary schools in towns of more than 100 families.

The significance of colonial education in New England was enormous, particularly in forming the traditions of public support for district schools, local autonomy, compulsory education, and distinct educational levels. Although New England's schools had, by modern standards, a rudimentary form, narrow curriculum, and weak support, they were the forerunners for what would eventually become the public education system in the United States.

In the years leading up to the American Revolution, education for the young was growing among the thirteen colonies, which had a total population of 2 million people. The ideas of the Revolution, such as those of Locke, were particularly influential. Locke believed that ideas came from experience and that the measure of truth of an idea is its correspondence with concrete, objective, commonsense reality. These beliefs helped lead to the growth of the kind of practical education programs supported by leaders such as Franklin.

The Revolution temporarily interrupted the momentum of education but eventually served to advance a unique form of American schooling. Though the formal bonds to Great Britain were broken, and with that any financial support previously provided, the United States began to define its own vision of public education. Among the primary architects of this vision were Noah Webster and Thomas Jefferson.

Webster, known as the "Schoolmaster to America," wrote the *Compendious Dictionary* in 1806, the first in a series of dictionaries that validated and disseminated an American lexicon. Also, Webster's *Elementary Spelling Book*, often referred to as the "Blue-Back Speller," was the most successful textbook ever produced in America, with an estimated almost 20 million sold by the time of his death in 1843. The book reflected Webster's strong nationalism and emphasis on the virtues of liberty, hard work, and morality. Accordingly, Webster vigorously supported legislative action leading to free schools in which U.S. children could learn these virtues.

Jefferson's impact on U.S. education was prodigious and mainly the result of efforts unrelated to his presidency. His support for the expansion of educational opportunity to ensure a wise populace that could protect democracy was evidenced with his 1778 proposal in the Virginia legislature known as the Bill for the More General Diffusion of Knowledge. The plan called for a state system of free elementary schools with local control of secondary schools supported by tuition and scholarships to help pave the way for poor boys. Although these provisions of the bill were not passed, it provided an often-imitated framework for future school systems, particularly the pattern of decentralized control and localization of financial responsibility. Jefferson's advocacy of the bill also served to help reduce the stigma of poverty as a barrier to receiving an elementary education and helped establish an American perception of educational equity, which is often at the center of today's education reform discussions.

The U.S. Constitution, ratified in 1789, did not explicitly mention education. The First Amendment's prohibition of government establishment of religion or religious practice did set a critical and oft-debated precedent separating state support for religious schools, though schools of all types continued to use religious material in instruction. The federal government supported the promulgation of schooling in the early republic through such acts as the Northwest Ordinance of 1785, which reserved a section in each township for schools and stated that schools and education should always be encouraged in the newly added regions covered by the act.

States emulated such support for provisions in their constitutions establishing funding for the creation of schools. The Pennsylvania Constitution, adopted in 1776, became a model for many states with its requirement that the state pay the salaries of public-school teachers. By the beginning of the 19th century most states had set up a system of schools with their constitutions. Formal education was not yet widespread, but the character and foundation of U.S. public education was established and ready to expand.

THE NINETEENTH CENTURY AND BEYOND

The first half of the 19th century in the United States saw social, economic, and political developments that led to the advancement of what is often referred to as the "common man." This increased adherence to the notion of equality led many citizens to believe that all should be able to read in order to a participate in government and improve their standing in society.

One important factor in the growth of public education during this time was the rise of industrialization. During the early stages of America's Industrial Revolution, efforts to promote public education suffered because so many children were part of the working force. For example, in New England during the 1830s, approximately 40 percent of children under the age of 16 were employed in industrial occupations. However, industrialization also required training and often led to a need for affordable activities for the children of working-class parents. In addition, many reformers viewed education as a means of combating the negative effects of industrialization, such as urban poverty.

Industrialization also led to a population boom in the United States, particularly in northern and eastern cities. Much of this growth was the result of huge waves of immigration from Europe. Schools were seen by many as an excellent tool to Americanize these newcomers, whose language and customs were different and often viewed as a threat to those of the native-born. Simultaneously, western settlers on America's frontier established one-room schoolhouses, often the only public building in a community, to educate their children. They were generally more reluctant than those in urban areas were to allow government influence over their educational institutions, reflecting an attitude that would be echoed decades later by advocates of homeschooling across the United States.

The emerging publicly supported common schools of the mid-1800s varied in size, organization, and curriculum. In rural areas, the one- or two-room schoolhouse was dominant. Progress in these schools was not marked by movement from one grade to another but rather by completing one text and beginning another. On the frontier, where there remained some distrust of too much education, the curriculum was limited to reading, writing, and arithmetic, while in larger cities the curriculum tended to be broader.[5] A wider variety of textbooks began to appear in common schools by the late 19th century, and the popular practice of rote learning, drill, and practice was beginning to be chipped away by early and sporadic measures of reform aimed at developing the individual talents of a child.

During the first half of the 19th century, states had gradually moved toward establishing educational systems. State superintendents, as educational officers were often called, of free schools, or common schools, usually had weak powers. Legal requirements for the collection of school taxes and compulsory attendance were often ignored as the tradition of parental and church responsibility for the education of children remained resilient.[6]

Two important leaders of this time who helped to propel state systems of education were Horace Mann and Henry Barnard. Mann was a Massachusetts legislator who led the effort to create a state board of education. When this measure was approved, he resigned to become the board's first secretary. During his 12 years in the post (1837–49), Mann was the most active leader of the common school education movement in the country. He succeeded in attaining state tax support for teacher salaries and new buildings, creating three of the first normal, or teacher training, schools in the country and establishing 50 new high schools. Attendance increased dramatically during Mann's tenure. Mann's educational philosophy influenced many other states and has had a profound impact on current mainstream thought.

Barnard, another important state education leader of the mid-19th century, had been a Connecticut state legislator before becoming secretary of the state board of education there and later in Rhode Island. Also like Mann, he espoused a democratic philosophy of education and was effective in spreading his message through the publication of the *American Journal of Education*.

The first half of the 19th century had also witnessed the emergence of the public high school. In 1821, the English Classical School was opened in Boston, becoming the first of its kind in the United States. High school growth remained weak over the course of the next few decades because of opposition to paying taxes for their support and the popularity of private academies, which had spread since the late 18th century and encompassed prestigious, exclusive institutions, as well as practical, religious, and military schools. By the 1860s there were only 300 high schools in the United States, one-third of which were in Massachusetts; however, the idea of free secondary education grew in popularity, particularly among the growing numbers of middle-class citizens who viewed a high school education as necessary to fully realize one's social and economic goals. In addition normal schools, named for the standard or normal curriculum that was followed, sprang up in the 1840s establishing a model for state-supported training of teachers.

Despite these advancements in U.S. public education, African Americans and Native Americans were almost always systematically neglected. Education for blacks during this time was limited in the North and almost nonexistent in the South. Formal education for Native Americans, guaranteed in the many treaties signed between the U.S. government and various Native tribes, was usually provided in the form of substandard mission schools that emphasized basic literacy and vocational and agricultural instruction. This educational negligence would reap generations of dissatisfaction still found at the center of some of the most intensely argued education reform issues, such as bilingual education, standards and assessments, and school choice.

The common school period came to a halt with the Civil War. The disruption inflicted on education was pervasive, particularly in the South where the damage done to an already-less-developed system was severe. Reconstruction-era efforts to build the southern education system, particularly attempts to instruct the more than 4 million newly freed slaves, were insufficiently supported or actively resisted. Proposed legislation in the U.S. Congress to boost education systems in areas devastated by war were also unsuccessful. In 1870, Massachusetts congressman George Hoar introduced a bill designed to establish a federal school system in southern states. This measure was defeated and served as a symbol of U.S. hesitance to cede too much autonomy on education matters to the federal government. The 1882, Blair Bill, named for its sponsor, New Hampshire senator Henry Blair, passed the Senate three different times but never passed in the House of Representatives. It proposed the application of almost $80 million for states to use as they saw fit to fight illiteracy.

Despite the difficulties experienced in the South, high school growth accelerated significantly following Reconstruction elsewhere. In 1875, fewer than 25,000 students were enrolled in public high schools, but that number jumped to more than 500,000 by 1900. Part of this growth was due to the legal precedent set by the 1874 Kalamazoo Michigan School Case (*Stewart et al. v. School District No. 1 of the village of Kalamazoo*), in which the state supreme court held that the state had the right to levy taxes to support high schools.

One problem confronting the rapid rise in high school enrollment was the standardization of curriculum. High schools offered traditional and practical programs, with emphasis usually on college preparatory curriculum, even though only about 10 percent of high school students in 1900 would attend college. The menu of courses from school to school varied extensively in scope and nature.

Two important events then took place to reform this lack of standardization: the creation of the National Education Association (NEA) in 1870 and that body's formation of the Committee of Ten in 1892. For decades, a variety of regional educational associations formed to deal with high school standardization issues such as curriculum, school day length, and quality of instruction. In 1870, the largest of these professional organizations—the National Teachers Association, the National Association of School Superintendents, and the American Normal School Association—merged to create the NEA, which quickly became recognized as the leading education group in the country.[7]

In 1892, the NEA convened the Committee of Ten to study and put forth recommendations relating to confusion over secondary schools' standards, curriculum, methods, and programs. The committee's name was a reflection of its composition: five college presidents, two headmasters, the U.S. education commissioner, a professor, and a high school administrator. Absent was any high school teacher.

The Committee of Ten's report reflected the group's college orientation, supporting an increased focus on general education subjects such as Latin, English, math, physical and biological sciences, history, and geography. Vocational and commercial subjects were largely ignored. The committee's recommendations further advanced the practice of studying each subject for one period each day, five days a week for a year. As a result of the report, the standard unit of credit for high school subjects, often referred to as a Carnegie unit, was established. The Committee of Ten also supported an eight-year elementary school followed by a four-year high school, though special subjects and methods were not suggested for students who did not expect a good college. Taken together, the Committee of Ten's efforts were critical in bringing a sense of unification to a national system of public education.

Vocational and manual training schools sought to fill the void that grew following the implementation of many of the Committee of Ten's recommendations, especially with the late 19th century's need for skilled workers, who often wanted a high school education but had no intentions of attending college. Some teacher training colleges designed programs for vocational educators, and the Industrial Education Association was formed in 1884.

Introduction to Education Reform

Along with the growth of schools came a marked increase in teacher training schools. The number of such public and private normal schools more than tripled between 1871 and 1900 (from 114 schools to 345).[8] Despite this growth, fewer than half of the trained teachers that were needed to staff public schools were provided by normal schools or other teacher training programs. Most classrooms continued to be taught by low-paid young women, often with little education beyond elementary school. These conditions in the teaching profession were cause for concern at the time, leading U.S. commissioner of education Henry Barnard to express what would become a frequently heard expression of frustration with teacher quality, preparation, and status. As reported in the July 13, 1867, *Boston Examiner*, Barnard explained:

> *Too many of those we have entrusted to guide and guard our nation's youth have little knowledge beyond that which they are attempting to impart. Indeed, we might well question whether their knowledge is superior to that of many of their fellow tradesmen. Not only is the depth and breadth of their knowledge of the curriculum matter a subject of concern, but where knowledge is possessed, there exists most often an absence of any training in pedagogy . . . teachers will not be elevated to that place in society and receive that compensation they so richly deserve until they are required to undertake a special course of study and training to qualify them for their new office.[9]*

Private schools also became more established in the late 1800s, even as their student body became more conspicuously composed of the wealthy, those gaining military training, and Catholics, who were often shunned in schools that were overwhelmingly Protestant and nativist. The 1875 proposal of the Blaine Amendment, named for its sponsor, Speaker of the House of Representatives James Blaine, sought to prohibit the use of state funds for "sectarian" schools. Though this legislation narrowly failed to pass in the U.S. Congress, supporters of the amendment turned their attention to the individual states, where they had much more success. Blaine amendments were critical in the development of an organized private, Catholic educational system in the United States, and they have contributed to the broad conception of the separation of church and state.

As the 19th century came to a close, education in the United States was far different from what it had been 100 years earlier. Well established was a de jure expression of belief in free opportunity for all citizens, and with that came a dramatic increase in school enrollment and prominence in society. Also well established was the foundation for future arguments of education reform, including the role of government and religion in schools, teacher quality, and standards and curricula. This rapid and meaningful pace of change witnessed in the 19th century would only accelerate in the 20th century.

Education Reform

THE EMERGENCE OF EDUCATION'S PROGRESSIVE MOVEMENT

In the early 1900s, most Americans felt pride in their public schools. Specifically, they believed that schools could enable children of humble origins to climb an educational ladder toward greater opportunity. Implicit in this widespread conception was the promise of a liberal education's role in providing access to knowledge previously only available to the elite. A movement was mobilizing, however, that would change the nature and purpose of American schools.

Central to the new education supported by the early 20th-century reformers was a focus on targeting instruction for practical subjects that would fit the future occupations of most students whose members were steadily climbing due to immigration, prosperity, and the implementation of laws preventing child labor. The primary proponents of such education were business leaders who wanted prepared and efficient workers and educators who would come to be known as progressive educators. Most of the progressives were teaching in the nation's burgeoning colleges of education and wanted the curriculum to serve the needs of society and the industrial age.

The leading colleges of education were Columbia University's Teachers College, Stanford, the University of Chicago, and Harvard. Teachers College professors were most prominent in combating many of what they considered conservative tendencies of a U.S. educational system that ignored the benefits of modern science. The establishment of these colleges of education played a significant role in wresting the authority of American education from school superintendents to professors in schools of education. From these schools came the ideas that powered the progressive education movement.

The progressive education movement had a variety of goals, including making school instruction more practical, introducing modern methods of teaching that recognize that students learn in different ways, and giving more attention to the health of students. It also sought to make education into a profession and in doing so, reduced the school-related influence of laypeople, especially in poor and immigrant neighborhoods. Toward these ends progressive reformers supported the creation of centralized school bureaucracies and civil service systems, particularly in urban districts. Progressive educators of the early 20th century often attacked the high school curriculum as rigid, elitist, and an obstacle to social progress, particularly for the masses of poor and immigrant students in urban schools.

The leading spokesman of progressive education was John Dewey during the 1890s and into the new century. At the age of 35, the former teacher and professor assumed the chairmanship of the University of Chicago's Department of Psychology, Philosophy, and Pedagogy. Two years later, Dewey opened the University of Chicago Laboratory School to test new approaches to education.

Dewey believed that education "must represent present life—life as real and vital to the child as that which he carries on in the home, in the neighborhood, or on the playground." He generally opposed the common practice of teaching by recitation. He advanced the notion that schools were instrumental to social reform, and he sought to create schools with "an active community life, instead of a place set apart in which to learn lessons."[10] For example, in Dewey's vision students should learn biology not by memorizing the technical names for different plants and their parts, but rather by observing the growth and considering the factors that affected their life. Dewey believed that the child should be viewed as a total organism and that education is most effective when it considers not only the intellectual but also the social, emotional, and physical needs of the child. He held that education was a lifelong process and that the school should be an integral part of community life, a concept that gave support to the development of the community school. Dewey wrote more than 500 articles and 40 books, and his imprint on education in the United States was unparalleled in the 20th century.[11]

Dewey's leadership brought cohesion and credibility to progressive education and helped the movement become the dominant doctrine in the new influential schools of pedagogy. The key ideas of the movement included the following:

- Education was a science, and the methods and results of education could be precisely measured.
- The methods and ends of education could be effectively derived from assessing the innate needs and nature of the child.
- The proper approaches and outcomes of education could be determined by assessing the needs of society and then fitting the student for his or her role in society.
- Education could effectively reform society.[12]

In order to determine the ways in which schools could advance society, progressive education theorists developed the concept of social efficiency. In this framework, the value of academic subjects was evaluated by the degree that they served the purpose outside the classroom. According to this standard, many academic subjects, or at least the traditional approaches to them, lacked relevance for the great majority of students, who would most likely become workers or homemakers after they left school.

A leading figure in the social efficiency movement was the Massachusetts commissioner of education David Snedden. He believed that students

should be assigned to different curricular tracks based on sociological criteria and that these differentiated curricula could be implemented for students
by the age of 14 by scientifically trained educational experts.

In line with notions of school efficiency was the development of industrial education. In 1907, this aspect of education reform was notably boosted
by President Theodore Roosevelt who stated, "our school system is gravely
defective in so far as it puts a premium upon mere literacy training and
tends therefore to train the boy away from the farm and workshop. Nothing
is more needed than the best type of industrial school, the school for me-
chanical industries in the city, the school for practically teaching agriculture
in the country."[13] Support such as this, the additional affirmations from the
NEA and other prominent professional educators, and the defections of
previous advocates of traditional academic education such as former Committee of Ten member Charles Elliott led to a marked shift in the orientation of U.S. public schools, particularly at the secondary level. With
remarkable speed, the meaning of public education had been redefined by
progressive theorists, from the relatively standardized academic ladder to a
variety of paths leading to different destinations, with future professionals
preparing for college, future farmers studying agriculture, future homemakers studying household management, and future industrial workers studying
metalworking and woodworking. The view that all students take college
preparatory courses was now usually seen as elitist, inappropriate, and un-
democratic.

Advancing these views was Ellwood Cubberley, a former teacher, school
superintendent, and education professor at Stanford. His books on education history and school administration describing the school's role in as-
similating immigrants and training workers were standard reading in
schools of education and remained so for many years. Also influential was
his support for vocational education and curricular differentiation.

High school enrollment continued to boom throughout the early 20th
century. In 1900, only 10 percent of those ages 14 to 17 attended high
school, but by 1920, the percentage had increased to 31 percent. The obvious heightened prominence of high schools combined with the momentum
of progressive educational thought led to the emergence of the school survey movement, designed to assess the efficiency of public schools.

The efficiency experts were largely the leading progressive theorists, and
their evaluations and recommendations given to school systems reflected
their support of changes, including intelligence testing and standardized
testing for the classification of students. The results of the school survey
movement was a continued rejection of the kind of broad education advocated at the turn of the century in favor of a socially efficient curriculum
strengthened by tax-supported improvements to facilities and programs addressing specific needs of students. The movement also helped open the

door to major battles over curriculum standards and the purpose and scope of testing that continue to rage to this day.

The reforms ushered in by the efficiency experts and progressive educators were essentially shut out of schools for African Americans. Black schools, particularly in the South, were woefully underfunded and inadequate compared to those for whites. Arguments about how best to educate black students included renowned scholar W. E. B. DuBois's belief in access to academic curriculum and educator Booker T. Washington's more accepted advocacy of the benefits of vocational education.

Critics of the progressive education movement, though dwindling in number, often spoke out against the proposed and implemented reforms. Among the critics were New York City superintendent William Henry Maxwell and University of Illinois education professor William Bagley. Bagley and Massachusetts education commissioner Snedden debated the merits of many progressive education reforms at a 1914 NEA conference, but it became clear to Bagley that he was fighting a futile battle, as evidenced in 1917, when the U.S. Congress passed the Smith-Hughes Act, establishing federal aid for vocational education. This act was the first federal program of any kind for public education.

In 1918, progressive education took another step forward with the publication of the *Cardinal Principles of Secondary Education.* This report was prepared by the NEA's Commission on the Reorganization of Secondary Education (CRSE), and it appeared exactly a quarter century after the Committee of Ten's report.

The *Cardinal Principles*, however, were very different in content and sensibility from the Committee of Ten's report. The composition of the CRSE was primarily made up of education professors who espoused the belief that high schools should promote different curricula for different groups depending on their likely future occupations. The CRSE explained that such reforms were necessary because schools needed to respond to new social realities, particularly increased industrialization; to support a larger and more diverse student population; and to apply advances in educational understanding.

Based on these assertions, the CRSE identified the main objectives of secondary education as:

1. Health
2. Command of fundamental processes
3. Worthy home membership
4. Vocation
5. Citizenship
6. Worthy use of leisure
7. Ethical character

Further, the CRSE noted that, "the purpose of democracy is so to organize society that each member may develop his personality through activities designed for the well-being of his fellow members and of society as a whole."[14]

The CRSE report was a critical milestone in the history of U.S. education. It crystallized and represented a new consensus about the direction of secondary education, one that emphasized social efficiency, socialization, and the authority of professional educators and education reformers.

Following the completion of World War I, education reform delved into an area that would prove to be a constant battleground: intelligence and standardized testing. This field of testing expanded during the war, and many educational theorists and practitioners believed that these kinds of testing procedures could be beneficial in constructing appropriate and effective public school curricula.

The group intelligence tests that had been administered in the U.S. Army during World War I were well suited for adaptation for schools, largely because they were relatively inexpensive, easy to administer, and resulted in the listing of group norms, which led to the assignment of students to the differentiated curriculum programs growing in popularity. The test quickly became a regular component of the public school experience, as evidenced by a 1925 U.S. Bureau of Education survey of 215 cities that reported that intelligence tests were used to classify students into homogenous groups by 64 percent of elementary schools, 56 percent of junior high schools, and 40 percent of high schools. These tests, a key component of what is sometimes called the measurement movement, allowed schools to classify, assign, and compare students, as well as diagnose learning difficulties and aptitudes. Opponents of widespread testing, then as now, decried the abuse of such assessment, arguing that the tests often led to faulty judgments about the quality of teaching and subjective judgments about students' potential.

Critics included William Bagley who warned of the "fatalistic inferences" of the tests and argued against the intentions of the testers, labeling them "educational determinists."[15] Popular newspaper columnist Walter Lippmann echoed such opinion during the 1920s, criticizing how these tests provided fodder to anti-immigrant sentiment and noted that the purpose of the school was to increase, not measure, a student's capacities. Despite such arguments, intelligence and standardized achievement testing took hold in public schools.

The 1920s also were a period in which a great deal of attention was given to creating curricula that would support progressive educational theory. The rising prominence of curriculum experts, steeped in scientific research, signaled growth in the transfer of educational influence away from parents and teachers and toward these specialists who had control over many districts' curriculum.

Introduction to Education Reform

Among the primary curriculum experts was John Franklin Bobbitt, author of *The Curriculum*, the first textbook of the theory of curriculum construction, which became a standard in teaching training institutions. Bobbitt likened his role to that of an educational engineer who could establish precisely what students needed to learn in order to function effectively in life and contribute to society. He sought to design curricula that could address deficiencies in the social order, believing, for instance, that if agricultural production dropped, it was the job of the school to provide better agricultural education.

Dewey's advocacy of the child-centered movement was another example of leading 1920s curricular thought. Inspired by Jean-Jacques Rousseau's book *Emile*, Dewey emphasized the value of what a student learns in the ordinary course of living. At his Laboratory School, Dewey sought to demonstrate how traditional subjects, often taught through unimaginative drudgery, could be exciting and meaningful through projects and activities that appealed to a child's interests and therefore unleashed his or her intellectual energies.

Other key curriculum experts included William Heard Kilpatrick, who helped popularize and extend progressive practice of project-based learning, curriculum integration, and whole child education, which sought to balance intellectual, physical, and emotional development, and Harold Rugg, who developed a new social studies curriculum intended to replace traditional instruction of history, geography, and civics. They, of course, had their critics, including steadfast supporters of traditional liberal and classical education, as well as Dewey, who feared that some proponents of child-centered education went too far by not providing sufficient adult guidance to instructional activities.

The Great Depression that struck the United States in October 1929 both interrupted the progressive education reform momentum and galvanized its proponents who viewed the crisis as an example of how schools needed to reform society. During this time, progressive education's left wing was articulated by leaders such as George Counts, a Teachers College educational sociologist, who, following a trip to the Soviet Union, promoted the abandonment of traditional American individualism and capitalism in the journal *The Social Frontier*. At the other end of the progressive education's ideological spectrum was Counts's colleague at Teachers College, Isaac Kandel, who ridiculed the notion that schools should be expected to build a new social order, noting the irony that the same progressive educators who had consistently opposed efforts at a planned curriculum now advocated a centrally planned society.

From 1920 to 1940, U.S. schools experienced another surge in enrollment, particularly in high schools, where the number of students attending rose from 2.2 million in 1920 to 4.4 million in 1930 and 6.6 million in

1940.[16] Many schools were built and additional teachers hired to deal with this new reality. Inside schools, the results of progressive education reforms were visible, often in the form of implementation of revised curricula. The vast majority of such changes reflected the progressive preference of experience-based over academic instruction.

One strand of curriculum revision, the activity movement, emphasized project-based learning evolving from students' interests. Many cities, including Ann Arbor, Michigan; Los Angeles; and New York City, launched ambitious activity programs in elementary schools. Even in these settings, however, the instructional result was often a modified version of traditional education, with the fundamental aspects of the classroom experience—the physical layout of the room, class size, rules, evaluation, and supervision—only marginally affected, despite the prolific use of progressive jargon.

The conflict between the needs of youth and academic curricula remained a volatile one during the late 1930s. The Progressive Education Association (PEA), an advocacy group for child-centered education, actively promoted the campaign contending that U.S. high schools needed to increase their emphasis of students' personal, emotional, and social problems and decrease their emphasis on academic studies and traditional forms of school structure. Formed in 1919, the PEA's guiding principles reflected the widespread beliefs of the increasingly influential movement. They included the following:

1. The child should be given the freedom to develop naturally.
2. Interest provides the motivation for all work.
3. The teacher should be a guide in the learning process, not the taskmaster.
4. The scientific study of pupil development should be promoted by the refocusing of information to be included on school records.
5. Greater attention should be given to everything that affects the child's physical development.
6. The school and home should cooperate to meet the natural interests and activities of the child.
7. The progressive school of thought should be a leader in educational movements.[17]

The PEA was joined in its efforts against the traditional academic curriculum by individuals and groups considered more mainstream, such as the NEA.

The academic curriculum remained a potent and steady force in U.S. schools, nonetheless, largely because achievement and academic coursework was still an essential measure determining college admission. In 1930, the PEA undertook what became known as the Eight-Year Study to demonstrate that such academic requirements for college admission were unnecessary. Results of the study, in which evaluations were made of college students admitted on the basis of following successful completion of required courses and exams and those admitted largely on the basis of recommendations, interests, and aptitude tests, supported their contention. Yet many observers questioned the reliability of the study and claimed that it lacked credibility because Ivy League schools did not participate. The academic curriculum survived but more than ever was associated primarily with the college bound and not with future farmers, housewives, and factory workers.

EVOLUTION, CRITICISM, AND CHANGE

The pervasive effects of progressive education were highlighted by a 1938 *Time* magazine cover article, entitled "Progressives' Progress," that noted, "No U.S. school has completely escaped its influence."[18] Yet efforts by critics of progressive education, led by Bagley and other essentialists who stressed rigorous standards and a common academically oriented curriculum, continued, even as public attention remained focused on the economic crises at home and growing conflicts overseas.

Other prominent critics of this period included Robert Maynard Hutchins and Mortimer Adler. Hutchins was a high-profile educator who in 1929, at age 30, became president of the University of Chicago. Adler was then brought to the university by Hutchins to advance his Great Books curriculum, which focused on an academically oriented examination of classic works, which they believed could help counter what they viewed as the anti-intellectual aimlessness of many progressive education reforms, such as child-centered education.

Largely in response to such criticism, progressive education's towering figure, John Dewey, published *Experience and Education* in 1938. In this book, his last major work on education, Dewey sought to temper the accusations of laissez-faire individualism and radicalism that sometimes were lobbed at progressive education by opponents. However, the tension among factions in education reform remained severe.

As the 1930s came to a close, the issue of teacher training and certification began to assume more prominence in the education reform debate. A leading advocate for national teacher testing was Teachers College professor Isaac Kandel. He defended the administration of the National Teachers Examinations, which were developed during the Great Depression when there were more teaching applicants than available teaching positions. The exams were first offered in 1940 in 20 areas, including such cities as Philadelphia, Atlanta, and Boston. The 10- to 12-hour exams, developed by the American Council on Education, assessed the teacher candidate's command of such fields as English expression, reasoning, quantitative skills, literature, science, history, fine arts, and current issues, as well as teaching methods and educational history, psychology, and philosophy.

Those opposed to these exams feared that they would lead to greater uniformity and would place too much emphasis on teachers' factual knowledge rather than their ability to teach. The conflict over teacher testing subsided when World War II created a teacher shortage, puncturing reliance on the test. However, the questions of who should teach, how these individuals are prepared, and how visions of curricular standards relate to strengthening public schools had established a prominent place on the education reform menu.

By the end of World War II, a half-century after the movement had begun, progressive education was the reigning ideology of U.S. public education. In the mid-1940s, the NEA published *Education for All American Youth*. The report, endorsed by the leading school administrators' and principals' organizations, defined the role of public schools as oriented toward effective career guidance. As a result of the report, increased emphasis was placed on aptitude and intelligence tests for college admissions and the classification of subjects such as physics, chemistry, history, and algebra as elective courses. Hollis Caswell, dean of Teachers College, helped advocate these and other curriculum reforms that sought to have a direct impact not only on theory but also on classroom practice.

The 1950s, though often characterized by its sense of societal conformity and political conservatism, was also an era of significant ferment in education reform, signaling many of the key battles of the coming decades. Critics of public schooling spanned the ideological and cultural range. Included among them were those who believed that a jargon-intensive education establishment, disconnected from parents and community, had lost sight of education's central purpose of developing the knowledge and intellect of students in favor of efforts to place young people within society according to their perceived personal needs. More religious and cultural conservative types worried that public schools would become too secular, undermining the nation's moral and spiritual foundation. Others, fueled by McCarthy-era fears of communist influence, blamed lax public school standards for such ills as diminished respect for authority and decreased school discipline, as featured in the popular 1955 film *Blackboard Jungle*. Largely as a result of such concerns, a push for increased recitation of the Pledge of Allegiance (with the words *under God* added in 1954) gained momentum, as did calls for more school prayer. However, proponents of prayer in public schools suffered a major setback when the U.S. Supreme Court ruled in 1962's *Engel v. Vitale* that public schools may not require the recitation of prayers.

A common complaint of 1950s public schools was that while schools of education required the study of teaching methods, they did not require teachers or administrators to be well educated. This, they asserted, was reflected in the de-emphasis of academic studies in high schools, and these critics pointed to statistics for support. High school enrollment in academic subjects such as physics, foreign languages, and geometry had significantly declined since the beginning of the 20th century.

Critics of public school standards enjoyed a breakthrough with the enormous popularity of Arthur Bestor's 1953 book, *Educational Wastelands*, and Rudolf Flesch's 1955 book, *Why Johnny Can't Read*. Flesch argued that modern reading approaches such as the look-see method found in the Dick and Jane readers often used in elementary schools were not as effective as traditional phonics instruction. Flesch noted that, "reading isn't taught at all. Books are put in front of the children and they're told to guess at the word or wait until the teacher tells them. But they're not *taught* to read."

Why Johnny Can't Read set off a national debate about literacy instruction and more broadly the common teaching practices of public schools. Most reviewers and the general public embraced its viewpoints, and it remained on the national best-seller lists for 30 weeks. But most prominent educators rejected its premise. The book spurred a Carnegie Corporation study led by Jean Chall of the Harvard Graduate School of Education and designed to determine the most effective method of reading instruction. Chall's three-year study concluded that both approaches were effective, with phonics instruction better suited for young readers and those from low socioeconomic backgrounds.

In response to Chall's report, most early to mid-1960s reading textbooks for early readers emphasized instruction in phonics. But, like the vast majority of other education reform issues, this trend was temporary, and the reading curriculum war would rage again later.

Progressive education encountered other challenges to its wisdom and authority during the late 1950s. In 1955, the PEA, unable to raise sufficient money or recruit members, closed its doors. Increasingly, the perceived excessiveness of the movement's methods and practices were mocked, as evidenced by satirist Tom Lehrer's song "New Math":

> *Hooray for new math,*
> *New-hoo-hoo-math,*
> *It won't do you a bit of good to review math.*
> *It's so simple,*
> *So very simple,*
> *That only a child can do it!*[19]

But the biggest blow to progressive education practice in the 1950s occurred outside the realm public schools. The Soviet Union's 1957 successful launch of the space satellite *Sputnik* struck fear in Americans and served as a symbol of the lagging quality of U.S. schools. In 1958, President Dwight Eisenhower and Congress passed the National Defense Education Act, which among other provisions, included unprecedented federal aid for school construction and for math, science, and foreign language curriculum support. Admiral Hyman Rickover reflected this shifting in the popular view of education's purpose and signaled future debate over standards in his 1959 book *Education and Freedom*, noting,

> *life in a modern industrial state demands a great deal more "book learning"*
> *of everyone who wants to make a good living for himself and his family . . .*
> *the schools must now . . . concentrate on bringing the intellectual powers of*
> *the child to the highest possible level. Even the average child now needs almost*
> *as good an education as the average middle and upper class child used to get*
> *in the college preparatory schools.*[20]

Defending public schools was former Harvard president James Conant, whose 1959 Carnegie Corporation–sponsored book, *The American High School Today*, became a national best seller. Among Conant's key points was that large comprehensive high schools that offered multiple curricula were most effective. He also asserted that every high school needed to have a high-quality counseling staff to help its students into the right program. He described the often-followed practice of requiring four years of English, three or four years of social studies, one year of science and math, with all other courses selected as electives, largely based on aptitude tests. Conant also endorsed social promotion in the required courses, which resulted in students moving on to the next grade based more on factors such as their age rather than academic achievement. *The American High School Today*, which did not refer to its recommendations as progressive education, was very influential in reducing the number of small high schools that could not provide a full array of academic, vocational, and general courses and in blunting the attacks of 1950s public school critics.

Among the most dissatisfied participants in public education during this time were African Americans and others who supported their access to education. The frustration over the substandard conditions of the largely segregated public school system could no longer be overlooked following the U.S. Supreme Court's unanimous, landmark 1954 decision in *Brown v. Board of Education*, which prohibited state-imposed racial segregation in public schools. However, despite the civil rights significance of this decision, education of black students still suffered. Resistance to the ruling in the South was widespread. In the North continued white flight to the suburbs contributed to the deterioration of public schools.

Educational researcher Kenneth Clark, whose work was a key factor in demonstrating the harmful effects of segregation in the *Brown* case, advocated an emphasis on raising standards in the now notoriously underachieving larger urban schools, most of which had a high concentration of blacks. Such calls were largely drowned out by the din of political struggles and crises that engulfed the nation and its public schools throughout the 1960s, although the standards debate would emerge a generation later.

The role of the federal government in education reform took a giant step forward in 1965 with the passage of the Elementary and Secondary Education Act. This legislation, providing the largest infusion of federal funding for public schools ever, was a key component of President Lyndon Johnson's Great Society program. The law's Title I provision of approximately $1 billion to help improve education in the nation's poorest areas represented an unprecedented and to many unwelcome commitment of federal government in local schools. While among many there was enormous optimism that poverty and its related ills, such as inadequate education, could actually be overcome, the late 1960s were a time of great discord and criticism for public education, creating fertile ground for the proposition of sometimes radical reforms.

In 1964, private school teacher John Holt published *How Children Fail*, ripping tests, grades, curricula, and other aspects of the schooling experience. His work is often credited with providing an articulation of the philosophical foundation for the homeschooling movement. Another important pen of reform was provided by teacher Jonathan Kozol, whose 1967 book, *Death at an Early Age*, won the National Book Award for its portrayal of the appalling conditions, including insensitive and unresponsive bureaucracy and incompetent and indifferent teachers, in the Boston public schools.

One proposed solution to the problems of urban schools and to the malaise of other public schools was the open education movement. The movement grew in popularity following the 1967 publication in *The New Republic* of a series of articles by American social critic Joseph Featherstone that described open education in Britain, in which the routine of the day "is left completely up to the teacher and the teacher, in turn leaves options open to the students." Partly as a result of this movement, multiage groups, activity centers, and other aspects similar to the child-centered movement of the 1930s became more common. Journalist Charles Silberman's popular book *Crisis in the Classroom* helped propel the movement, and by the early 1970s many schools had been modified to fit the tenets of open education. However, this movement fizzled almost as quickly as it grew. Many ambitious but poorly planned open education experiments failed miserably, as depicted in Massachusetts principal Roland Barth's book *Open Education and the American School.*

In 1969, a Gallup poll of Americans listed "lack of discipline" as the school's leading problem.[21] The real and perceived problems that resulted from the late 1960s and early 1970s, namely the easing of graduation requirements, bilingual education programs, dress codes, and disciplinary rules, led to a groundswell of support for a back-to-basics movement in education. This growing contingent of citizens who believed that schools had lost their focus of teaching young people in a morass of ill-conceived programs, services, and curricular trends would find hospitable terrain in the more conservative political environment of the early 1980s.

SEEKING SECURITY IN A NATION AT RISK

In 1983, the debate over education reform was redefined with the publication of *A Nation at Risk*. The controversial report issued by the National Commission on Excellence in Education, whose members had been appointed by President Ronald Reagan's secretary of education, Terrell Bell, warned of the dire consequences of U.S. educational decline. It charged that lax academic standards in American schools were clearly related to the drop in behavioral standards and that the failure to address these conditions could result in educational catastrophe. The report stated, "if an unfriendly foreign power had attempted to impose on America the mediocre educational performance that exists today, we might well have viewed it as an act of war."[22]

A Nation at Risk asserted that four aspects of schooling needed to change: content, expectations, time, and teaching. The report claimed that high school content had been, "homogenized, diluted, and diffused" to the point that it was a "cafeteria-style curriculum in which the appetizers and desserts can easily be mistaken for the main courses." *A Nation at Risk* continued to claim that expectations had been unacceptably watered down by grade inflation and weak promotion policies such as those found in the majority of states requiring only one year of math and science for high school graduation.

The report also compared the length of the school day and the school year in the United States and other industrialized nations and found that American students spent an insufficient amount of time pursuing academic study. In addition, the report argued that standards for teachers were in need of significant improvement by criticizing the relatively low academic achievement of teacher candidates and the heavy methods orientation of teacher education programs. Among the report's recommendations were the standardization of high school graduation criteria, including the requirement of successful completion of the "new basics": four years of English, three years of math, science, and social studies, and a half year of computer science.

Intense and ideologically diverse debate over the best ways to address the deficiencies of U.S. public schools followed the highly publicized release of *A Nation at Risk*. A first wave of reform resulted in top-down types of measures, including state legislation enacting higher graduation requirements, standardized curriculum mandates, increased testing of students and teachers, raised certification requirements for teachers, minimum standards for participation in athletics, and in some cases the lengthening of the school day and school year. A second wave of reform focused on bottom-up changes, such as increased local control of schools and site-based management, teacher empowerment, parental involvement, and various forms of school choice.

Two significant curricular schools of thought during this period were the modern tradition of progressive education of Ted Sizer and the academic curriculum emphasis of E. D. Hirsch. Sizer, former dean of the Harvard Graduate School of Education, published *Horace's Compromise* in 1983. In it, he melded traditional progressive education principles while shedding some of the more discredited notions of the movement. The book decried the low expectations and dull routine of most U.S. high schools. To counter this, Sizer advocated for increased authority for the teachers, administrators, and parents at local schools. For students, he recommended a greater emphasis on demonstrations of mastery rather than reliance on standardized tests. He created the Coalition of Essential Schools to advance reform ideas.[23] Among these schools was Central Park East School in Harlem, led by prominent education reformer Deborah Meier. By 2000, more than 1,200 schools were part of this coalition.

In the early 1980s, E. D. Hirsch was an English professor at the University of Virginia, and was not particularly well known outside Charlottesville. However, in 1987 his book *Cultural Literacy* was published and quickly became an education reform lightning rod. Supporters of the book lauded its purpose of transmitting "the basic information needed to thrive in the modern world" and backed Hirsch's claim that the understanding of a common, explicit curriculum was "the only way of combating the social determinism that condemns [students] to remain in the same social and educational condition as their parents."[24] Critics disparaged Hirsch's dictionary-like collection of information as trivia, but well over 1 million purchasers of the book found it to be relevant.

One common thread running through the major education reforms of the 1980s was a focus on academic standards. Increased economic globalization and rapidly advancing technology led many, particularly in the business community, to worry that American students would not be sufficiently prepared to lead the U.S. economy in a more competitive environment. Critical input from within the education community on the standards debate was provided by American Federation of Teachers president Albert Shanker. As the leader of the nation's largest teachers' union, Shanker exerted his considerable influence through regular newspaper op-ed pieces advocating clear standards and assessments that would strengthen the meaning and consequences of schooling for students. Soon elected officials were promoting standards as well, leading to President George H. W. Bush's 1989 Education Summit with the nation's governors to promote national education goals. This culminated in 1994 with President Bill Clinton signing the *GOALS 2000: Educate America Act.*

Despite the apparent middle ground consensus on curriculum standards, battles, particularly relating to U.S. history, raged. In 1994, University of California Los Angeles's Center for History in the Schools prepared a federally funded project of National History Standards. Even before the release, they were the focus of severe criticism. Lynne Cheney, former chairwoman of the National Endowment for the Humanities, attacked them for political bias, noting how the standards mentioned such shameful figures as Joseph McCarthy 19 times and the Ku Klux Klan 17 times yet omitted figures generally regarded as heroic, such as Paul Revere and Thomas Edison.[25] Although many, including the editorial boards of the *New York Times* and *Los Angeles Times,* endorsed the standards and their reflection of a multicultural curriculum emphasis, public sentiment was largely opposed to them. The U.S. Senate passed a resolution condemning them 99-1 (the one opponent wanted a harsher condemnation). President Clinton's secretary of education, Richard Riley, distanced the administration from them saying, "this is not my view of how history should be taught in America's classrooms . . . our schools should teach our students to be proud of the Americans."[26] The National History Standards were eventually revised but also largely ignored by states and districts, highlighting the historic difficulty of reaching a meaningful consensus in education reform in light of consistently deep ideological divisions.

CURRENT ISSUES IN EDUCATION REFORM

The impact and implications of education reform's history have merged with key current issues since the 1990s and into the 21st century. Following is an examination of the most prominent present-day issues in education reform, including choice, vouchers, and charter schools; privatization; homeschooling; accountability, standards, and assessments; and teacher quality, school environment, and school financing.

CHOICE

School choice initiatives are based on the premise that allowing parents to choose which schools their children attend is not only the fair thing to do but also an important strategy for improving public education. Instead of a one-size-fits-all model, choice programs are designed to offer parents various alternatives from which to pick the educational settings that they believe work best for their children.

The earliest expression of this critical and increasingly prominent aspect of education reform is often credited to the free-market champion author of the 1776 book *Wealth of Nations*, Adam Smith. In that book, Smith argued that parents are in the best position to decide how their children should be educated and that the state should give parents the money to hire suitable teachers. The view that the state should provide funding for poor families to secure a basic education for their children was also endorsed by famous patriot and writer Thomas Paine toward the end of the 18th century.

However, circumstances in 19th-century America would lead to a general consensus against the embryonic notions of school or education vouchers. Especially damaging was the prevalent anti-Catholic bias that existed in the United States following the large influx of largely Catholic immigrant groups. Because of what he viewed as the intolerable resistance of non-Catholics, New York City bishop John Hughes asked the Public School Society of New York for state aid for Catholic schools in 1840. After his request was denied, Hughes built his own system with private funds. Three decades later, President Ulysses Grant helped certify the United States' educational separation of church and state by explaining, "Not one dollar . . . shall be appropriated to the support of any sectarian schools."[27]

Vouchers

The push for vouchers remained essentially dormant for almost a century. Despite support for voucher programs from advocates such as economist Milton Friedman, who first proposed vouchers in 1955, popular and legal opposition to the practice of using public funds for private religious education was formidable. The period of the 1960s and 1970s were witness to a series of Supreme Court cases, including 1971's *Lemon v. Kurtzman*, that struck down attempts to provide state aid to religious schools in the form of teachers' salaries and instructional materials. During this time different forms of school choice began to emerge, including public school choice, in which students were able to attend schools outside their neighborhood but within their public school district.

Like many other education reforms, the choice movement owes a debt of gratitude to the 1983 report *A Nation at Risk*. This highly critical evaluation of U.S. public schools both reflected and initiated concern about the failure of schools and helped create an environment in which more radical approaches could be encouraged. A new openness to vouchers for private schools was evident in the 1983 Supreme Court case *Mueller v. Allen*. In a

5-4 decision, the Court supported the concept of tuition tax credits, holding that a state government (in this case Minnesota) could allow taxpayers to deduct expenses incurred due to "tuition, textbooks, and transportation" at religious, elementary, and secondary schools.[28]

Momentum for vouchers also grew in 1990 following the release of John Chubb and Terry Moe's book *Politics, Markets, and American Schools*, in which they claimed that "choice, all by itself, has the capacity to bring about a transformation in public education." A dramatic expansion then took place throughout the 1990s in the use of public school choice and in the more controversial private and religious school choice programs based on vouchers. The most renowned and contested of these programs were the Milwaukee Parental Choice Program, the Cleveland Scholarship Program, and the Florida A+ Plan.

There are three different types of options that fit the umbrella term of *school choice*. The least disputed and most common of these is intradistrict choice. This is the kind of public choice that allows parents to select among schools within their home district. Magnet schools, which typically focus on a specialization, such as technology or fine arts, are examples of intradistrict choice, as much or all of their enrollment is made up of students from all parts of the district and admission is based on lottery and/or the demonstration of academic achievement.

A less frequent but similarly oriented choice plan is statewide or interdistrict choice. Under these programs, students are allowed to attend public schools outside their home district. Minnesota led the way for such initiatives in 1988 and five other states (Arkansas, Iowa, Nebraska, Oklahoma, and Wisconsin) currently have them.

The issue of vouchers is most associated with private school choice. These programs, which usually are at the center of arguments about choice, permit parents to use public funds to send their children to private schools and, in many cases, religious schools.

Few issues in education, if any, are as intensely debated as private school vouchers. Supporters of the practice often argue that private school vouchers encourage equity by enabling students from families of low socioeconomic status, like their wealthier peers, to escape the troubled and inadequate public schools. In addition, these proponents also claim that private school vouchers will create competition that will spur innovation, accountability, and improvement in a public school system that serves as a monopoly providing poor services to its most vulnerable clients.

Opponents of private school vouchers generally contend these programs endanger the ideal of offering every student access to high-quality education by treating learning as a commodity rather than a public good. They point out how this competitive conception does not always work in the interest of the consumer. At best, they claim, private school vouchers are a kind of lifeboat that may help the fortunate few while leaving the majority of others stranded in a public system with depleted resources. In addition, voucher foes assert that allowing private schools to take public money with little oversight may lead to mismanagement or corruption.

Although the ideological divisions in the voucher debate are clear, they often do not fall along the common political or demographic lines. Vouchers are generally presented as something that conservatives and business types support and liberals and teachers' unions oppose. While that is often true, some of the strongest support for vouchers has come from individuals and groups that rarely endorse policies considered conservative. For instance, studies have indicated that African Americans have typically posted higher levels of support for some form of private school vouchers than the general public.[29]

Momentum for support of school voucher programs appears to have crested. According to the 2002 Phi Beta Kappa/Gallup Poll on the Public's Attitudes Towards the Public Schools, the general public was split but increasingly supportive of the notion. In the poll, 52 percent of those surveyed said that they oppose allowing students to attend private school at "public expense." However, support for private school vouchers jumped 12 percentage points in just one year—from 34 to 46 percent. When this same question dropped the phrase "public expense," instead stating "the government would pay all or part of the tuition," 52 percent of respondents supported private school vouchers, an increase from 44 percent in 2001.[30]

Reasons for this increase of support may include the Supreme Court's pro voucher decision in the 2002 case *Zelman v. Simmons-Harris* and a high approval rating at the time of the survey for President George W. Bush, who publicly endorsed private school vouchers. However, in years since then, private school vouchers advocates have suffered both at the ballot box, where voters in California and Utah recently rejected voucher programs, and in state supreme courts, where judges have cited state constitution provisions to rule against voucher programs in Maine and Florida. In March 2009, this trend continued when the U.S. Congress voted to end funding for a voucher program in Washington, D.C.

The key questions of the voucher debate involve a wide range of legal, fiscal, social, and practical issues with potentially far-reaching implications: Are vouchers constitutional? Do they work? Do vouchers drain money from public schools? And, is there capacity to handle potentially expanded voucher programs?

The most vigorous arguments about vouchers often revolve around their constitutionality, specifically whether they infringe on church-state separation. Supporters of vouchers, who often draw comparisons between these programs and the enormously popular 1944 GI Bill, which provided educational support for veterans, claim the government has allowed public money in the past to go to private religious education and continues to do so, when, for instance, a student attending Notre Dame receives financial aid.[31] Proponents also point to some state and Supreme Court rulings that have allowed more lenience in the application of public funds toward religious institutions.

Opponents of vouchers consistently assert that such mingling of public money and sectarian groups is a clear violation of the First Amendment's establishment clause, prohibiting government establishment or endorsement of religion. They often counter arguments that parents, not the government, actually would pay religious schools under voucher plans as legally irrelevant because public funds could still be used for religious instruction. As for claims that voucher funding would only pay for secular subjects, opponents argue that this would be impossible to enforce and further, that the public funds could actually violate discrimination laws in schools that make personnel decisions based on such factors as religious faith and sexual orientation.

The academic effectiveness of voucher programs is a particularly muddled aspect of the voucher debate. Despite the growing national dialogue about vouchers, many education reform experts explain that there are few studies about them that have been conducted by objective researchers with sound methodology. In addition, because there have been so few voucher programs, and those that exist have been in place for a relatively brief amount of time, reliable statistics demonstrating whether students and schools actually benefit from these programs are in short supply. Not surprisingly, many of the studies that are referenced point out that voucher programs are either great saviors or horrific failures.

Advocates on both sides of the voucher issue also argue about whether these programs are fiscally fair. Supporters believe that they are because they enable students from poor families to gain resources that can help them attend better and safer schools. They claim that voucher programs are designed to provide additional money for educational support so that they do not poach already determined spending allocations. Regarding charges that broader voucher plans would unfairly deplete funding available to public schools, supporters explain that if public schools receive the same amount of money per pupil they will not suffer.

Opponents argue that even the most ambitious and supportive voucher plans usually are not able to cover a student's entire tuition, making such plans useful for the wealthy and perhaps the middle class but not for the poor, whom the programs are ostensibly designed to help. They usually believe that money that could go toward the establishment and maintenance of a voucher program would be more wisely spent on measures designed to improve instruction in struggling public schools, such as initiatives to reduce class size and to improve reading instruction.

Voucher combatants also disagree on the fundamental question of whether voucher programs are socially practical. Supporters assert that they are, pointing out that vouchers will lead to public school improvement, and over time, fewer transfers to private schools. This will help allow private schools to absorb more easily incoming students, and if there are too many students leaving public schools, more private schools will be created.

Those opposed to voucher programs argue that such plans undermine society's commitment to public education by establishing an unfair framework in which public schools will be required to accept all students while private schools will be free to reject students for a variety of reasons, including the ability to provide special education services and student noncompliance with often stricter codes of conduct.

Until recently, voucher opponents held the upper hand in this education reform battle, as there were few and isolated private school voucher programs across the United States. But the course of this issue, and perhaps the nature of public education in the United States, changed on the morning of June 27, 2002, when the U.S. Supreme Court delivered its decision for *Zelman v. Simmons-Harris*, allowing the Cleveland voucher program to continue and calling it "true public choice . . . [providing] benefits to a wide spectrum of individuals, defined only by financial need and residence in a particular district."[32]

Just days after this decision, state legislators in California, Pennsylvania, Minnesota, and elsewhere organized plans for what they believed would be a new era of school choice. However, despite the crucial Supreme Court victory, voucher programs were by no means a fait accompli. Thirty-seven state constitutions contained language that prohibits state aid from going to religious schools. Even if such provisions were not insurmountable, they were at least likely to stall voucher plans.[33] Despite the important *Zelman* victory for choice advocates, by 2009 only 14 states and Washington, D.C. had some form of voucher legislation. Together, these programs served only approximately 160,000 students.

There are several reasons to explain why vouchers have not enjoyed the expansion many might have expected following *Zelman*. Voucher programs have traditionally struggled to gain widespread support at the ballot box when they have been brought to voters. In addition, difficult economic times, like much of the first decade of the 21st century, have led many states to fight just to maintain previous levels of spending, making the fiscal growth caused by vouchers enormously hard to implement.

Furthermore, teachers' unions, which have led the effort to halt vouchers, have remained steadfastly opposed, especially after the Supreme Court's decision, in *Zelman*. Less than one week after the ruling, NEA president Bob Chase said, "And to the voucher ideologues we make this promise: we will expose your false promises. We will lay bare your lies . . . we will defeat you!"[34]

Charter Schools

Another form of choice that exploded in popularity over the past 20 years was charter schools. Under the charter school concept, a group of teachers or other would-be educators applied for permission from their local education authority to open a public school, operating with taxpayer dollars just like a regular public school. The difference is that charter schools are freed from many of the rules and regulations governing regular public schools that many feel cripple learning and stifle innovation. The schools operate under a contract, or "charter," with a local school board, state, or university(ies). In exchange for exemption from most state and local regulations, the schools, usually with a smaller, limited enrollment designed to enhance attention to student needs, must educate students according to an agreed-upon standard and must prove their success in order to gain renewal of the charter.

The rise of charter schools has been rapid and influential. At the beginning of 1991 there was not a single charter school in the United States. Ten years later, there were almost 2,500 serving more than one-half million students.[35] By the 2009–10 school year, the number of charter schools operating in the United States had risen to more than 5,000. One key reason for the rapid growth of charter schools is that they are a form of school choice that most stakeholders generally embrace in a broad, bipartisan fashion. Most Republicans like the emphasis on choice, competition, and deregulation, and most Democrats appreciate the fact that they are public schools, open to all, nonreligious, and accountable to public authorities. Political disputes over charter schools usually focus on which candidate is most committed to them, rather than which candidate supports them.

Charter schools do have their critics, however. One common charge against charter schools is that they create a kind of educational balkanization by usually serving students concentrated in low socioeconomic areas. Charter boosters often respond to this by explaining that they serve the same demographic characteristics as exist in the public school community in which they are located. Further, they assert that the disproportionate percentage of minorities enrolled in charter schools is a reflection of the traditional public schools' failure to meet the needs of these groups.

Charter opponents also claim that, even after nearly two decades of existence, they have not demonstrably improved the achievement of their students or the performance of other public schools. Along with this, many believe that the innovations promised in charter school applications are often not delivered. Charter supporters answer this by pointing to studies that provide evidence that students and schools are improving because of the competition and accountability encouraged by charter schools. They also explain that charter schools respond to local conditions, meaning that what may be considered innovative in one area (such as block scheduling of classes, year-round schooling) may be common in another area.

Perhaps the most serious criticism of charter schools is that they need to be more accountable to the taxpayer, whose money supports their creation and maintenance. In defense of charter schools, advocates explain that in the rare cases when charter schools fail to meet their detailed goals, they can be sanctioned or even closed. Regular public schools, they argue, are the ones lacking accountability because if they fail to meet goals, which often are not articulated, they can and do remain open, continuing to poorly serve their students.

Although charter school advocates enjoy the overwhelming support of parents, businesspeople, and politicians, they often feel that teachers' unions are uncertain allies. The NEA and the American Federation of Teachers (AFT), which staunchly oppose private school vouchers, state their support of charter schools, albeit with a number of conditions. The NEA, for instance, insists that charter schools should have no negative impact on the regular public school program, hire only licensed teachers, and not contribute to racial or ethnic segregation. Both unions also favor state caps on the number of charter schools. Former AFT president Sandra Feldman explained in 2000, "I'm in favor of charter schools that are accountable and adhere to the same standards as all public schools. We're not for charter schools that can just go off and do their own thing."[36] Charter proponents have also charged some union leadership with seeking to weaken state charter legislation through what they view as excessive restrictions on their number, authorizer eligibility, and regulatory independence.

The passage of the No Child Left Behind Act of 2001, reauthorizing the Elementary and Secondary Education Act, included provisions for both public school choice and charter schools, further signaling the prominence of choice in current education reform. Although private school vouchers were not supported in the act, legal momentum and state legislation significantly increased the scope and influence of charter schools in the first decade of the 21st century. Evidence of this is seen in the numbers of charter schools operating in the United States. With broad support among policy makers in both major political parties, the number of charter schools operating has grown over 300 percent between 2000, when there were fewer than 1,300 charter schools, and 2010, when there were more than 5,000. Although tides of reform can change meaningfully and quickly, the push for charter schools remains vital and, far more than the stagnating choice movement, appears to enjoy a brighter future.

PRIVATIZATION

Closely related to aspects of school choice is the issue of privatization in public education. The notion of turning the operation of public schools over to private companies is a controversial idea based on the widely accepted premise that what makes improving public schools so hard is that they are bogged down in a bureaucratic mire.

Advocates of privatization in public schools see the move as being an opportunity to provide the best of government and business. They contend that government's oversight function and its responsiveness to the needs of its citizens can be retained while taking advantage of private enterprise's ability to be more efficient, cut costs, and maximize production—in this case, student achievement. Advocates also point out that, like other major public services such as health care and defense, public schools have been and will always be partly about business.

Opponents of privatization and public education argue that, while this appears good on paper, it will not work efficiently in reality. Through privatization they see the individual needs of students, particularly those with special and often costly requirements, being sacrificed for the needs of corporate shareholders. They worry that the pressure for profit will replace student achievement as the driving force within schools. Many skeptics also do not accept the premise upon which the privatization plans are based, pointing out that private managers can be as inefficient or incompetent as public managers, if not more so.

Privatization efforts have had the most conspicuous impact on charter schools, as entrepreneurs recognized the business opportunity in working with the teachers and community activists who founded charter schools and were running an enterprise for the first time. Data varies on the proportion of the nation's charter schools that are run by for-profit companies, though estimates are usually placed at about 10 percent.

The most prominent for-profit school management company is Edison Schools (originally named the Edison Project). It was started in 1992 by entrepreneur Christopher Whittle, whose goal was to demonstrate how the market can improve the outcomes and efficiency of the public schools. The conditions for this venture were promising, coming at the beginning of a simultaneous wave of economic prosperity and education reform activity. Whittle proceeded to raise tens of millions of dollars and hired a well-respected team, including former Yale president Benno Schmidt, Jr., to design an exemplary school model.

When the first four Edison-managed schools opened at the beginning of the 1995–96 school year, the company began implementation of "the Edison design." This 10-point framework, still used today, emphasizes fundamentals such as varied instructional programs (including project-based learning and direct instruction), a longer school day and longer school year (198 days as opposed to the standard 180 days), a focus on technology integration (including providing every teacher with their own laptop computer), and a detailed standards-based, academically oriented curriculum. By the 1999–2000 school year, Edison was managing 79 schools and could boast that it had never lost a contract. Although still controversial and opposed by many traditional educators and teachers unions, Edison was enjoying mainly favorable media coverage and looked forward to an even greater academic and fiscal future.

Some of the same market factors that led to Edison's early success, however, contributed to its later struggles. Precipitous drops in the stock market witnessed a plunge in Edison's stock price from $36 a share in early 2001 to as low as 14¢ a share in mid-2002, and as of December 2002, it was selling at approximately $1.70 a share.[37] (Edison was taken private in a 2003 buyout valued at $180 million, approximately $1.76 a share.) Edison did demonstrate success in its mission of delivering effective education and improving academic achievement in its schools, which were overwhelmingly located in impoverished areas, but these results often did not meet initial claims of Edison's boosters. This, as well as highly publicized failures in Edison-managed schools in New York City and Philadelphia, which resulted in lost contracts, has led to a decline in Edison's impact and an increase in the questioning of the market's ability to effectively run public schools. The complaints from school districts and charter school boards lodged against Edison are familiar ones often heaped upon traditional public school management—low test scores, high teacher turnover, and unsatisfactory "bang for the buck."

Edison Schools changed its name to EdisonLearning in 2008 to identify itself with its growing presence in online education. It remained involved with the management of "brick and mortar" schools but focused mainly on supplementary educational services, such as testing, summer school management, and tutoring. Edison's rocky history in the educational management field reflected that of many private enterprises, which struggled in the perilous political and professional thicket of education reform in the United States.

HOMESCHOOLING

The ultimate form of school choice is the decision to educate one's own child at home. The homeschooling movement, like vouchers, charters, and privatization, has grown enormously over the past 30 years. Once generally considered to be the domain of highly religious parents and those from counterculture, homeschooling has garnered steadily increasing measures of mainstream acceptance as a viable option for frustrated parents concerned that the public schools are not effectively educating or protecting their children.

Homeschooling in practice takes many different forms. For many it means duplicating school at home, complete with textbooks, report cards, and standardized tests. At the other end of the homeschooling spectrum is the practice of "unschooling," in which students pursue their studies according to their own interests and according to their own pace. Most homeschooling reflects a middle course in which parents mix methods and curricula.[38] Increasingly, homeschooling families are organizing co-ops to share resources and increase student socialization and are participating in Internet-based distance learning programs. The consensus among those who follow homeschooling is that there are at least 1.5 million U.S. students currently being educated at home. Reliable numbers are difficult to ascertain because states define and track homeschoolers in different ways and some parents do not comply with state rules requiring them to register their homeschooled children.

Homeschooling's appeal emanates from spiritual, financial, academic, and social concerns. Many of the earliest homeschooling families were seeking a way out from secularized public schools, which following legal and social development of the 1960s and 1970s were viewed as increasingly intolerant of religious expression. Enrollment in religious schools usually remained an option for such families, but many have decided that schooling their children at home makes too much financial sense to refuse, as the cost of supplies for a home school curriculum is consistently significantly less than the average cost of tuition at a private school.

Academic considerations also play a crucial role in homeschooling's growth. Many of the criticisms found in *A Nation at Risk* are echoed by homeschooling families: frustration with inefficient school bureaucracies, lack of time for quality academic instruction, and declining standards of achievement and discipline in schools.

Related to this is the well-established concern among homeschooling parents that schools are simply not a safe environment. This trend in thought spiked dramatically following a spate of school shootings by students, including the 1999 murder of 12 students and one teacher at Columbine High School in Littleton, Colorado.

Despite the rising popularity of homeschooling, the movement has many critics. In the view of many professional educators and others, homeschooling remains a dangerously deregulated enterprise with an unacceptable lack of quality control. A resolution passed by the NEA argues that, "homeschooling programs cannot provide the student with a comprehensive education experience."[39]

Another concern is that some parents may be keeping their children out of school not because of the commonly stated reasons but rather because they do not want them to mix with children of other races or backgrounds or even so that they can work in a family business. In line with this argument is the contention that homeschooling seriously undermines the social development of a young person. Homeschooling supporters often counter that students too often develop poor and sometimes dangerous socialization traits in public schools. Critics respond, however, that the skills required to deal with the real world are rarely acquired within the walls of a home and that the sheltered isolation of homeschoolers may ultimately be detrimental to them and society.

The academic merits of homeschooling have received national attention, particularly in light of the success and disproportionately high participation of homeschooled students in national spelling and geography bee competitions. In addition, most studies of homeschoolers' academic performance suggest that they generally achieve above national norms on standardized tests and in postsecondary academic endeavors. However, such studies cannot examine how those students would have performed had they stayed in public school, and they usually are unable to provide credible data regarding homeschoolers' social and emotional development.

By 1986, homeschooling had graduated from a fringe movement to a legally recognized activity practiced in all 50 states.[40] Disputes still often occur, nonetheless, between parents and state or local education officials about enforcement of homeschooling laws, which vary considerably across the country. Most states do not require parents to have specific qualifications for teaching their children at home, but most states do have provisions requiring that homeschooled students have regular evaluations or take standardized tests.

Recent trends have featured a significant increase in the homeschooled population. According to the National Center of Education Statistics, there were approximately 850,000 homeschooled students in the United States in 1999. That figure jumped to 1.1 million in 2003 and reached 1.5 million in 2007. This represented an increase of 74 percent in just eight years and 36 percent in the last four-year period. Of this group, it was determined that 84 percent spent their entire school day at home. This increase in the homeschooled population has been accompanied by the evolution of the homeschooling industry, with the proliferation of for-profit companies and nonprofit organizations providing curricular materials specifically designed for homeschooling families. As the homeschooling movement has become larger and more accepted, relationships with public schools, such as homeschooled students' participation in public school extracurricular activities, have increased, seemingly benefiting both the homeschooled and the public school system. Whether such relationships also threaten these educational stakeholders remains to be seen.

ACCOUNTABILITY

Accountability—the concept of holding schools, districts, teachers, and students responsible for academic achievement—has become the most essential element affecting the variety of current education reform efforts. Across the United States, policy makers have moved decisively toward rewarding achievement and punishing failure in an effort to ensure that students receive a high-quality education and that the public's tax money is used efficiently.

All 50 states test students to determine what they have learned, and 45 states publish report cards on individual schools, based largely on test scores. More than half of the states publicly rate their schools, or at least identify low-performing ones, and 15 states have the legal authority to close, take over, or replace the staff and schools that have been identified as failing.[41]

This recent push for accountability is a modern manifestation of the history of education reform battles, in this case specifically seeking to prove what needs to be taught and how to measure whether this material has been effectively learned. This pursuit, combined with the back-to-basics sensibility of *A Nation at Risk*, has led to the formation and influence of accountability measures, the two most relevant of which are standards and assessments.

Standards

The underlying assumption of standards-based reform is one that harkens back to the early 20th-century conception of the educational ladder that offered all students the opportunity to meet high goals. For many supporters of standards, they represent the most effective means by which glaring gaps in student performance and expectations can be addressed, leading to a foundation of excellence and equity throughout the public school system.

Within this framework are different types of standards. Academic standards describe what students should know and be able to do in the core academic subjects at each grade level. Content standards describe basic agreement about the body of education knowledge that all students should know. Performance standards describe what level of demonstrated skill is sufficient for students to be ranked advanced, proficient, or below basic.

Public support for standards is strong, although surveys typically find higher levels of approval for the adaptation of standards among business leaders than among teachers. Despite the widespread setting of academic standards, significant obstacles stand in the way of making them effective tools for educational progress. Standards advocates and critics often worry that standards are too vague to be truly meaningful. Many are also concerned about a "Goldilocks phenomenon," which often finds educators thinking that standards are set properly while many parents, business leaders, policy makers, and others find them to be either too easy or too difficult.

Introduction to Education Reform

Assessments (Testing)

The role of standards and the accountability discussion is inexorably linked to the more controversial issue of assessments. The testing policies established in every state are designed largely to find an accurate way to measure students' success as well as to hold schools accountable for results. The implementation and far-reaching implications of these tests are at the heart of accountability, and they have become an increasingly essential feature of education reform.

Assessment advocates often view statewide testing as a way to raise expectations and to help guarantee that students are held to the same high standards. Critics respond that testing too often narrows student learning to what is tested, leading instructors to "teach to the test" and cover only a sample of what students should know. In addition, they lament that tests tend to focus on what is easiest to measure rather than assessing the critical thinking skills students need to develop.

One of the key issues in the assessment debate concerns alignment, or how well state tests match state standards. Developing a clear and meaningful alignment between state standards and state assessments requires time, expertise, and money. Some states have invested in developing tests designed for alignment, while others have opted for partial alignment or "off the shelf" tests that do not necessarily reflect state standards. Since 1969, the National Assessment of Educational Progress (NAEP) has administered periodic national tests in reading, math, science, writing, history, and geography, providing data on the achievement of students over time and across the country.

Another area of concern is the quality of state assessments. Many reform-minded testing experts are aiming to create assessments that elicit higher order critical-thinking, problem-solving, and communications skills rather than or in addition to the traditional multiple-choice approach that is considered effective at measuring more basic content knowledge. Assessments that measure the higher order skills are typically more open ended, with teachers judging students on written essays, on the process they used to solve a problem, and in some cases on a portfolio of their work over the course of the school year. Currently, almost all states include multiple-choice items in their assessments, most states include short answer items, approximately one-third include performance-based assessments in subjects other than English, and only two use portfolio assessments.

State assessments, particularly following the increased reliance on them in recent years, have brought to the surface another contentious aspect that has been associated with testing for years—bias. Although African Americans and most other minorities have recently demonstrated relative and absolute gains in standardized test scores, they still score much lower than whites as a group. Many educators and parents believe that this "achievement gap" is partially, if not largely, because the embedded cultural bias of standardized tests that draw primarily upon the experiences and sensibilities of middle-class white students. Critics also question what they consider to be the emphasis on these tests and the high stakes attached to them.

Social Promotion

State assessments are increasingly being applied to determine whether students advance to the next grade, attend summer school, and in some cases graduate. Led by reform efforts in the Chicago public schools during the mid-1990s, many school systems and states are implementing policies designed to restrict or end the practice of social promotion, instead basing student advancement to the next grade on whether he or she meets predetermined assessment benchmarks. Supporters of such policies argue that this is a way to raise expectations and convey the importance of academic achievement. Detractors claim that these policies are unfair because the schools implementing them often do not provide the held-back students with the tools they need to succeed, such as high-quality instruction, a strong curriculum, and support services. Further, they argue that retention, while perhaps successful in sending a message, does not actually help the student grow academically or socially.

Reconstitution

Procedures are also in place for schools that fail to meet collective assessment goals. One such method growing in frequency is reconstitution, in which a governing authority, usually a state, though sometimes a district, can replace any or all of a low-performing school's staff. This drastic strategy to improve persistently failing schools was explicitly endorsed in the No Child Left Behind Act of 2001.[42] Under this law, districts must implement corrective actions, such as replacing staff members if a school fails to make adequate progress for four consecutive years. After five consecutive years of inadequate progress, a district is required to set up an alternative governance structure, such as reopening the school as a charter school or turning operation of a failing school over to the state.

Supporters of reconstitution hail its intolerance for the culture of failure within many schools and its recognition of the inability of such schools to help themselves without severe intervention. Opponents of reconstitution worry that the approach wrongly blames teachers and school staff for conditions largely out of their control. Further, they argue that deficiencies in some school communities are so endemic that changing the staff in an attempt to improve a school will do little good and may in fact cause harm.

Because reconstitution is a relatively recent measure, it is still unclear whether it has been an effective approach to strengthening the weakest of America's public schools. What is clear is that reconstitution represents another of the dramatically increased efforts to ensure accountability that have taken hold over the past 25 years.

Bilingual Education Programs

Adding to the complexity of this issue is the issue of how to properly address standards and assessments for students enrolled in bilingual education programs. The original objective of bilingual education was to ensure that students would not fall behind academically because of a poor command of the English language and to gradually teach them English as a second language. Proponents claimed that if language-minority students were taught some subjects in their native tongue, they potentially could learn English without sacrificing content knowledge. The bilingual education's critics disagreed, arguing that this approach keeps students in a cycle of native language dependency and inhibits their progress toward English-language mastery.

Bilingual education programs gained traction in the 1970s and expanded into the 1990s. However, public sentiment against bilingual education has been growing and may threaten its existence as previously practiced. In 1998, California voters overwhelmingly approved Proposition 227 (organized by software entrepreneur Ron Unz), which largely eliminated bilingual education from the public schools. A similar campaign succeeded in Arizona in 2000, and public sentiment against bilingual education programs has remained steady since then. Most significant, the No Child Left Behind Act transformed 1968's Bilingual Education Act into the English Language Acquisition Act, semantically reflecting a new emphasis on teaching English language learners with English-intensive curricula. Federal money under No Child Left Behind is spent and awarded to support accountability provisions, such as judging schools by the percentage of English language learners reclassified as fluent in English each year.

TEACHER QUALITY

In the final analysis, any effective education reform will need to positively influence the instruction that occurs inside a classroom. With this in mind, many recent education reform efforts have been focused on strengthening the background, training, and professional development of teachers.

Research consistently shows that teachers who have been trained in the subjects they teach perform better than teachers who lack subject-matter preparation. Yet on average, about one-third of teachers in public schools are assigned at least one class a day for which they have not been trained. This occurs even more frequently in low-performing schools. In addition, most research also demonstrates that teachers are more effective when they possess at least a few years of classroom experience, yet more than 20 percent of new teachers leave the profession within five years. This high rate of turnover has had a destabilizing effect on schools and the profession as a whole.

To address high attrition rates, many districts have introduced induction and mentoring programs for new teachers. In addition, many states and districts are attempting to raise teacher compensation to make the profession more attractive to new workers and experienced educators. Experiments with such practices as forgiving student loans for future teachers have not been widespread but have demonstrated some success as an incentive to attract potential teachers.

Another way that states and districts have sought to improve teacher quality is by establishing stronger minimum requirements for initial licensure. Part of this approach has included increasing student teaching experience for prospective teachers and requiring the passage of professional exams. As of 2009, 41 states required prospective teachers to pass a basic skills test, and many others required candidates to master a test of subject knowledge and/ or pass a subject-specific pedagogy exam in order to be able to teach.

Among all the teacher-quality reforms, none is more controversial within the education community than alternative certification, which allows teachers into the classroom without the traditional teacher training usually required. Proponents of alternative certification explain that Albert Einstein would not have been able to teach a high school physics class in a U.S. public school because he had not completed the pedagogical coursework required by state certification agencies. This mindset, they assert, is not only foolish but also a luxury that schools cannot afford, particularly in light of an anticipated teacher shortage that, according to a 2009 study by the National Commission on Teaching and America's Future, will claim more than a third of the nation's 3.2 million teachers.

One program leading the way in alternative certification has been Teach For America (TFA). Founded in 1990 by recent Princeton graduate Wendy Kopp and based on the Peace Corps model, TFA is a national corps of recent college graduates from a variety of academic backgrounds who commit to two years of teaching in public schools in low-income communities struggling with persistent teaching shortages. TFA, a largely privately supported organization, narrowly survived fiscal crises in the mid 1990s and as of 2009 had placed more than 24,000 teachers in U.S. classrooms where they have taught more than 3 million students.

The federal government has also become more vocal in advocating alternative certification programs as well as speaking out in favor of a de-emphasis on pedagogy in traditional teacher training programs. Commenting on his 2002 *Annual Report on Teacher Quality*, Secretary of Education Rod Paige stated:

Many schools of education have continued business as usual, focusing heavily on pedagogy . . . when the evidence cries out that what future teachers need most is a deeper understanding of the subject of the teaching, of how to monitor student progress, and how to help students who are falling behind.

The report also complained that while 45 states had set up alternative routes into the profession, many did not allow prospective teachers to skip "burdensome" education courses or student teaching, leading Paige to insist that "we must tear down barriers preventing talented men and women from entering the teaching profession."

Representatives of teachers and teacher preparation programs took exception to the secretary's comments, claiming that his plans would lower the quality of teachers without addressing the root causes of existing teacher shortages, such as inadequate salaries and unappealing working conditions. The NEA's former director of teacher quality, Gayla Hudson, said, in 2002 "We see this as an insult to the teaching profession. . . . we have a nursing shortage, and nowhere is there any recommendation for six week courses for nurses."[43]

Despite such disenchantment among prominent education leaders, similar rhetoric continued into the administration of President Barack Obama. In October 2009, Secretary of Education Arne Duncan addressed an audience at the prestigious Teachers College at Columbia University and said, "By almost any standard, many if not most of the nation's 1,450 schools, colleges and departments of education are doing a mediocre job of preparing teachers for the realities of the 21st century classroom." Duncan conceded that concern over the quality of teacher training programs has existed for decades but stressed that the federal government now has more power to effect improvement, primarily through economic stimulus funding of more than $4 billion. These funds will be applied in competitive innovation grants and other programs, such as one that seeks to establish longer periods for training teachers, similar to medical residency programs.

SCHOOL FINANCING

It is often said that schools would function more effectively and improve more consistently if only they had access to more money. This common notion has led to a recent emphasis in the education reform field of school financing.

The manner in which school budgets are financed varies from state to state. Although the federal government has had an increasingly influential role in public schools over the past 40 years, it accounts for less than 10 percent of the more than $500 billion spent on public schools annually.

States generally use a combination of income taxes, corporate taxes, sales taxes, and fees to provide about half of public schools' budgets. Local districts typically contribute 40 to 55 percent, drawn mostly from local property taxes, and the remaining portion of the budget comes from the federal government. However, every state creates school budgets slightly differently, and the amount of funding tends to vary dramatically, depending on fluctuating property values.

Critics of the commonly applied property tax–based system of school financing argue that it is inherently inequitable, saddling the poorest areas with the fewest financial resources. Supporters contend that it is fair, as wealthier residents pay more for higher-quality public schools and that even in states with the greatest funding gaps the difference accounts for only about a $10 a day difference in per-pupil spending.

However, attacks on the funding gap are accelerating. One recent example is the settlement by California in the 2004 case *Williams v. State of California*. In this case, the plaintiffs cited the deplorable conditions in school districts across the state and asked the court to require the state to ensure the provision of certain educational basics such as qualified teachers, safe facilities, and textbooks. Rather than go to trial, the state of California agreed to create new standards for measuring whether schools have the basic conditions students need to learn, such as textbooks, well-trained teachers, and clean and safe school facilities, and consented to accountability measures to show how well schools are meeting these standards.

Related to the reform of school financing is the issue of school construction. This is the focus of many educational reformers because of the burden shouldered by local districts to pay for repairs to and construction of school buildings, particularly in this era of rising student enrollment.

Advocates in this discussion often argue for a greater state role in contributing to much-needed repairs and construction of schools. They point to a 2000 NEA report placing a whopping $268 billion price tag on the cost of needed school repairs and construction. In the mid- to late 1990s, the number of bills passed by state legislatures increased significantly as did the number of states making meaningful changes to their school construction financing system toward equalized funding, though progress in this area was stalled by weakened economic conditions across the United States in recent years.

SCHOOL ENVIRONMENT

A great deal of recent education reform activity has focused on factors affecting the culture of learning. In an effort to create schools in which students' academic, emotional, and social needs are respected and nurtured, many policies have been implemented to reduce class size and ensure safety.

Introduction to Education Reform

Class-size Reduction

In recent years, reducing class size has become a leading school improvement strategy. More than 40 states now have class-size reduction initiatives in place. The reasoning behind such initiatives is rather direct: With fewer students, teachers will be able to provide each of them with more individual attention that will result in greater interest in achievement in school.

Class-size reduction has a wide range of supporters including teachers' unions and the federal government, which in 2000 created a federal class-size reduction program, giving states funding to recruit, hire, and train new teachers. Under the No Child Left Behind Act of 2001, that program was consolidated into a more general teacher-quality block grant program funded by almost $3 billion for 2002.

Research has tended to find consistent benefits of small class size, particularly for students living in poverty. However, reducing class size is more expensive than many other school improvement ideas. Another concern is that, with many districts already facing shortages of qualified teachers, the additional classes created will be filled by unprepared teachers.

Such a situation was experienced in California following its class-size reduction initiative, which began in 1996. In the first year of implementation, more than 20 percent of the new teachers hired in that state had only emergency credentials. Hit especially hard were schools serving predominantly poor and minority students. To further complicate matters, the ensuing search for new instructional space led administrators to carve classrooms out of closets and to erect portable classrooms on playgrounds.

California's experience has led some researchers to investigate other potentially more cost-effective strategies, such as improved professional development for teachers. Such research became even more important in the context of the economic downturn of much of the early 21st century, which led several districts facing budget shortfalls to consider eliminating part or all of these programs. Although the No Child Left Behind legislation has been in place for several years, data to indicate its effects have only recently been produced, and the continuing controversy over the law's benefit suggests that it is far from conclusive.

School Safety Policies

Another set of reforms intended to improve the school environment has focused on ensuring students' protection from violence and threats of violence. Installing metal detectors, practicing hostage drills, and conducting anger management training were certainly not imagined by Horace Mann or John Dewey when they helped build the U.S. public school system, but they are often a reality in the public schools of today.

Education Reform

The tragic rash of school shootings across the United States during the 1990s led to a public perception that school violence was on the rise. An April 2000 Gallup poll found 63 percent of parents with children in school believing that it was very likely or somewhat likely that a Columbine-style shooting could occur in their community. Although studies by the U.S. Departments of Education and Justice indicated that overall violent crime rates in schools had actually dropped throughout the 1990s from their peak in 1993, many schools and districts added policies designed to ensure students' safety.

Among these measures are zero-tolerance policies for students who engage in violent acts, students found with weapons on school grounds, or students who have made threats of violence against teachers or other students. Supporters of such policies appreciate the straight, no-nonsense approach that conveys the seriousness of infractions. However, several cases of zero-tolerance policy implementation have struck many in the public as clearly running counter to common sense.

An example is a 2002 Texas case in which a 16-year-old honors student with no disciplinary record was found with a bread knife in the back of his truck. His explanation that it belonged to his grandmother and must have fallen out when he was transporting boxes for her was vouched for by his parents and believed by school administrators. Nevertheless, under the zero-tolerance policy, the student was expelled for one year and ordered to attend a juvenile education program for one year. Although the student's penalty was later reduced to a five-day suspension, the case illustrated the complex intersection of confusing legal mandates, fear of liability, and fair and effective means of protecting students.[44]

Many educators, administrators, and students feel that preventive measures can be effective in creating a healthier learning environment. Among the methods often implemented are service learning and character education curriculum, conflict resolution programs, and other support systems that seek to address the root causes of school violence including student isolation, disengagement from learning, and home stress.

A highly publicized approach to create secure and orderly learning environments centers on the implementation of dress codes, often requiring school uniforms. In 1996, President Bill Clinton endorsed the idea in his State of the Union address, and the popularity of such policies jumped. School uniforms appeal to many because they bring to mind visions of more orderly public schools of the past, and in areas of high gang activity, they may help avoid conflicts that arise over opposing colors or symbols. School uniform advocates cite reports from Long Beach, California, the first large urban school district in the nation to institute a mandatory uniform policy. Studies there indicate that between 1994, when uniforms were first required for all students up to ninth grade, and 1998, there was a significant drop in school crime, assaults committed on school property, and incidents of school vandalism, and a surge in average attendance to an all-time district high.

Critics decry the way that school uniform policies repress freedom of expression and dispute data, including findings from studies of Long Beach's policy in the 1990s, linking these policies to a reduction in school violence. They claim that such data are overblown in significance and may be the result of many other factors. Although many schools and districts maintain a school uniform policy, the focus on the implementation of such policies has declined significantly in recent years.

THE FUTURE OF EDUCATION REFORM

The dominating force in education reform during the first decade of the 21st century, the No Child Left Behind Act, has attracted much praise, intense criticism, and the near-constant attention of teachers, administrators, and educational policy makers. Because it directly and indirectly affects almost every aspect of elementary and secondary education in the United States, it remains poised to continue its central role in education reform in the near, and perhaps distant, future.

The ultimate fate and legacy of No Child Left Behind will likely be determined by how the following critical areas of controversy are addressed:

- **Standards:** Are the 50 states, each of which devises its own annual tests and curriculum standards, setting the bar at the appropriate level for students, and if not, what should be done about it?
- **Accountability:** Is adequate yearly progress (AYP) a fair criteria to measure learning and raise academic achievement in schools, districts, and states?
- **Curriculum:** Is the curricular focus on reading and math distorting and narrowing education at the expense of other subjects, such as history, technology, and the arts?
- **Improving Failing Schools:** Are the directives aimed at failing schools having the intended impact? What is the right role for local, state, and the federal government in fixing bad schools?

STANDARDS

In a 2009 article in *Time* magazine, journalist, author, and education reform advocate Walter Isaacson described the possibility of national standards as "the third rail of education politics." Isaacson explained the political dynamic and its damaging effects by noting, "The right chokes on the word *national,* with its implication that the feds will trample on the states' traditional authority over public schools. And the left chokes on the word *standards,* with the intimations of assessments and testing that accompany it. The result is a K–12 education system in the U.S. that is burdened by an incoherent jumble of state and local curriculum standards, assessment tools, tests, texts and teaching materials."[45]

He and many other education reform leaders advocate the creation of such national standards to avoid what is widely considered a confusing and often debilitating muddle of standards that stymie teachers, students, parents, and administrators. In 2009, newly appointed U.S. secretary of education Arne Duncan echoed this sentiment, saying, "If we accomplish one thing in the coming years, it should be to eliminate the extreme variation in standards across America. I know that talking about standards can make people nervous, but the notion that we have 50 different goalposts is absolutely ridiculous."

One of the key tools Duncan and the administration of President Barack Obama have at their disposal to meet this goal is more than $4 billion in "Race to the Top" funding from the 2009 economic stimulus package. This "Race to the Top" money will be distributed on a competitive basis to states that create programs designed to make "dramatic progress" in education, including improving standards. According to provisions of the legislation, states that fail to give assurances that they will improve standards risk losing education funding from other parts of the stimulus bill.

Despite such incentives and significant support, actually constructing such national standards remains a formidable challenge, both politically and practically. Congress is not inclined to take on this challenge, nor is there much desire for Congress to do so. Instead, bipartisan groups of policy makers, mainly governors and other state education officials, are working with universities and education organizations to advance the cause and creation of national standards. This expressed priority of the Obama administration will be among the most important and closely watched developments in education reform and could play a decisive role in other plans envisioned to improve American schools.

While it remains to be seen whether the United States will join most other leading nations by creating a series of national standards, states are responsible for setting standards for their students. Supporters of this practice praise how the standards evolve from the unique perspectives and needs of the state's people, but critics have charged that these standards lead to distorted information and undesirable outcomes.

A study by the nonprofit Thomas B. Fordham Foundation found that between 2000 and 2006, the quality and rigor of educational standards declined in 30 states, and 37 states received a grade of C- or lower, with only three states earning an A. No Child Left Behind requires all of a state's students (with the exception of approximately 3 percent with special issues) to be proficient in reading and math by 2014. Disturbingly, four states expected to reach this requirement were among those with declining standards.[46] Critics have accused states of watering down standards in order to meet No Child Left Behind mandates—of engaging in a "race to the bottom." How this problematic aspect of standards and No Child Left Behind compliance is resolved is also likely to attract a great deal of attention from education reform advocates.

ACCOUNTABILITY

Another No Child Left Behind cornerstone nearly certain to remain a center of attention in the future is its provision that schools demonstrate adequate yearly progress (AYP) in order to avoid penalties. Supporters of AYP laud its demanding and clear expectation of success, while its opponents contend that it is too inflexible, arbitrary, and punitive.

Among the most criticized aspects of AYP is that students and schools can be labeled as failing even if they are making significant improvement in assessed areas. This is a complaint particularly among leaders and teachers in schools that serve students from the most impoverished neighborhoods. Since passage of No Child Left Behind, there have been several examples of schools that have made huge strides in AYP categories but remained on the "needs improvement" list and therefore were required to provide help for students who desired a transfer.

The emphasis on AYP also has led to a great deal of disenchantment at wealthier and relatively high-achieving schools. Because AYP focuses on students who are just above or just below grade-level proficiency, many top students find that they are lacking in attention and programs to challenge them. In addition, many parents, particularly those of the children as young as seven who are taking the high-stakes assessments that determine AYP, are concerned that their children are prematurely exposed to the pressurized approach of testing and that this developmentally inappropriate emphasis on achievement adversely affects their love of learning at a critical time. Some, such as Washington, D.C., superintendent of schools, Michelle Rhee, dismiss that concern, explaining, "People say, 'Well, you know, test scores don't take into account creativity and the love of learning. . . . Creativity is good and whatever. But if the children don't know how to read, I don't care how creative you are. You are not doing your job."[47]

Although AYP remains a solid part of No Child Left Behind, many education practitioners hope that it will become more flexible and move toward what some have described as a "growth model." With a growth model, students and schools would have an incentive to demonstrate steady growth rather than to meet specific—and, many contend, unrealistic—benchmarks.

CURRICULUM

A consistent concern regarding No Child Left Behind legislation, even among its proponents, is its strong emphasis on reading and math. Studies conducted since the passage of No Child Left Behind show a marked and continuing drop in the amount of time dedicated to subjects such as history, science, physical education, and the arts as schools and teachers devote more time and resources to the subjects that will determine whether they are in compliance with No Child Left Behind mandates. Among these studies is a 2007 Center on Education Policy survey of 300 school districts, in which 71 percent of local administrators admitted that reading and math were broadening their already leading instructional time at the expense of other subjects.[48] A common practice, praised by some pedagogic leaders for its creativity and adaptability if not for its effectiveness, has been to incorporate history and science into reading and math activities.

A related concern is that No Child Left Behind is causing pressured instructors to "teach to the test," focusing only on topics and skills likely to be covered on high-stakes assessments, rather than exposing their students to important information and developing much-needed thinking skills. Just as these practices have increased in the No Child Left Behind era, their future will likely be determined by the status of the requirements included in the law.

IMPROVING FAILING SCHOOLS

Although No Child Left Behind supporters point to several studies indicating meaningful academic gains, they typically concede that many of the law's interventions have not gained sufficient traction. Specifically, provisions allowing students to transfer from schools that do not meet AYP measures two years in a row and requiring funded tutoring services for students who request it in schools that fail to meet AYP for three consecutive years have often gone ignored or—even worse, claim critics—simply have not been funded. By 2005, approximately 20 percent of students eligible for tutoring took advantage of it and only about 1 percent of eligible students transferred schools. In some cases parents are not aware of these options, and in other cases they simply choose not to transfer their students because the other options within their district are also failing schools. These interventions, as well as the most severe of reconstitution for schools failing to make AYP for five consecutive years, are ambitious but expensive. For such measures to work in the future, they will need to be effectively administered and sufficiently funded.

One aspect of school improvement that has enjoyed broader support and steadier success has been charter schools. The growth of charter schools is perhaps the most prominent development in education reform since the publication of *A Nation At Risk*. Evidence of their influence can be seen in the almost universal agreement among national political leaders of their efficacy as well as a review of their numbers. Since the 1999–2000 school year, when there were just under 1,300 charter schools in the United States, there has been a nearly 400 percent increase to a total of more than 5,000 in the 2009–10 school year.[49] Most of this growth occurred during the administration of Republican president George W. Bush, but it has continued into the presidency of Democrat Barack Obama, whose choice for secretary of education, Arne Duncan, was a strong booster of charter schools while CEO of the Chicago Public Schools.

Another enduring education reform that is showing signs of continued vitality is the expansion of power wielded by big city school leaders who have been handpicked by mayors. Joel Klein has been enormously influential in advancing vast reforms in New York City. In Chicago, Paul Vallas ushered in a major reform, which several other cities emulated, before he moved on to lead the school systems in Philadelphia and New Orleans. In June 2007, Michelle Rhee was appointed by Washington, D.C.'s mayor to lead that city's troubled school system, even though she had never headed a district or even served as a principal.

Rhee, a Teach For America alumnus who had taught in inner-city Baltimore, has garnered much praise and criticism for her bold style, particularly relating to her purge of many teachers and administrators considered substandard or incompetent. She has sought to fight tenure rules allowing teachers to hold their positions regardless of the performance of their students and has worked to implement merit pay provisions based on student achievement. Rhee and others leading school districts large and small will likely play a critical role in determining the future course of improving failing schools in particular and in molding the shape of education reform in general.

Other important historical and recent issues in education reform, such as vouchers, privatization, homeschooling, school financing, bilingual instruction, and efforts to improve the school environment, continue to push forward, though the powerful scope of No Child Left Behind has diminished their prominence. However, as the history of education reform in the United States has repeatedly proven, issues and movements tend to ebb and flow, and each of these issues has strong advocates still working to support them in the public and policy spheres.

In fact, as the question at the beginning of this book suggests, the most certain prediction about education reform's future is that there will be steady and spirited concern and debate, and often action. All of it will focus, as it always has, on strengthening the ability of bright American children to grow into productive American adults capable of advancing their nation for the next generation.

1 L. Dean Webb, Arlene Metha, and K. Forbis Jordan. *Foundations of American Education*. Upper Saddle River, N.J.: Merrill, 2000, p. 147.

2 Sir William Berkeley, quoted in John D. Pulliam and James Van Patten. *History of Education in America*. Englewood Cliffs, N.J.: Prentice Hall, 1995, p. 24.

3 Pulliam and Van Patten. *History of Education in America*, p. 28.

4 Pulliam and Van Patten. *History of Education in America*, p. 31.

5 Webb, Metha, and Jordan. *Foundations of American Education*, p. 181.

6 Pulliam and Van Patten. *History of Education in America*, p. 52.

7 Diane Ravitch. *Left Back: A Century of Battle over School Reform*. New York: Simon & Schuster, 2000, p. 41.

8 Pulliam and Van Patten. *History of Education in America*, p. 99.

9 Henry Barnard, quoted in Webb, Metha, and Jordan. *Foundations of American Education*, p. 167.

10 John Dewey, quoted in Ravitch. *Left Back: A Century of Battle over School Reform*, p. 57.

11 Webb, Metha, and Jordan. *Foundations of American Education*, p. 209.

12 Ravitch. *Left Back: A Century of Battle over School Reform*, p. 60.

13 Theodore Roosevelt, quoted in Ravitch. *Left Back: A Century of Battle over School Reform*, p. 79.

14 See Appendix A for extract from the CRSE's *The Cardinal Principles of Secondary Education*.

15 William Bagley, quoted in Ravitch. *Left Back: A Century of Battle over School Reform*, p. 147.

16 Ravitch. *Left Back: A Century of Battle over School Reform*, p. 239.

17 Webb, Metha, and Jordan. *Foundations of American Education*, p. 211.

18 *Time*, January 21, 1938, quoted in Ravitch. *Left Back: A Century of Battle over School Reform*, p. 237.

19 Tom Lehrer, quoted in *That Was the Year That Was*, Reprise Records (1965).

20 Hyman Rickover, quoted in Ravitch. *Left Back: A Century of Battle over School Reform*, p. 362.

21 Ravitch. *Left Back: A Century of Battle over School Reform*, p. 399.

22 See Appendix C for extract from *A Nation At Risk*.

23 See Chapter 8 for contact information about the Coalition of Essential Schools.

24 E. D. Hirsch, quoted in Ravitch. *Left Back: A Century of Battle over School Reform*, p. 419.

25 Ravitch. *Left Back: A Century of Battle over School Reform*, p. 434.

26 Richard Riley, quoted in Ravitch. *Left Back: A Century of Battle over School Reform*, p. 435.

27 Ulysses Grant, quoted in "School: The Story of American Public Education." Available online. URL: http://www.pbs.org/kcet/publicschool/roots_in_history/choice.html.

28 Austin Cline. "Supreme Court Decisions on Religious Liberty." Available online. URL: http://atheism.about.com/library/decisions/religion/bl_l_MuellerAllen.htm.

29 Lynn Olson. "Redefining 'Public' Schools." *Education Week*, April 26, 2000, p. 1.

30 Linda Jacobson. "Polls Find Growing Support for Publicly Funded Vouchers." *Education Week*, September 4, 2002, p. 7.

[31] Matthew Miller. "A Bold Experiment to Fix Public Schools." *Atlantic Monthly*, July 1999, p. 15.

[32] See Appendix F for an extract from the U.S. Supreme Court ruling of *Zelman v. Simmons-Harris.*

[33] John Gehring. "Voucher Battles Head to State Capitals." *Education Week*, July 10, 2002, p. 1.

[34] Bob Chase, quoted in "Statement of Bob Chase, President of the National Education Association on the U.S. Supreme Court Decision on Private School Tuition Vouchers." June 27, 2002. Available online. URL: http://www.nea.org/nr/nr020627.html.

[35] See Appendix E for a state charter school legislation and enrollment chart (2001).

[36] Sandra Feldman, quoted in Lynn Olson. "Redefining 'Public' Schools." *Education Week*, April 26, 2000, p. 1.

[37] Morningstar Web site. Available online. URL: http://quicktake.morningstar.com/stock/Price 2.asp?Country=USA & Symbol=EDS Downloaded May 28, 2003.

[38] Kathy Ishizuka. *The Unofficial* Guide to Homeschooling. Foster City, Calif.: IDG Books, 2000, p. 22.

[39] NEA resolution, quoted in "Homeschooling." January 15, 2003. *Education Week on the Web*. Available online. URL: http://www.edweek.com/context/topics/issuespage.cfm?id=37.

[40] See Chapter 2 for a detailed description of homeschooling state legislation.

[41] "Assessment." January 16, 2003. *Education Week on the Web*. Available online. URL: http://www.edweek.com/context/topics/issuespage.cfm?id=41.

[42] See Chapter 2 for a detailed description of the No Child Left Behind Act of 2001.

[43] Gayla Hudson, quoted in Bess Keller and Michelle Galley. "Paige Uses Report As a Rallying Cry to Fix Teacher Ed." *Education Week*, June 19, 2002, p. 25.

[44] "Violence and Safety." *Education Week on the Web*. Available online. URL: http://www.edweek.com/context/topics/issuespage.cfm?id=39.

[45] Walter Isaacson. "How to Raise Standards in American Schools." *Time*, April 27, 2009, p. 32.

[46] Michelle Rhee, quoted in Amanda Ripley. "Can She Save Our Schools?" *Time*, December 8, 2008, 36.

[47] Claudia Wallis, and Sonja Steptoe. "How to Fix No Child Left Behind." *Time*, June 4, 2007, p. 34.

[48] Kenly Walker. "Schools Boost Focus on Math and Reading." CBS News. Available online. URL: http://www.cbsnews.com/stories/2007/07/25/national/main3096192.shtml?source=RSSattr=U.S._3096192. Posted July 25, 2007.

[49] The Center for Education Reform. "Charter School Growth over Ten Years." Available online. URL: http://www.edreform.com/_upload/CER_charter-numbers.pdf. Posted November 2009. See also Appendix G, "Statistics on State Charter Enrollment and Operation."

CHAPTER 2

THE LAW AND
EDUCATION REFORM

This chapter describes federal, state, and local laws and court cases that have significantly influenced education reform. Extracts for some of these laws and court decisions appear in the appendices.

FEDERAL LEGISLATION

ELEMENTARY AND SECONDARY EDUCATION ACT OF 1965

Background

In the early 1960s, momentum increased for government programs designed to aid those who did not share in the post–World War II economic prosperity. As a result of this growing concern with poverty, the administrations of Presidents John Kennedy and Lyndon Johnson successfully supported federal legislation to subsidize low-income housing, improve access to health care, expand welfare services, and provide job training.

In his 1964 State of the Union address, President Johnson, a former teacher, announced, "This administration today, here and now, declares unconditional war on poverty in America." Central to this War on Poverty were programs specifically intended to strengthen U.S. public schools, particularly those in poor areas. Among the early measures passed during Johnson's presidency was the Economic Opportunity Act of 1964. Included in this legislation was the creation of Project Head Start, which Johnson claimed would "strike at the basic cause of poverty" by boosting the disadvantaged preschool child.

Key Aspects of Legislation

On April 11, 1965, President Johnson signed the Elementary and Secondary Education Act (ESEA) of 1965. The ESEA was the most far-reaching piece of federal education legislation in the history of the United States, providing more than $1 billion in federal funds to education.

The ESEA consisted of five major sections, or titles, which provided financial assistance for

- Title I—Local Educational Agencies to Educate Students from Low-Income Families
- Title II—School Library Resources and Instructional Material
- Title III—Supplementary Education Centers and Services
- Title IV—Educational Research and Training
- Title V—Strengthening of State Departments of Education

Among these, by far the most influential on public schools was Title I. The purpose of Title I was to give schools with the highest concentrations of poverty the funds to provide special aid for students who are not achieving well academically or who are at risk of educational failure. Title I's key provisions included an expansion of Head Start, creation of bilingual education programs, establishment of guidance and counseling programs, and a significant increase in the number and scope of reading instruction programs.

Title I has been reauthorized by Congress many times, including in 1981 when it became known as Chapter I. Since its inception, Title I and Chapter I funding has eclipsed more than $175 billion spent by the federal government in an effort to support the education of the poorest Americans.

Impact

The implementation of the ESEA was the seminal event in the history of federal involvement in education. Although the funds were largely controlled by state and local agencies, the financial resources allocated by this act and the more than two dozen other major pieces of legislation affecting education passed later in the 1960s represented a significant increase in federal involvement in public education.

In 1963–64, federal funds for elementary and secondary education schools totaled almost $900 million, and by 1968–69, that amount jumped to $3 billion. In addition, the federal government's share of the financing of education rose from 4.4 percent to 8.8 percent during that time period.

The ESEA has been consistently reauthorized by Congress, including the 1966 addition of Title VI for programs for Native American children, children of migrant workers, and the disabled and the 1968 addition of Title VII for programs addressing students with limited English-speaking ability. The Goals 2000: Educate America Act of 1994 and No Child Left Behind Act of 2001 are also reauthorizations of the original ESEA.

Education Reform

GOALS 2000: EDUCATE AMERICA ACT OF 1994

Background

Following the 1983 publication of *A Nation at Risk*, political leaders became more vocal in advocating education reform efforts. This was evident during the presidential campaign of 1988, in which Republican candidate George H. W. Bush promised that, if elected, he would be the "education president."

Soon after his inauguration in 1989, Bush organized the National Education Summit in Charlottesville, Virginia, the first-ever gathering of all 50 state governors, convening for the sole purpose of improving U.S. elementary and secondary education.

Bush articulated his vision at the summit, explaining, "From this day forward let us be an America of tougher standards, of higher goals . . . and our goals must be national, not federal." To this end, the president and the governors, led by then Arkansas governor Bill Clinton, crafted the National Education Goals.

Goal number one stated that by the year 2000, "all children in America will start school ready to learn." This emphasis on the concept of school readiness was further delineated by a 1991 National School Readiness Task Force report that highlighted the educational importance of physical health, self-confidence, and social competence, in addition to academic knowledge and skills. The report also noted the relationship between school readiness and developmentally and culturally appropriate instruction, class size, access to technology, and staff development.

Key Aspects of Legislation

The National Educational Goals established at the 1989 summit provided the framework for the GOALS 2000: Educate America Act, signed into law with broad bipartisan congressional support on March 31, 1994, by President Bill Clinton. The language of GOALS 2000 recognized that education is a state and local responsibility, but that it must also be a national priority.

GOALS 2000 encouraged states to develop challenging standards for students and provided grants for schools, communities, and states to support their own approach to student achievement. It also sought to promote flexibility by providing authority for the secretary of education to waive certain regulations to states and communities implementing school improvements.

Six original education goals were codified into law by GOALS 2000. These concerned school readiness, school completion, student academic achievement, leadership in math and science, adult literacy, and safe and drug-free schools. Two additional goals supporting teacher professional development and parental participation were included in 1996.

GOALS 2000 also established a National Education Standards and Improvement Council to examine and certify national and state content, student performance, opportunity-to-learn standards, and assessment systems voluntarily submitted by states. A National Skill Standards Board was also established to facilitate development of occupational standards. The goal of the board was to identify broad occupational clusters and standards that would lead to portable, industry-recognized credentials indicating mastery of skills in specific occupational areas.

Impact

Funding for GOALS 2000 began with $94 million in 1994 and climbed to $490 million by 1999, thanks largely to vigorous support from business and education groups. Eventually, GOALS 2000 provided $2 billion to promote standards-based reform. At first, some states declined the GOALS 2000 funding on the grounds of preserving states' rights, but within two years of its initiation 48 states accepted GOALS 2000 grants. The program would ultimately provide more than 5,000 of the nation's 15,000 school districts with grants.

Despite this significant infusion of money and effort, those hoping for a broad scope and lasting influence as a result of GOALS 2000 were largely disappointed. One key difficulty the program experienced was that most of the money was required to be spent at the district level, which led to little available funding for building state capacity to help districts in the greatest resource needs. Another problem was creating strong and sustainable support for implementation—preparing teachers to use new standards and develop instructional materials, particularly in small districts and those with high rates of poverty. Although high-poverty districts were typically aware of programs designed to support them, they often lacked personnel with the opportunity or expertise to provide technical assistance on standards-based reform. Similarly, smaller districts often were not sufficiently connected to resources of expertise that might have helped them more efficiently enact GOALS 2000 reforms.

NO CHILD LEFT BEHIND ACT OF 2001

Background

In the 2000 presidential election, the Republican candidate, Texas governor George W. Bush, touted his record as a leader able to usher in bipartisan and successful education reform laws that strengthened the academic performance of Texas schools. Three days after taking office, Bush announced the plans for the No Child Left Behind Act (NCLBA). Describing the legislation as "the cornerstone of my administration," the president noted that despite the nearly $200 billion in federal spending since the passage of the Elementary and Secondary Education Act of 1965, "too many of our neediest children are being left behind." The title of the act was taken from the slogan of the ideologically left-leaning Children's Defense Fund, but its measures were largely popular within the Republican Party, particularly provisions for accountability and choice. The bill was approved with broad bipartisan support by the Congress and was signed by President Bush less than a year after his inauguration.

Key Aspects of Legislation

Significant provisions of the NCLBA include

- **Student Assessment:** Title I assessment provisions are significantly expanded by the NCLBA. Participating states are required to implement standards-based reading and math assessments for students in each of grades 3–8 by the 2005–6 school year. In addition, states will have to develop and implement assessments at three grade levels in science by the 2007–8 school year. All states are required by the NCLBA to participate in National Assessment of Educational Progress (NAEP) reading and math tests for fourth and eighth grade, to be administered every two years, with the costs paid for by the federal government. The bill requires students who have been in U.S. schools for at least three years to be tested for reading in English, and it requires states to annually assess the English-language proficiency of their limited English proficient (LEP) students. Assessment results and other data for individual public schools, local educational agencies (LEAs) or districts, and states must be reported to parents and the public through "report cards." These report cards are to include information on student performance, broken down by race, ethnicity, gender, disability status, English proficiency, and status as economically disadvantaged.

- **Adequate Yearly Progress Requirements:** Requirements for state-developed standards of adequate yearly progress (AYP) are substantially increased under the NCLBA. These standards will be applied to all students in each public school, district, and state and will be specifically applied to students who are economically disadvantaged, LEP, and disabled. Each state must define what constitutes AYP in increasing student achievement toward the goal of all students reaching proficient levels on the state assessments by 2014. Each state must establish a "starting bar," or measuring point, for the percentage of students who must be at the proficient level, which may be based upon the lowest achieving schools or lowest achieving demographic subgroup in the state (whichever is higher). Once the starting bar and target year are set, the state must "raise the bar" in gradual but equal increments to reach 100 percent of students performing at the proficient level by the target year, which must be 2014.

- **Corrective Actions:** Schools that fail to meet AYP for two consecutive years must be identified as needing improvement. For such schools, technical assistance is to be provided and public school choice must be offered to their students by the next school year, unless prohibited by state law. Districts are generally required only to offer public school choice options within the same district. However, if all public schools in the district to which a student might transfer have been identified as needing improvement, then districts "shall, to the extent practicable," establish cooperative agreements with other districts to offer expanded public school choice options. If a school fails to meet the state AYP standard for three consecutive years, students for low-income families must be offered the opportunity to receive instruction for a supplemental services provider of their choice. States are to identify and provide lists of approved providers of such supplemental services, which may include public or private schools or commercial firms, and monitor the quality of services they provide. Schools that fail to meet AYP for four consecutive years must undergo at least one of the noted "corrective actions," including replacing school staff, implementing a new curriculum, decreasing management authority at the school level, appointing an outside expert to advise the school, extending the school day or year, or changing the internal organizational structure of the school. "Restructuring" will occur for schools that fail to meet AYP standards for five consecutive years. Such restructuring must consist of one of more of the following "alternative governance" actions: reopening as a charter school, replacing all or most school staff, or state takeover of school operations (if permitted by state law). Similar procedures are set to be applied in the NCLBA for districts that fail to meet AYP requirements.

- **Staff Qualifications:** Each state receiving Title I funds must develop a plan to ensure that all teachers teaching core academic subjects are "highly qualified" by the end of the 2005–6 school year. Teachers hired and teaching in a program supported with Title I, Part A funds had to be "highly qualified" starting the first day of the 2002–3 school year. All paraprofessionals hired and working in a program supported with Title I, Part A funds are required by the NCLBA to have completed at least two years of college or to have met a "rigorous standard of quality."

61

Education Reform

- **Flexibility Measures:** Under the NCLBA, states may transfer up to 50 percent of the funds received for state-level activities for specified Title I programs including preparing, training, and recruiting high-quality teachers and principals; technology; safe and drug-free schools; 21st-century community learning centers; and innovative programs. Districts may also transfer up to 50 percent of the funds received for local activities for specified programs. However, if a district is in school improvement, it may transfer only 30 percent of its funds, and these funds must be used for school improvement. If the district is in corrective action, it may not transfer funds.

- **Performance Bonuses and Sanctions:** The NCLBA includes provisions for the U.S. secretary of education to establish a peer review process to determine whether states are meeting their AYP standards and to report the results of this review to Congress. The Department of Education would provide technical assistance to states that fail to meet their AYP requirements for two consecutive years.

- **Voluntary School Choice Programs:** As a means of achieving education reform through school choice, states may use specified funding for the planning, design, and implementation of charter schools. Districts may use specified funding to support school choice by using it for magnet schools and for the planning, design, and implementation of charter schools. Districts may also apply specified funding to promote, implement, or expand public school choice and for supplemental educational services, including transportation supporting public school choice, tuition transfer payments, enhancements in schools receiving transfer students, and for public education campaigns about public school choice.

- **Mandatory School Choice Provisions:** Each state receiving NCLBA funding will be required to allow students who attend chronically unsafe schools and those who are victimized on the grounds of an elementary or secondary school to transfer to a safe public school.

- **Reading Initiatives:** The Reading First program (Title I, Part B) of the NCLBA provides funds to help states and districts implement comprehensive reading instruction. It replaces the Reading Excellence Act and is designed to help teachers identify students at risk of reading failure in order to provide them with effective early instruction leading to reading proficiency. Funds are allocated according to a poverty-based formula. Although states must apply to the U.S. Department of Education for funding, every state with a satisfactory application will receive a grant. States may retain up to 20 percent of their allocations to develop and implement professional development for teachers of kindergarten through third grade, provide technical assistance, administer the program, and fund eligible, alternative providers of reading instruction chosen by parents. States must use at least 80 percent of the funds to make five-year grants on a competitive basis to local school districts, with a priority to school districts with at least 15 percent of families in poverty.

Funded districts may only serve schools that have a high percentage of students in grades K–3 below the poverty line or schools that have a high percentage of students reading below grade level. Funds may be used to provide eligible services including identifying students who have difficulty with reading, providing research-based reading instruction, providing professional development for teachers, and expanding access to engaging reading material. The Reading First program is funded at $900 million, compared to $286 million for the Reading Excellence Act in the 2001–2 school year. Funds for the Early Reading First program are distributed directly to local school districts and public and private organizations that serve children aged three to five (such as Head Start and family literacy programs).

- **School Library Programs:** The NCLBA's Improving Literacy Through School Libraries program awards grants to states in order to provide students with access to up-to-date and technologically advanced school library media resources and well-trained, professionally certified school library media specialists.

- **Teacher and Principal Training and Recruiting Funding:** Title II, Part A of the NCLBA, the Teacher and Principal Training and Recruiting Fund, replaces the Eisenhower Professional Development program and the Class Size Reduction program with a new state formula grant program authorizing a broad array of teacher-related activities for states and local school districts.

Among the state activities included in the more than $3 billion appropriation for this program are supporting teacher and principal professional development, reforming teacher and principal certification requirements, assisting local districts in recruiting and retaining highly qualified teachers and principals, reforming tenure systems, helping teachers use state standards and assessments to improve instruction and student achievement, helping teachers meet certification and licensure requirements, and training educators in integrating technology into instruction. To receive these funds from the state, districts must submit a plan that addresses a range of key issues, including a description of the professional development that will be made available to teachers and principals. Districts may use funds for permitted activities, including hiring highly qualified teachers; providing professional development for teachers, principals, and paraprofessionals, including training for improving classroom behavior and teaching students with different learning styles; developing and implementing educator recruitment and retention strategies; testing teachers in their subject area; establishing partnerships with institutions of higher learning; developing teacher advancement plans to emphasize multiple career paths and pay differentiation; and establishing programs for exemplary teachers.

- **Technology Programs:** The NCLBA's Title II, Part II Enhancing Education Through Technology program consolidates several technology programs authorized under prior law. Participating states and districts must have new or updated long-range technology plans, and districts must use at least 25 percent of its funding for professional development in the integration of advanced technologies into curriculum and instruction. Other authorized activities for districts include using technology to connect schools and teachers with parents and students, preparing teachers to serve as technology leaders in their schools, and acquiring, expanding, implementing, repairing, and maintaining technology. States may use funds for such activities as supporting innovative strategies to deliver courses and curriculum through technology including distance learning and developing performance measures to determine the effectiveness of educational technology programs.

- **Safe and Drug-Free Schools and Communities:** State and local agencies are funded for programs to prevent student violence in and around schools and the illegal use of alcohol, tobacco, and drugs. Funding is available for many new purposes, including permitting states to require expelled or suspended students to perform community services during their time away from school, assisting districts to improve school security by creating a school security center, establishing school hot lines and other safety procedures, and allowing eligible groups to assist in creating and supporting mentoring programs for students in need.

- **Twenty-First-Century Community Learning Centers:** The NCLBA provides grants for districts, community-based organizations, and other public and private groups to conduct after school activities for students and their families, although activities are narrower in scope than previously permitted.

Impact

Less than 10 years after its passage, the effects of the No Child Left Behind Act are still not entirely clear, though it is certainly evident that it has had an enormous impact on the framing and nature of the education reform discussion in the United States. Proponents of the law laud several independent measures of academic improvement, particularly in the subjects of reading and math and in the schools considered the most desperate. Further, they claim, No Child Left Behind has sent a strong message to administrators, teachers, parents, and students, that success in the classroom is a meaningful priority to the federal government.

Critics, including those who generally support the law but want to see it amended, point out several shortcomings. Among the most prominent of these charges is that the federal government issued mandates to schools and then failed to sufficiently provide the funding for states to effectively implement them. Another common criticism is that No Child Left Behind required each state to ensure that its students achieve proficiency in reading and math but allowed each to define what that meant. The result was that many states made their job easier by setting the bar lower.

An often-referenced case is found in Mississippi, which has historically ranked near the very bottom in most elementary and secondary education measures. According to the standards Mississippi set for itself, 89 percent of its fourth-graders were proficient or better in reading, making them the best in the nation. Yet according to the random sampling done every few years by the National Assessment of Educational Progress (NAEP) test, a mere 18 percent of the state's fourth-graders were proficient, making them the worst in the nation.

STATE AND LOCAL LEGISLATION

CHICAGO SCHOOL REFORM ACT OF 1988 (AND AMENDMENTS OF 1995)

Background

In 1987, U.S. secretary of education William Bennett pronounced the Chicago public schools to be "the worst in the nation," and there was much evidence to support his claim. The poor performance of the Chicago public schools, including a fiscal crisis that required a financial bailout, chronically low test scores, a high dropout rate, and consistent labor strife, led a coalition of parents, activists, and business leaders to press the Illinois legislature to pass the Chicago School Reform Act of 1988. The law shifted significant powers and responsibilities from the central administration to local school communities.

Key Aspects of Legislation

Among the important provisions of the Chicago School Reform Act were

- **Creation of Local School Councils (LSCs):** LSCs consisted of the principal, six parents, two community members, two teachers, and, in high schools, one student. Responsibilities of the LSCs included writing and approving the principal's contract, evaluating the principal's performance, and helping to create the school's budget and school improvement plan.

- **Reorganization of Central Authority:** The 11-member Board of Education was abolished and replaced with a 15-member board nominated by a community-driven nominating commission and approved by the mayor.

- **Revision of Principal's Authority:** The principal became able to fill vacant educational positions with the applicant of his or her choice, regardless of seniority. The principal's authority was also extended to allow him or her to keep a set of keys to the building and reduce remediation time for unsatisfactory teachers from one year to 45 days.

- **Implementation of Accountability Procedures:** Subdistrict councils were established to propose actions to remedy low-performing schools, including drafting remediation plans and placing schools on probation.

- **Use of State Chapter I Funds:** This required the distribution of money directly to schools based on their enrollment of poor children only for programs that supplement the basic curriculum, including reduced class size, early child education, and enrichment activities

- **Expansion of School Choice:** Students were able to attend schools within the district based on a lottery admissions process, providing busing for low-income students and complying with desegregation regulations. Magnet schools were exempted from this provision.

In 1995, Democratic Chicago mayor Richard M. Daley teamed up with primarily Republican leaders in the Illinois legislature to pass many amendments to the Chicago School Reform Act of 1988. Focusing on finding an effective way to deal with chronically underperforming schools, these reforms have come to be known as "the Chicago Model" and have recently been emulated in many large cities throughout the United States. As a result of the 1995 amendments:

- The mayor was allowed to appoint a five-person Chicago School Reform Board of Trustees without needing city council approval, as well as a seven-member regular board to serve four-year overlapping terms. Together these entities would be known as the superboard. In addition, the mayor became responsible to appointing a chief executive officer (CEO) to assume the powers of the superintendent.

- The CEO was given the duty to appoint a chief operating officer, a chief financial officer, a chief purchasing officer, and a chief educational officer, with approval of the new superboard. The CEO also took over all powers of the subdistricts and subdistrict councils. These included initiating action against failing schools, breaking LSC deadlocks over principal selection, and evaluating principals in conjunction with LSCs.

- School board policies were revised to allow the hiring of outside, privatized contractors to do work currently done by board employees. Policies placing restrictions on nepotism and conflicts of interest were also adopted.

- LSCs were endowed with new powers to approve receipts and expenditures for schools' internal accounts. They also were required to undergo three days of training within six months of taking office or be removed.

- The teacher and principal dismissal process was streamlined, although principals were still required to document cases against teachers and LSCs needed to document cases against principals. Written warnings were no longer required for conduct that is "cruel, immoral, negligent, or criminal or which in any way causes psychological or physical harm or injury to a student."

- The Chicago Schools Academic Accountability Council was developed to carry out an evaluation system of schools. Intervention and reconstitution procedures for "chronically underperforming schools" were established, allowing the CEO to select a new principal to guide the school and select all staff. In addition, 5 percent of a school's Chapter I money was allocated for employee performance incentives.

- The principal gained the authority to supervise, evaluate, and otherwise discipline his or her school's maintenance and lunchroom staffs. The principal could also "determine when and what operations shall be conducted" within school hours and to schedule staff within those hours. Assistant principals were no longer allowed to be represented by the teachers' union, giving principals more freedom to select and change assistants.

- The board had more flexibility in the use of state Chapter I money, allowing the amount in the "general education" block grant to be used for "any of the board's lawful purposes."

- Regulations against corruption, waste, and financial mismanagement were expanded through the protection of whistle-blowers and the expansion of the powers of the district's inspector general.

Impact

The Chicago School Reform Act and its 1995 amendments had an enormous impact on Chicago's schools as well as on the education reform debate, particularly in big cities, throughout the country. In Chicago, the act gradually gave schools money that was previously controlled by the city schools' central administration. It also gave principals the ability to select teachers to fill vacancies rather than having them delivered by seniority and allowed them to choose their own vice principals.

These laws are also credited with ushering in new systems of school accountability. By 1996, more than 100 schools (about a fifth of Chicago's total) were put on probation for having less than 15 percent of its students scoring at or above national norms on the Iowa Test of Basic Skills (ITBS) for elementary students and Tests of Achievement and Proficiency (TAP) for high school students. Probation managers, usually former public school administrators and principals, were quickly recruited to work with these schools, and more than $20 million was paid to "outside partners," mainly university professors, to help these schools correct their problems. Reports on the effectiveness of the managers and partners vary, but in subsequent years the number of schools requiring such remediation dropped significantly.

Less than a year after announcing probation, the Reform Board of Trustees added the procedure of reconstitution for the schools deemed to be the most egregious failures. In some cases, reconstitution involved removing principals and teachers and reorganizing the entire structure of the school. In addition, a promotion policy was instituted requiring students in third, sixth, eighth, and ninth grades to hit test-score targets in reading and math in order to advance to the next grade. This stance against the policy of social promotion has also included sending failure warning notices to parents and requiring summer school for low-achieving students, including first graders who lag behind. Although debate and research disagree about the cause-effect relationship of these reforms, test scores in the Chicago public schools have risen steadily since the implementation of the act, particularly in elementary schools (24 percent in 1989, to 34 percent in 2000, to 67 percent in 2008 meeting or exceeding state standards in reading; 28 percent in 1989, to 44 percent in 2000, to 71 percent in 2008 meeting or exceeding state standards in math).

Nationally, the Chicago School Reform Act and its amendments have been influential in framing discussion of education reform issues, particularly social promotion, school accountability, and local control. Similar reform laws, investing primary power over public schools to the mayor, have since been implemented in Boston, Detroit, Cleveland, New York City, and Washington, D.C., and are being seriously considered in many other cities.

MILWAUKEE PARENTAL CHOICE PROGRAM (1990)

Background

Frustration with the struggling condition of Milwaukee's public schools led Republican Wisconsin governor Tommy Thompson and the Democratic-controlled state legislature to enact the Milwaukee Parental Choice Program (MPCP) in 1990. The program allowed a maximum of 1 percent of the Milwaukee public schools' enrollment—about 1,000 students—to attend religious schools. The cap was raised to 1.5 percent in 1993. In response to growing program support, the Wisconsin legislature and governor raised the cap to 15 percent and allowed low-income parents to choose among religious and nonreligious schools.

Opponents of the MPCP have twice challenged the constitutionality of the law and have failed both times. During the three-year challenge to the 1995 amendments to the law, the Wisconsin Supreme Court delayed the participation of religious schools in the program but ultimately upheld its constitutionality in 1998. In November 1998, the U.S. Supreme Court declined to hear an appeal of the Wisconsin Supreme Court's 1998 decision, and the expanded program was allowed to continue.

Key Aspects of Legislation

The MPCP legislation includes specific descriptions of key participation factors, including

- **Student Eligibility:** A student qualifies for the MPCP on the basis of his or her residency in the city of Milwaukee, household income, and where and if the child was enrolled in school in the prior school year. For the 2002–3 school year, the child's household income had to be at or below the specified amounts of $26,140 for a household of three and $36,932 for a household of five. Additionally, in the prior school year the child must have been enrolled in the Milwaukee public schools; participated in the MPCP; enrolled in kindergarten or first, second, or third grade in a private school in Milwaukee but not in the choice program; or not enrolled in school anywhere.
- **Admissions Procedures:** A parent or guardian must fill out a MPCP student application form and submit it to the school during the open application period(s) for the program. Parents will have to prove the child's residency in Milwaukee and their income status. Choice schools must inform parents how many choice program slots are open by grade level; the date, if necessary, of a lottery to select choice students if more applications are received than there are choice slots available; and within 60 days of receiving the student's completed application, whether the child has been accepted into the choice program.
- **Related Fees:** The private school cannot charge MPCP students tuition for instructional purposes. A student in the program can be charged reasonable fees for personal items such as gym clothes or uniforms, or social and extracurricular activities if the activity is not a part of the required curriculum.

- **Receipt of State Aid Payments:** The state issues checks payable to the parent or guardian of an MPCP student and sends the checks to the school where the child is enrolled four times a year. The parent or guardian must sign the checks over to the school and cannot cash the checks.

- **Aid-Per-Student Provisions:** In the 2002–03 school year, the state aid for a student enrolled full-time in the choice program at a particular school (defined as enrolled in the choice program on both the third Friday in September and the second Friday in January) is estimated to be $5,785 or the private school's operating and debt service cost per student, whichever is less.

- **Requirements Regarding Religious Participation:** If a choice student's parent or guardian submits to the student's teacher or the school's principal a written request that the student be excused from any religious activity, the teacher and school must honor that request.

- **Special Needs Services:** A private school may not discriminate against a child with special educational needs in the admission process for the program. However, as a private school, an MPCP school is required to offer only those services to assist students with special needs that it can provide with minor adjustments.

- **Student Suspensions and Expulsion:** State law does not require private MPCP schools to have any procedures in place regarding student suspensions or expulsions. Milwaukee public schools involved in the program must abide by a state law that describes actions punishable by suspension or expulsion and allows a pupil or the parent or guardian to appeal a suspension to the school administrator. These expulsions are determined by the school board and may be appealed to the state superintendent and circuit court. Private schools are not required to have such procedures in place.

Impact

The MPCP has been watched more closely and for a longer period of time than any other voucher program in the United States. Its leadership and survival have encouraged choice advocates across the country and spurred calls of inequity and inefficiency from opponents.

Studies by Wisconsin's Legislative Audit Bureau as well as research by Harvard and Princeton Universities have found some statistical support that the reforms brought on by the program may be positively influencing academic achievement. Fourth graders scoring at or above proficiency on the Wisconsin Knowledge and Concept Examination have increased in all core academic areas, and high school students have either demonstrated gains or smaller decreases than usually seen on standardized exams in reading and math. However, the cause-effect relationship of such results is a complex one and should not be solely attributed to individual factors such as the voucher program.

The law's impact has been clearly evident where Milwaukee's students have attended school. In 1990–91, the first year of the program, only seven schools and 341 schools participated. That number stayed relatively steady until the 1997–98 school year when 235 schools and 1,545 students took part. Following the Wisconsin Supreme Court decision allowing expansion of the MPCP, 86 schools and more than 6,000 students participated. Those figures grew to 106 schools and 10,882 students for the 2001–02 school year. For that year, 34 percent of the program's students attended nonreligious schools, and 66 percent were enrolled in religious schools. By mid-September of the 2009–10 school year, total enrollment in MPCP grew to more than 21,000 students.

FLORIDA A+ PLAN FOR EDUCATION (1999)

Background

Education reform as a political issue, increasingly prominent on the federal level, over the past 20 years has been even more salient on the state and local level due to the nature of funding and history of U.S. public schools. Evidence of this is seen with the evolution of the A+ Plan for Education. In 1998, Republican candidate for Florida governor, Jeb Bush, proposed the A+ Plan to be the nation's first statewide school voucher program. Bush was elected and signed the bill into law on June 25, 1999.

The A+ Plan survived the near-immediate legal challenges that followed its passage. In October 2000, the First District Court of Appeals for Florida declared the plan constitutional, and in April 2002 the Florida Supreme Court declined to review that decision. However, on August 6, 2002, a circuit court judge in Florida ruled that the A+ program's provision that allows students in failing schools to get scholarships to move into other schools, including private and religious institutions, violates the religious Establishment Clause of the state's constitution. In 2006, the Florida Supreme Court upheld that decision and struck down the A+ Plan.

Key Aspects of Legislation

Florida's A+ Plan included many measures designed to improve the academic achievement of the state's students and schools. Among the law's provisions were a revision of the state curriculum standards; expansion of student assessment requirements, including the administration of the Florida Comprehensive Achievement Test annually from third to 10th grade;

and expanded funding for school safety enhancements, truancy reduction, and teacher training and recruitment initiatives. Funding was also provided to districts for the elimination of social promotion through summer school programs, after school instruction, tutoring, mentoring, and extended-day programs.

However, the most influential and controversial measures revolved around the A+ Plan's requirement that all schools receive a report card detailing how well they perform. This report card, featuring a letter grade, provided the foundation for such measures as incentives for school achievement and improvement and to the provisions of Opportunity Scholarships.

The incentives featured financial rewards of up to $100 per student for schools that received an "A" and those that improved at least one grade based on student achievement and dropout rate. Under the plan, the highest-performing and improving schools also were deregulated and encouraged to manage their own budgets and use innovative strategies to continue their improvement.

Opportunity Scholarships were provided for students at failing schools. Under the A+ Plan, a school receiving an "F" was given two years to improve, during which time it would receive assistance from the school district and state Department of Education. If a school failed to improve beyond an "F" in the second year, parents had an opportunity to send their children to any public or private school with a state rating of "C" or better within or adjacent to their home district.

The amount of the voucher was based on the local district's per-pupil cost or the private school's tuition, whichever was less. Selection of eligible transfer students needed to be random, though the siblings of students already enrolled were given preference. Participating private schools needed to be in compliance with specified civil rights laws and health and safety codes and were required to demonstrate fiscal soundness. Transportation for students who attended another public school inside their district could use the transportation provided by local school districts, but parents choosing to use an Opportunity Scholarship to send their child to a private school would have to make their own arrangements. Participating private schools were required to administer the standardized tests given in public schools and report the results to the state.

Students with learning disabilities were also covered in A+ legislation under the McKay Scholarship, named for Republican state senator John McKay, who sponsored the legislation. With a McKay Scholarship, any parent of a learning-disabled student who was dissatisfied with the progress his or her child was making in a public school could transfer the child to a participating program school.

Another closely watched, hotly debated provision of the A+ program was its plan allowing corporations to donate up to 75 percent of what they would pay in state taxes to fund low-income public school students to transfer to private schools.

Impact

Because of the A+ Plan's Opportunity Scholarships, Florida took the lead in state efforts to advance school vouchers. The state paid the private school tuition of more than 25,000 students, which far outnumbered the combined amount of students enrolled in the highly publicized Cleveland and Milwaukee voucher programs.

The newest of the A+ provisions, the corporate tax program for school vouchers, attracted enormous interest from Floridians. Under the program, students qualifying for free and reduced-price lunches could receive up to $4,500 for private school tuition. Its first-year capacity of 15,000 students was reached quickly, with more than 25,000 eligible applications rejected because the program selected students on a first-come first-served basis.

The establishment of the Opportunity Scholarship program and of the publication of many reports lauding its positive effects led state legislators in Illinois, California, Texas, and elsewhere to begin exploring limited or statewide voucher programs. The program continued while voucher proponents appealed for the trial court's ruling that vouchers for private or religious schools violate the state's constitution. The Florida Supreme Court reviewed this decision in 2006 and ruled that it violated the states constitution. Its ultimate demise played a significant role in slowing momentum for choice programs in other states.

ARIZONA CHARTER SCHOOL LAW (1994)

Background

The charter school movement traces its roots to a number of other reform ideas, from alternative schools, site-based management, and magnet schools to public school choice, privatization, and community-parental empowerment.

The term *charter* may have originated in the 1970s when New England educator Ray Budde suggested that small groups of teachers be given contracts, or "charters," by their local school boards to explore new approaches. Albert Shanker, a former president of the American Federation of Teachers, then publicized the idea, suggesting that local boards could charter an entire school with union and teacher approval.

In 1991, Minnesota passed the first charter-school law based on three basic values: opportunity, choice, and responsibility for results, with California following suit in 1992. By 1995, 19 states had signed laws allowing for the creation of charter schools, and by 1999, that number increased to 36 states, Puerto Rico, and the District of Columbia. Charter schools are one of the fastest-growing innovations in education policy, enjoying broad bipartisan support from governors, state legislators, and past and present secretaries of education. President Bill Clinton also supported them, calling in his 1997 State of the Union address for the creation of 3,000 charter schools by the year 2000 and delivering remarks for the 1999 Charter Schools National Conference.

Since 1994, the U.S. Department of Education has provided grants to support states' charter school efforts, from $6 million in fiscal year 1995, to almost $100 million in fiscal year 1999. President George W. Bush requested and received approval for $200 million for the creation of almost 2,000 new charter schools in fiscal year 2003. By 2010, federal funding for charter schools had grown to $256 million.

The Arizona state legislature passed the Charter School Law on September 16, 1994. This legislation was among the earliest state charter laws and is often recognized as the strongest in the nation.

Key Aspects of Legislation

The Arizona Charter School Law is the blueprint by which all charter schools in the state operate, regardless of their sponsorship. Major provisions of the bill address the purpose of charter schools, application and maintenance requirements, academic policies, financial procedures, and employment regulations.

- **Purpose:** The expressed goal of Arizona's charter school legislation is to "provide additional academic choices for parents and pupils" through the establishment of "public schools that serve as alternatives to traditional public schools." A charter school in Arizona may consist of a new school or any portion of an existing school.

- **Application and Maintenance Requirements:** Under Arizona's charter school law, there are three types of boards that may sponsor a charter school, including the state board of education, the state board for charter schools, and any local school district governing board.
  The Board for Charter Schools consists of the following members:

  1. The superintendent of public instruction or the superintendent's designee.
  2. Six members of the general public, at least two of whom shall reside in a school district where at least sixty percent of the children who attend school in the district meet the eligibility requirements established under the national school lunch and child nutrition acts . . . for free lunches, who are appointed by the governor . . .

3. Two members of the business community who are appointed by the governor . . .

4. Three members of the legislature who shall serve as advisory members and who are appointed jointly by the president of the senate and the speaker of the house of representatives.

There is no restriction on the number of charters any of these three entities may sponsor, although since July 1, 2000, school districts may only sponsor schools located within the geographic boundaries of the district. The initial charters that are granted run for 15 years and must be reviewed by the sponsoring body every five years.

Application eligibility for potential sponsors is very open under Arizona's charter school legislation. Existing public and private schools may submit proposals. However, private schools must agree to the laws that govern charter schools in the state, including having a nonselective and nondiscriminatory admission policy as well as rules prohibiting the charging of tuition. A religious organization may organize a charter school, although the school charter must ensure that the school is "non-sectarian in its programs, admission policies, and employment practices and all other operations."

Once granted a charter, new charter school operators are required to hold a public meeting at least 30 days prior to opening, posting notices of the meeting in at least three different locations within 300 feet of the proposed school site.

- **Academic Policies:** Arizona's charter law addresses student admission by explaining:

> *A charter school shall enroll all eligible pupils who submit a timely application, unless the number of applications exceeds the capacity of a program, class, grade level or building. A charter school shall give enrollment preference to pupils returning to the charter school in the second or any subsequent year of its operation and to siblings of pupils already enrolled in the charter school. A charter school that is sponsored by a school district governing board shall give enrollment preference to eligible pupils who reside within the boundaries of the school district where the charter school is physically located. If capacity is insufficient to enroll all pupils who submit a timely application, the charter school shall select pupils through an equitable selection process such as a lottery except that preference shall be given to siblings of a pupil selected through an equitable selection process such as a lottery.*

Other academic policy mandates include the provision of a comprehensive program of education aligned to the Arizona Academic Standards, although such instructional programs may emphasize a particular learning philosophy, style, or subject area and the annual issuance of school report cards reflecting the academic progress of a school. A charter school may have any grade configuration as long as it provides a comprehensive program of education for at least one grade from among kindergarten through 12th grade.

- **Financial Procedures:** Charter schools in Arizona are subject to the same financial requirements as a school district, including the Uniform System of Financial Records for Charter Schools, procurement rules, and audit requirements. However, exceptions to these rules may be requested by the party applying for a charter and granted by the charter's sponsor. A school district is not financially responsible for any charter school that is sponsored by the state board of education or the state board for charter schools. Arizona's charter legislation also provides a stimulus fund providing:

  financial support to charter school applicants and charter schools for start-up costs and costs associated with renovating or remodeling existing buildings and structures. The fund consists of monies appropriated by the legislature and grants, gifts, devises and donations from any public or private source. The department of education shall administer the fund.

- **Employment Regulations:** Teachers in Arizona's charter schools do not have to be certified, although federal regulations require that special-education programs be supervised by a certified teacher. The legislation protects employment benefits of teachers through a provision stating:

  A teacher who is employed by or teaching at a charter school and who was previously employed as a teacher at a school district shall not lose any right of certification, retirement or salary status or any other benefit provided by law, by the rules of the governing board of the school district or by the rules of the board of directors of the charter school due to teaching at a charter school on the teacher's return to the school district.

Impact

The Arizona Charter School Law has served as a model for other states with far-reaching charter school legislation, including Florida and Texas. Furthermore, Arizona has more charter schools (523 as of fall 2009) than any other state and represents just over 10 percent of the national charter school enrollment, despite a population that is only 2 percent of the national total.

The state experienced some difficulties in implementing the legislation, including cases of financial misappropriation and ineffective oversight. However, Arizona boasts many other successes with its charter schools, including comparatively higher academic achievement among charter students, disproportionately high percentages of minority students, and higher pay for its teachers.

LOUISIANA RECOVERY SCHOOL DISTRICT LAW (2003)

Background

The momentum of education reform in states and local districts throughout the United States took a significant step into the South in 2002, when the Louisiana legislature overwhelmingly passed an amendment that would allow the state to take over schools that have "failed" under the state's accountability program. On November 6, 2003, that amendment was approved by Louisiana voters.

This new Louisiana Recovery School District Law provided the state with greater powers in education than it had ever previously possessed. It also represented the broader trend of increased influence of state and local educational entities over schools that had continued to struggle reaching high achievement in such areas as graduation rates and scores on standardized assessments.

Key Aspects of Legislation

The Louisiana Recovery School District Law included several key components, including provisions for memorandums of understanding, receivership, school recovery plans, and oversight and funding.

- **Memorandums of Understanding:** A key component of Louisiana's Recovery School District Law is the establishment of memorandums of understanding (MOU). These binding agreements between a local school district and the Louisiana Department of Education outline necessary actions that must be implemented at a failing school in order for it to avoid placement in the Recovery School District (RSD).

  If the district fails to comply with the terms of the MOU or fails to make progress toward the implementation of the school recovery plan during the first year of the agreement, the Louisiana Department of Education may exercise the option of placing the school in the RSD. According to the law, a school can be placed under the control of the Recovery School District in the following circumstances:

When a city, parish, or other local public school board or other public entity: (a) fails to present a plan to reconstitute the failed school to the state board, as required pursuant to such an accountability program, or (b) presents a reconstitution plan that is unacceptable to the state board, or (c) fails at any time to comply with the terms of the reconstitution plan approved by the state board, or (d) the school has been labeled an academically unacceptable school for four consecutive years, the school shall be removed from the jurisdiction of the city, parish, or other local public school board or other public entity and transferred to the jurisdiction of the Recovery School District.

The degree of oversight involved in each school's MOU varies and is based on the level of intervention state education officials deem necessary for the school to succeed.

- **Receivership:** Under provisions of the Louisiana Recovery School District law, schools that fail to meet required benchmarks may be placed into receivership—typically by an outside corporation or organization—while they are being reorganized.

- **School Recovery Plan:** Under the law, schools placed into the Recovery School District must create a school recovery plan to indicate how it plans to become an academically acceptable school. The plan describes what reorganization will occur at the school and how it will be implemented, and it also details how and why the proposed changes will lead to improved student performance.

- **Oversight and Funding:** The State Board of Elementary and Secondary Education (BESE) serves as the oversight board for the RSD. Louisiana schools that are placed in the Recovery School District must remain there for a minimum of five years in order to fully establish the instructional practices and expectations necessary for success prior to reentry into the local school board. This requirement was based on research that indicated that it takes about five years to turn around a failing school. The RSD receives both the state and local portions of foundation funding and any federal funding that would follow the children who attend the schools in the district. In addition, grant funding and the support of national foundations, specific to the RSD, further support the efforts to reform the schools in this district.

Impact

The initial indications of the Recovery School District Law's impact have been obscured somewhat and enormously influenced by Hurricane Katrina, which struck the Gulf Coast and devastated New Orleans in fall 2005, less than two years after final passage of the law.

Prior to Katrina, there were five schools under RSD control. A special expansion of the RSD law helped move scores of schools damaged by the hurricane into RSD management. By fall 2009, there were 112 RSD schools in Orleans parish alone, which includes Louisiana's largest city, New Orleans, though about a third of those schools were still being rebuilt and were not yet open. A slim majority of the RSD schools that were operational were charter schools, and RSD superintendent Paul Vallas, who ushered in major school reform in Chicago in the 1990s, has encouraged the continued growth of charters within New Orleans and choice among all its public schools.

The data suggesting the academic impact of the RSD law were beginning to emerge by fall 2009, and most of it was encouraging. One report from the Louisiana Department of Education, which analyzed 60 New Orleans schools that had failed for four consecutive years to meet minimum achievement standards and had been moved to RSD control, found that almost half of them had surpassed that measure. In addition, the overall performance of New Orleans schools on the School Performance Scores assessment had increased more than 6 percent in just one year, from 2008 to 2009.

Perhaps the Recovery School District's greatest impact, however, will be as a supporting tool for a region that was suffering educationally before being battered by one of the worst natural disasters in American history, through its emphasis on charter school creation, new building construction, and academic accountability.

SAMPLING OF STATE HOMESCHOOLING-RELATED LEGISLATION

Background

Although the roots of homeschooling in the United States trace back to its founding, when most children were educated at home by parents or tutors, the surge in the popularity of the homeschooling movement is a relatively recent development.

The challenge to traditional institutions commonly seen in the 1960s extended to public schooling as well. John Holt, a former teacher and left-wing education reformer, advocated homeschooling as an alternative to conformist and failing public schools, although his views were usually viewed as fringe. Homeschooling's voice became a bit louder in the 1970s and early 1980s following the publication of additional research and books, usually from conservative activists, that supported the movement. The 1972 Supreme Court decision in *Wisconsin v. Yoder*, which struck down compulsory education laws, and the 1983 publication of *A Nation at Risk*, which portrayed the dangerous weaknesses of the U.S. public school system, also added momentum to homeschooling.

However, homeschooling remained extremely rare until the 1980s and 1990s when mainly well-organized evangelical Christians adopted it as a way to combat what they saw as the disorder and oppressive secularism of public schools. Over the past 20 years, homeschooling has emerged as perhaps education reform's most influential, if often overlooked, movement.

The most recent federal study, completed in 2007, points to almost 1.5 million homeschooled students. This total represents an almost 75 percent increase since 1999. Although the largest estimates place the homeschooled population at about 4 percent of the entire K–12 population, that total still outnumbers the combined enrollment of all students in Alaska, Delaware, Hawaii, Montana, New Hampshire, North Dakota, Rhode Island, South Dakota, Vermont, and Wyoming. In light of this rampant growth, homeschooling legislation has become more prominent throughout the United States.

Key Aspects of Legislation

Provisions included in homeschooling legislation vary significantly from state to state. Following is a description of laws that cover the range of states with almost no regulation, to low, moderate, and high regulation of homeschooling.

Texas homeschooling law provides an example of a state with no requirement for parents to initiate contact with the school district, submit to visits by state authorities, gain approval of a curriculum, or have any specific teacher certification. Home schools only need to have a written curriculum, conduct it in a bone fide manner, and teach math, reading, spelling, grammar, and good citizenship. This hands-off policy followed a 1987 class-action lawsuit filed on behalf of more than 80 homeschooling families who were criminally prosecuted for truancy. The case *Leeper v. Arlington Independent School District* resulted in a key victory for homeschooling that was subsequently upheld by the Texas court of appeals and the Texas Supreme Court. The *Leeper* decision stated:

> *The evidence establishes that from the inception of the first compulsory attendance law in Texas in 1915, it was understood that a school-age child who was being educated in or through the child's home, and in a bona fide manner by the parents . . . was considered a private school.*

In 1989, the Texas legislature exempted private and parochial schools from new state requirements for schools and in the process, confirmed that the term *private school* includes home schools. Other states with similar legislation include Alaska, Idaho, Illinois, Indiana, Michigan, Missouri, and Oklahoma.

Many states have home school laws with low regulation. An example of this is California, where families interested in homeschooling their children have four options:

1. The individual home school could qualify as a private school* by filing an annual private school affidavit certifying that
   a. The instructors must be capable of teaching;
   b. The instruction must be in English;
   c. The instruction must be in the several branches of study required in public schools;
   d. Attendance must be kept in a register; and
   e. A private school affidavit must be filed with the county superintendent between October 1 and October 15 of each school year.
2. The home school could have instruction provided by a certified private tutor.
3. The child could be enrolled in an independent study program at home, using the public school curriculum. Under this option, the child is considered a public school student and has to abide by the rules and policy of the public school.
4. Homeschoolers could enroll in a private school satellite program and take "independent study" through that private school, as long as the private school independent study program (ISP) complies with California law. Many home school families have organized these private ISPs, which enroll anywhere from two to several hundred families.

Under California law, teacher certification is necessary only if the home school parent chooses to qualify as a private tutor and standardized testing of homeschooled students is not required. Other states with similar low-regulation laws include Alabama, Arizona, Kansas, Kentucky, Mississippi, Montana, Nebraska, New Mexico, and Wisconsin.

Georgia is an example of a state whose homeschooling legislation reflects moderate regulation. Under Georgia law,

- Parents must submit a declaration of intent to home study to the local superintendent within 30 days after the establishment of the home study

---

* The establishment of home schools as private schools was supported by the 1992 U.S. District Court of the Southern District of California decision *Institute of Creation Research v. Honig*, which ordered, "a private K–12 school is not within the jurisdiction of the State Department of Education for the purpose of approval of courses or course content or issuance of regulations, except as provided by law."

program and by September 1 every year thereafter. This declaration must include the names and ages of students, the location of the home school, and the time the parents designate as their school year.

- The home school must provide "a basic academic educational program."
- Each school day must be at least four and one-half hours long.
- Attendance records must be kept and submitted to the superintendent each month.
- Parents must write an annual progress report and retain it for three years.
- Parents or guardians may teach only their own children in the home study program provided they have a high school diploma or GED, but the parents or guardians may employ a tutor who holds at least a baccalaureate college degree.

Homeschooled students must take a national standardized test every three years beginning at the end of third grade, though these test scores are not required to be submitted to public school authorities. Other states considered moderate in their regulation of homeschooling include: Arkansas, Colorado, Connecticut, Florida, Iowa, Louisiana, Maryland, New Hampshire, North Carolina, Ohio, Oregon, South Carolina, South Dakota, Tennessee, and Virginia.

Finally, many states have homeschooling laws that require parents to provide a relatively high degree of notification to, and approval from, the state. Pennsylvania is one such state. Its home school statute requires

- Parental filing of a notarized affidavit with the local superintendent prior to the commencement of the home education program and annually thereafter by August 1. The affidavit must include
  a. The name of the parent/supervisor, name and age of children, address, and telephone number;
  b. Assurance that subjects are taught in English;
  c. "Outline of proposed education objectives by subject area";
  d. Evidence of immunization;
  e. Receipt of health and medical services required by law; and
  f. A certification that the supervisor, all adults living within the home, and persons having legal custody of the children have not been convicted of certain criminal offenses within the past five years.
- Annual parental maintenance and provision to the superintendent of education with certain documentation, including

  a. A portfolio of records and materials, including a "log . . . which designates reading materials used, samples of any writing, work sheets, workbooks or creative materials used by the student."

b. An annual written evaluation of the student's educational progress by (1) a licensed psychologist, (2) a teacher certified by the state, or (3) a teacher or administrator (who must have at least two years' teaching experience in the last 10 years in public or nonpublic schools). The evaluation shall be based on an interview and review of the portfolio and "it shall certify whether or not an appropriate education is occurring."

A 1990 federal district court decision in *Stobaugh v. Wallace* ruled that a superintendent cannot "arbitrarily choose to flout state law" by requesting to see the portfolio midyear when he has no evidence of noncompliance. If the superintendent determines an appropriate education is not taking place, the parent-supervisor has 20 days to submit additional documentation. If there is still a problem, the family has a right of appeal to an impartial hearing examiner and then to the secretary of education or the court.

Parents may also teach their children at home if they qualify as a "properly qualified private tutor," which is defined as "a person who is certified by the Commonwealth of Pennsylvania to teach in the public schools of Pennsylvania." The private tutor must file a copy of their Pennsylvania certification and the required criminal history record with the student's district of residence superintendent.

In addition, parents may teach their children at home if the home is an extension or satellite of a religious day school. Such a day school must provide a minimum of 180 days of instruction or 900 hours of instruction per year at the elementary level or 990 hours per year of instruction at the secondary level. Specific requirements regarding courses of study at the elementary and secondary levels are also noted. Other states with similarly high regulation statutes include Maine, Massachusetts, Minnesota, Nevada, New York, North Dakota, Rhode Island, Utah, Washington, and West Virginia.

Impact

One result of the rapid rise in homeschooling has been a strain on public schools' financing. For instance, in Florida the homeschooled population has quadrupled between 1991 and 2001. Although less than 2 percent of students were homeschooled, that flight from public schools represented a loss of nearly $130 million in the state's public education budget. Of course, this means that the schools have fewer students to teach, but the damage to the image of schools as well as a loss of often high academic achievers has been significant. In addition, property taxes, which provide a large chunk of most school systems' budgets, have been tougher to approve in communities whose reliance on public schools has diminished.

Homeschooling advocates often claim that the proliferation of home-schooling legislation has led to a higher academic achievement for home-schooled students, and they point to testing results for evidence. Indeed, the average homeschooled student does rank higher than the average public school student in most studies. However, not all home school students take standardized tests, and it is difficult to assess how a homeschooled student would have done in a traditional school.

One trend that has emerged from recent homeschooling legislation is an increase in crossover efforts between public schools and home schools. By mid-2009, 24 states had laws or court rulings that permitted homeschooled students to participate in extracurricular activities and advanced placement classes. Such laws are often referred to a "Tebow Laws" because of Tim Tebow, a homeschooled student in Florida who led his high school football team to a state championship. He went on to attend the University of Florida, where he helped his college team win two national championships, and he won the 2007 Heisman Trophy. Such arrangements allow home-schooled students to gain access to resources unlikely to be available to them otherwise, and school districts are able to recoup a portion of the per-pupil funding lost by counting homeschooled students in their programs. Although more than 20 percent of homeschooled students participate in such forms of traditional school activities, the home school debate remains a highly contentious one whose future will affect millions of students and the perception of the role of public schools.

COURT CASES

BROWN V. BOARD OF EDUCATION, 347 U.S. 483 (1954)

Background

In the 1940s and 1950s, the National Association for the Advancement of Colored People (NAACP), the leading civil rights organization in the coun-try, organized legal challenges to the "separate but equal" doctrine estab-lished by the U.S. Supreme Court in *Plessy v. Ferguson* (1896).

In *McLaurin v. Oklahoma State Regents* (1950), the Supreme Court unan-imously struck down University of Oklahoma rules that had permitted a black man to attend classes but required that he be separated from his white classmates. On the same day as its *McLaurin* decision, the Supreme Court ruled in *Sweatt v. Painter* that a makeshift law school created by the state of Texas to avoid admitting blacks into the University of Texas Law School was unconstitutional.

Encouraged by these legal decisions, the NAACP and its chief legal counsel, Thurgood Marshall, brought five cases before the Court specifically designed to challenge segregation laws requiring separate public schools for blacks and whites. The case took its name from the lawsuit brought on behalf of Linda Brown, a student enrolled in the Topeka, Kansas, school system. She had been denied admission to the all-white elementary school a few blocks from her house. Instead, she had to travel 21 blocks to an all-black school.

Legal Issues

The NAACP argued that segregating students on the basis of race denied them the equal protection guarantees of the Fourteenth Amendment. Many of the arguments they presented were based on social and psychological research material gathered by professor Kenneth Clark.

The Topeka Board of Education argued in favor of the decades of law and custom, as well as the tradition of states' rights, which permitted the segregation of public schools by race. They further contended that it was not the intention of the Fourteenth Amendment to abolish segregation.

Decision

Chief Justice Earl Warren issued *Brown's* unanimous and historic ruling on May 17, 1954. In it, he reflected the growing belief in the importance of public education in American society, explaining,

> *Today, education is perhaps the most important function of state and local governments. Compulsory school attendance laws and the great expenditures for education both demonstrate our recognition of the importance of education to our democratic society. It is required in the performance of our most basic public responsibilities, even service in the armed forces. It is the very foundation of good citizenship. Today it is a principal instrument in awakening the child to cultural values, in preparing him for later professional training, and in helping him to adjust normally to his environment. In these days, it is doubtful that any child may reasonably be expected to succeed in life if he is denied the opportunity of an education. Such an opportunity, where the state has undertaken to provide it, is a right which must be made available to all on equal terms.*

Warren proceeded to address the Court's view on the legal justification for, and societal impactions of, public school segregation:

> *We come then to the question presented: Does segregation of children in public schools solely on the basis of race, even though the physical facilities and other "tangible" factors may be equal, deprive the children of the minority group of equal educational opportunities? We believe that it does. . . . To*

separate them (minority group children in public schools) from others of similar age and qualifications solely because of their race generates a feeling of inferiority as to their status in the community that may affect their heart and minds in a way unlikely ever to be undone. The effect of this separation on their educational opportunities was well stated by a finding in the Kansas case by a court which nevertheless felt compelled to rule against the Negro plaintiffs: "Segregation of white and colored children in public schools has a detrimental effect upon the colored children. The impact is greater when it has the sanction of the law; for the policy of separating the races is usually interpreted as denoting the inferiority of the negro group. A sense of inferiority affects the motivation of a child to learn. Segregation with the sanction of law, therefore, has a tendency to retard the educational and mental development of negro children and to deprive them of some of the benefits they would receive in a [racially] integrated school system." Whatever may have been the extent of psychological knowledge at the time of Plessy v. Ferguson, this finding is amply supported by modern authority. Any language in Plessy v. Ferguson contrary to this finding is rejected.

We conclude that in the field of public education the doctrine of "separate but equal" has no place. Separate educational facilities are inherently unequal.

Impact

The Supreme Court's unanimous decision in *Brown* was a landmark in constitutional history and has served as an enduring symbol for the cause of civil rights. Its more particular influence on public education is also significant. The case served as the most important catalyst leading to the end of sanctioned segregation in public education. The years immediately following the decision led opponents to resentment, delay, and occasionally conflict with legal authorities, most notably at Little Rock Central High School in 1957.

Implementation of the decision also represented the growth in judicial activism of the Supreme Court regarding education issues. Over the course of ensuing decades, education reformers of various ideological persuasions increasingly viewed the courts as an outlet for the promotion of their agendas.

LEMON V. KURTZMAN, 403 U.S. 602 (1971)

Background

The Supreme Court case known as *Lemon v. Kurtzman* is actually three separate cases (including *Easrley v. DiCenso* and *Robinson v. DiCenso*) that were joined together because they all concerned public assistance to private schools, some of which were religious. The cases concerned a Pennsylvania law that allowed the public payment of teachers' salaries as well as assistance for the purchase of teaching supplies and textbooks in parochial schools and a Rhode Island law that allowed state payment of up to 15 percent of private school teachers' salaries. In each of these cases, the teachers were teaching secular subjects.

Prior to being argued before the Supreme Court, a federal court upheld the Pennsylvania law and a separate district court had ruled that the Rhode Island law fostered "excessive entanglement" of church and state.

Legal Issues

The complex and controversial relationship between religion and public education had long been an area of constitutional contention, particularly in the 30 years leading up to the Lemon case. A clearer separation of church and state gathered momentum following Supreme Court decisions in *McCollum v. Board of Education* (1948), disallowing the practice of having religious education take place in public school classrooms during the school day, and *Abington Township School District v. Schemp* (1963), which prohibited the forced recital of Bible verses and the Lord's Prayer in public schools.

Decision

On June 28, 1971, the Supreme Court ruled unanimously that direct government assistance to religious schools was unconstitutional. Chief Justice Warren Burger wrote to the majority's decision, establishing what has become known as the "Lemon Test." This three-part analysis was established to determine whether a policy or activity violates the First Amendment's Establishment Clause. It notes:

> *Every analysis in this area must begin with consideration of the cumulative criteria developed by the Court over many years. First, the statute must have a secular legislative purpose; second, its principal or primary effect must be one that neither advances or inhibits religion; finally, the statute must not foster an excessive government Entanglement with religion.*

The payment of public school teachers' salaries under the control of religious officials and in a religious institution was found to be in violation of this new criteria. Further, the Court explained that to ensure that teachers play a nonideological role, the state would have to become directly involved in the management of the teachers and, hence, become entangled with the church.

Education Reform

Impact

The *Lemon* decision has served as the seminal case relating to government aid to religious schools. However, the trend following this case of increasing distance between church and state has narrowed in recent decades as a result of Supreme Court decisions marginalizing or ignoring the Lemon Test.

This shift is most evident in the Supreme Court's decision in *Mitchell v. Helms* (2000), which allowed federal and state support for private and religious schools' purchase of library and media materials as well as computer software and hardware. The Court decision that aid to religious groups can be made so long as it furthers some legitimate secular purpose and is granted in the same manner to nonreligious groups caused alarm in certain quarters: Critics were concerned about the potential impact that increased government financing of religious institutions, including schools, might have on the separation of church and state. However, recent years have not resulted in such an increase outside of the parameters noted in *Mitchell v. Helms*.

WISCONSIN V. YODER, 406 U.S. 208 (1972)

Background

This case concerned three Amish families who sued the state of Wisconsin over a requirement that children be enrolled in school until the age of 16. The parents refused to comply by removing their children from school after they completed eighth grade and continued their education at home, with an emphasis on domestic and farming skills. The parents claimed that further education would present their children with too much exposure to the "evil world."

Legal Issues

The Amish families involved in the suit argued that their rights to freely exercise their religion were not being respected by the state's compulsory attendance laws. Before the suit reached the U.S. Supreme Court, the Wisconsin Supreme Court had ruled in favor of the parents.

Decision

On May 15, 1972, the U.S. Supreme Court ruled 6-1 that the compulsory education law in Wisconsin violated the Constitution's Free Exercise Clause.

Justice Warren Burger wrote in his majority opinion that the Amish have a legitimate reason for removing their children from school prior to their attending high school, because qualities emphasized in high school, such as scientific accomplishment, are contrary to their mission and values.

The Court further determined that the beliefs of the Amish were religiously based and rejected the state's arguments that the Free Exercise Clause extends no protection because the case involved "action" or "conduct" rather than "belief." Additionally, the Court asserted that the governmental interest of providing education was met, with the Amish attending public schools through the eighth grade and then continuing with the home-based, primarily vocational instruction.

Impact

The primary impact of the *Wisconsin v. Yoder* decision has been seen in the growing prominence of homeschooling over the past 40 years. Reliable national estimates note an almost 100 percent increase in the homeschooled population since 1999, to a total of more than 1.5 million.

The Court's decision prevented states from asserting any absolute right to institute compulsory high school education, as parents' rights to teach their religion were deemed more important than governmental interest in educating all children. Since this decision, legal scholars and parents have often successfully argued that people with more individualistic choices based on secular grounds should be granted the same consideration in school attendance matters, significantly expanding homeschooling options.

SAN ANTONIO INDEPENDENT SCHOOL DISTRICT V. RODRIGUEZ, 411 U.S. 1 (1973)

Background

On May 16, 1968, approximately 400 students at Edgewood High School in San Antonio, Texas, held a walkout and demonstration, marching to the district administration office to protest insufficient supplies and lack of qualified teachers in their school. The walkout induced parents to form the Edgewood District Concerned Parents Association to address the problems highlighted by the student protest. A few weeks later, one of the students' parents, Demetrio Rodriguez, and seven other Edgewood parents filed a class-action lawsuit on behalf of Texas schoolchildren who were poor or resided in school districts with low property tax bases, claiming a notable unfair disparity in the per-pupil expenditures among school districts. On December 23, 1971, a federal district court agreed with the plaintiffs and declared the Texas school finance system unconstitutional.

Education Reform

Legal Issues

The primary issue of this case was inequity in school financing. The plaintiffs argued that although their school district had one of the highest tax rates in Bexar County, it was only able to raise $47 per student, while Alamo Heights, the county's wealthiest district, was able to raise $413 per student. They argued that this common public school funding strategy was unconstitutional under the Equal Protection Clause of the Fourteenth Amendment.

Decision

On March 21, 1973, the Supreme Court ruled 5-4 that the system of school finance at the center of contention did not violate the U.S. Constitution and that the issue should be resolved by the state of Texas. The Court also held that the state would not be required to subsidize poorer school districts, which produced additional legal barriers to funding equalization.

In his majority opinion, Justice Lewis Powell explained:

Wealth did not constitute a suspect class and thus the strict scrutiny test, which was appropriate when state action impinged on a fundamental right or operated to the disadvantage of a suspect class, was not applicable in this case. The financing method employed did not impinge on any fundamental right so as to call for the application of the strict judicial scrutiny test. In addition, the Court did not view education as a fundamental right which afforded explicit or implicit protection under the Constitution.

The Court then applied the traditional standard of review which requires a showing that the state's action had a rational relationship to legitimate state purposes. It found that the financing method used satisfied this test, namely in the areas of fiscal policy and educational requirements. This result was achieved despite the inherent and somewhat obvious imperfections in the current system. However, it was not up to the Court to measure the quality of system, only its constitutionality.

Impact

The Supreme Court's decision in the *Rodriguez* case allowed states a more relaxed standard for justifying their funding policies. In addition, it asserted that the Fourteenth Amendment's Equal Protection Clause permits any kind of school finance system as long as it provides a minimum education for every student. As a result, the issue of per-pupil expenditure has been the frequent focus of challenges in state courts, which often rule against the funding policies established by state legislatures.

The Law and Education Reform

LAU V. NICHOLS, 414 U.S. 563 (1974)

Background

In the early 1970s, parents of Chinese-speaking students in the San Francisco Unified School District (SFUSD) filed a class-action lawsuit alleging that the district's failure to provide equal educational opportunities for students who did not speak English was a violation of the Fourteenth Amendment to the U.S. Constitution.

A federal district court and the ninth court of appeals denied the plaintiffs' claims before the case came to the U.S. Supreme Court. The Court was not asked to determine a specific remedy but rather to direct the SFUSD to apply its expertise to the problem.

Legal Issues

The Supreme Court avoided addressing the arguments relating to the Fourteenth Amendment's Equal Protection Clause, instead relying on the much narrower grounds of the regulations issued under Title VI of the Civil Rights Act of 1964, which prohibits federally funded programs from discrimination on the basis of race or national origin.

Decision

On January 21, 1974, the Supreme Court ruled in favor of the plaintiffs; however, the Court carefully refrained from dictating a particular methodology, leaving the pursuit of remedies for the local level. Writing for the majority, Justice William Orville Douglas noted:

> *Where inability to speak and understand the English language excludes national origin minority group children from effective participation in the educational program offered by a school district, the district must take affirmative steps to rectify the language deficiency in order to open its instructional program to these students.*

While concurring the decision, Justice Harry Andrew Blackmun (joined by Justice Warren Burger) added a caveat that has proven to be significant as school districts confront increasingly diverse student populations:

> *Against the possibility that the Court's judgment may be interpreted too broadly, I stress the fact that the children with whom we are concerned here number about 1,800. This is a very substantial group that is being deprived of any meaningful schooling because the children cannot understand the language of the classroom. We may only guess as to why they have had no exposure to English in their preschool years. Earlier generations of American*

ethnic groups have overcome the language barrier by earnest parental endeavor or by the hard fact of being pushed out of the family or community nest and into the realities of broader experience.

I merely wish to make plain that when, in another case, we are confronted with a very few youngsters, or with just a single child who speaks only German or Polish or Spanish or any language other than English, I would not regard today's decision . . . as conclusive upon the issue whether the statute and the guidelines require the funded school district to provide special instruction. For me, numbers are at the heart of this case and my concurrence is to be understood accordingly.

Impact

Lau v. Nichols is the most important Supreme Court case concerning students with limited English proficiency. Key words and phrases in the decision have led to heated debate and varying interpretations among educators and policymakers, particularly "effective participation," "affirmative steps," "rectify the language deficiency," and "open its instructional program."

The volatile dispute over the best approach to educating limited-English-proficient students was left unresolved by *Lau*. The Office of Civil Rights set forth a series of principles, known as the Lau Guidelines, outlining procedures to follow for districts enrolling 20 or more limited-English-language-proficient students. However, it soon became apparent that these guidelines did not have the force of law.

In the decades since the *Lau* decision, California has been the primary battleground over the issue of bilingual education. Its leadership in implementing the far-reaching Chaco-Mosconi Bilingual Bicultural Education Act of 1976, which mandated bilingual education, was emulated in many states throughout the country. However, by the mid-1990s, criticism of these programs became widespread. Prominent reports suggested that bilingual education programs had done little to boost the academic achievement or competitiveness of a limited-English-proficient students.

In June 1998, California's Proposition 227, designed to all but end the state's bilingual education programs, passed with more than 60 percent support from the state's voters. The proposition, headed by software mogul Ron Unz, has survived legal challenges and has led to similar efforts across the country.

GOSS V. LOPEZ, 419 U.S. 565 (1975)

Background

The student protests that broke out on many college campuses in the 1960s spread to many high schools by the early 1970s. In February and March

The Law and Education Reform

1971, race-related student riots at Columbus, Ohio's Central High School led to the suspensions of 75 students for disruptive behavior and damage to school property.

One of the suspended students, Dwight Lopez, insisted that he was an innocent bystander, but he was not allowed to get a hearing to tell his side of the story. Lopez and eight other students, through their parents, sued the school board for violation of their civil rights.

Legal Issues

At issue in the *Goss* case were two provisions of the Fourteenth Amendment: the Equal Protection Clause and the Due Process Clause, requiring states to recognize the rights of all citizens facing legal action. Specifically, the Supreme Court examined whether these protections necessarily extend past the schoolhouse doors.

Decision

On January 22, 1975, the Supreme Court ruled 5-4 in favor of the plaintiffs, striking down the Ohio law as a violation of students' limited rights to due process.

In his majority opinion, Justice Byron White noted:

> *Among other things, the State is constrained to recognize a student's legitimate entitlement to a public education as a property interest which is protected by the Due Process Clause and which may not be taken away for misconduct without adherence to the minimum procedures required by that Clause. The Due Process Clause also forbids arbitrary deprivations of liberty. "Where a person's good name, reputation, honor, or integrity is at stake because of what the government is doing to him," the minimal requirements of the Clause must be satisfied. School authorities here suspended appellees from school for periods of up to 10 days based on charges of misconduct. If sustained and recorded, those charges could seriously damage the students' standing with their fellow pupils and their teachers as well as interfere with later opportunities for higher education and employment. It is apparent that the claimed right of the State to determine unilaterally and without process whether that misconduct has occurred immediately collides with the requirements of the Constitution.*

The decision explained that students were entitled to the following due-process rights: oral or written notice of the charges; if a student denies the charges, an explanation of the evidence the school will use against him or her; and an opportunity for the student to present his or her side of the story. The Court ruled that in an emergency situation, students could be sent home immediately and a hearing held at a later date. The Court did not rule, however, that students had a right to an attorney, to cross-examine witnesses, to call witnesses in their defense, or to a hearing before an impartial person.

Impact

More than 35 years of law or court case rulings have elaborated these procedural protections for a wide range of situations, from short-term suspensions in interscholastic athletics to lengthy expulsions from school.

Zero-tolerance policies for certain types of student conduct, and legal challenges to them, proliferated in the wake of the 1999 Columbine High School killings committed by two students in Littleton, Colorado. However, in recent years, focus on such policies have diminished significantly, in part because of high-profile cases in which it was perceived that students were being disproportionately punished for technical violations. Such incidents included a nine-week suspension and mandatory attendance at an alternative school for behavioral treatment for a Delaware first grader. He had brought his Boy Scout utensils, which included a small knife, to use while eating his lunch. (The punishment was reduced to less than a week's suspension.) To avoid similar problems, many schools have instituted more flexible policies that allow for greater discretion, situation-based solutions, and student-based programs, such as peer mediation and support groups.

HONIG V. DOE, 484 U.S. 305 (1988)

Background

On November 6, 1980, a 17-year-old student (referred to in the case as Doe) at the Louise Lombard School in San Francisco, a developmental center for learning disabled students, responded to the taunts of a fellow student by choking the student to the degree that abrasions were left on the student's neck. Doe then kicked out a school window as he was being escorted to the principal's office.

Doe admitted his misconduct and the school suspended him for five days. The principal referred the matter to the San Francisco Unified School District (SFUSD), recommending expulsion. The district agreed and notified Doe's mother that he would not be allowed to come to school until the expulsion hearing was held. Doe's family sued, alleging that the suspension and proposed expulsion violated the Individuals with Disabilities Education Act (IDEA). A district judge granted an injunction, and Doe reentered school.

A similar incident within the SFUSD occurred almost simultaneously involving another student, who was expelled for stealing, extorting money from fellow students, and making sexual comments to female classmates. The student's family joined in the Doe family suit.

A district judge agreed with the students' families and prevented the school district from taking any disciplinary action other than a maximum five-day suspension against any disabled student for disability-related misconduct or from effecting any other change in the educational placement of any such students without parental consent pending completion of any IDEA proceedings.

The Court of Appeals for the Ninth Circuit affirmed the orders of the district judge with slight modifications. The case was referred to as *Doe v. Maher* at the district and appeals levels. When California superintendent of education Bill Honig petitioned the Supreme Court for review of the case, it became known as *Honig v. Doe.*

Legal Issues

Honig v. Doe provided the intersection of two critical education-related constitutional issues: the rights of the disabled and the protection of the student population by school authorities. Honig argued that a "dangerousness" exception exists in the "stay-put" provision of IDEA though not explicitly noted in the law, explaining that Congress either excluded it because it was too obvious to be included or inadvertently failed to provide such authority.

Decision

On January 20, 1988, the Supreme Court in a unanimous decision ruled that suspensions of disabled students, particularly those with emotional disabilities, was a form of exclusion and therefore a violation of the student's right to a "free and appropriate education" guaranteed by IDEA. The Court ruled that such students could not be suspended for more than a total of 10 days in one school year and that such suspensions should be reviewed by multidisciplinary teams to determine if they constituted a change in the placements prescribed in the student's individualized educational plan (IEP).

Justice William Brennan's majority opinion explained:

Our conclusion that 1415(e)(3) means what it says does not leave educators hamstrung. The Department of Education has observed that, "[w]hile the [child's] placement may not be changed [during any complaint proceeding], this does not preclude the agency from using its normal procedures for dealing with children who are endangering themselves or others." Such procedures may include the use of study carrels, time-outs, detention, or the restriction of privileges. More drastically, where a student poses an immediate threat to the safety of others, officials may temporarily suspend him or her for up to 10 school days.[8] This authority, which respondent in no way disputes, not only ensures that school administrators can protect the safety of others by promptly removing the most dangerous of students, it also provides a "cooling down" period during which officials can initiate IEP review and seek to persuade the child's parents to agree to an interim placement. And in those cases in which the parents of a truly dangerous child adamantly refuse to permit any change in placement, the 10-day respite gives school officials an opportunity to invoke the aid of the courts . . .

Impact

The years since the *Honig* decision have been a turbulent period in the area of student discipline. Initially, lower courts were reluctant to grant preliminary injunctions. In 1997, Congress passed amendments to IDEA to clarify what constitutes removal of students and offered schools other options for dealing with disruptive behavior.

The generally hands-off approach to offenses committed by special education students ran counter to the wave of zero-tolerance policies for rules infractions within public schools. This perceived double standard in treatment of special education and regular education misconduct came under increased scrutiny following highly publicized school shootings that followed the kinds of taunting that Doe had responded to a generation earlier. Despite this scrutiny, in recent years the provisions for the discipline of students with disabilities as prescribed in *Honig* have remained in place, with schools relying on the student's IEP to determine the specific steps taken in particular cases.

DAVIS V. MONROE COUNTY BOARD OF EDUCATION, 97 U.S. 843 (1999)

Background

LaShonda Davis was a fifth-grade student at Hubbard Elementary School, in Monroe County, Georgia, during the 1992–93 school year. She claimed that a male classmate, referred to as "G.F.," repeatedly tried to touch her in a sexual manner and made sexual comments despite her reporting of the incidents to her mother, principal, teacher, and other teachers at the school. G.F. was subsequently charged with sexual battery, which he did not deny.

Frustrated with the school's failure to effectively respond to this harassment, Davis's mother sued the Board of Education of Monroe County. The U.S. District Court for the Middle District of Georgia dismissed the suit for failing to state a claim upon which relief could be granted. Davis appealed and a panel for the Court of Appeals for the Eleventh Circuit reinstated the claim but then rejected it. Davis then filed a petition for certiorari, asking the Supreme Court to review the decision of the lower courts.

Legal Issues

The salient issue of the *Davis* case concerned whether Title IX of the Education Amendments of 1972 covers peer sexual harassment and if so, what the standard of liability is for school districts. Specifically, Title IX provides that "no person in the United States, shall, on the basis of sex be excluded from participation in, be denied the benefits of, or be subjected to discrimination under any education program or activity receiving federal financial assistance."

Decision

On May 24, 1999, the Supreme Court in a 5-4 ruling reversed the lower court's decision and remanded the case to the district court.

Justice Sandra Day O'Connor explained in the majority decision:

A private Title IX damages action may lie against a school board in cases of student-on-student harassment, but only where the funding recipient is deliberately indifferent to sexual harassment, of which the recipient has actual knowledge, and that harassment is so severe, pervasive, and objectively offensive that it can be said to deprive the victims of access to the educational opportunities or benefits provided by the school.

The decision went on to assert:

Applying this standard to the facts at issue, the Eleventh Circuit erred in dismissing petitioner's complaint. This Court cannot say beyond doubt that she can prove no set of facts that would entitle her to relief. She alleges that LaShonda was the victim of repeated acts of harassment by G.F. over a 5-month period, and allegations support the conclusion that his misconduct was severe, pervasive, and objectively offensive. Moreover, the complaint alleges that multiple victims of G.F.'s misconduct sought an audience with the school principal and that the harassment had a concrete, negative effect on LaShonda's ability to receive an education. The complaint also suggests that petitioner may be able to show both actual knowledge and deliberate indifference on the part of the Board, which made no effort either to investigate or to put an end to the harassment.

Impact

The *Davis* decision established that lawsuits can be filed against school officials who knowingly and deliberately ignore student-on-student harassment. This has resulted in a dramatic increase in harassment in school litigation. Fearing liability, many schools and districts have developed polices and procedures mandating intervention in such cases, including the highly publicized and legally contentious enactment of zero-tolerance policies.

ZELMAN V. SIMMONS-HARRIS, 200 U.S. 321 (2002)

Background

In the early 1990s, the Cleveland public schools were in dismal condition. Most of the more than 75,000 students enrolled in the system performed below proficiency on state exams, and more than two-thirds of high school students dropped out or failed before graduation. In 1995, the city's school system was placed under state control.

In 1995, the Ohio legislature adopted the Ohio Pilot Scholarship Program, which provided two kinds of assistance: tuition aid for kindergarten through third-grade students to attend a participating public or private school of their parents' choosing and tutorial aid for students who chose to remain in public school. Provisions for school participation included location within district boundaries and nondiscrimination on the basis of race, religion, or ethnic background. Tuition aid was distributed to parents according to financial need.

The program began at the start of the 1996–97 school year. In the 1999–2000 school year, 56 private schools participated in the program, and 46 of these (82 percent) had a religious affiliation. None of the adjacent public schools eligible to participate chose to do so.

In January 1996, Doris Simmons-Harris, a parent of a public school student, and others challenged the program in state court on the grounds that it violated both the state and federal constitutions. The case eventually reached the Ohio Supreme Court, which determined that the voucher program violated Ohio's "one subject" rule because the voucher bill was an addition to a state budget bill.

In June 1999, the Ohio legislature reenacted the voucher program as a freestanding measure. A month later, Simmons-Harris and others sued the state department of education in federal court alleging violation of the First Amendment's Establishment Clause. Some parents and religious schools then intervened in the suit to defend the program.

In December 1999, a federal district court ruled in favor of the plaintiffs' claim that the voucher program was unconstitutional. The state's appeal to the Court of Appeals for the Sixth Circuit was denied, and the state then appealed the case to the U.S. Supreme Court, which agreed to hear the case.

The Law and Education Reform

Legal Issues

The central legal issue of the *Zelman* case was the major conflict embroiling advocates of each side of the voucher issue. Does the First Amendment's Establishment Clause prohibit a voucher plan in which participating students in the program attend religiously affiliated schools?

Decision

On June 27, 2002, the Supreme Court ruled in a 5-4 decision that the Ohio Pilot Project Scholarship Program did not violate the Establishment Clause of the First Amendment, reversing the decisions of the lower courts. Writing for the majority, Justice William Rehnquist noted:

We believe that the program challenged here is a program of true private choice, . . . and thus constitutional. As was true in those cases, the Ohio program is neutral in all respects toward religion. It is part of a general and multifaceted undertaking by the State of Ohio to provide educational opportunities to the children of a failed school district. It confers educational assistance directly to a broad class of individuals defined without reference to religion, i.e., any parent of a school-age child who resides in the Cleveland City School District. The program permits the participation of all schools within the district, religious or non-religious. Adjacent public schools also may participate and have a financial incentive to do so. Program benefits are available to participating families on neutral terms, with no reference to religion. The only preference stated anywhere in the program is a preference for low-income families, who receive greater assistance and are given priority for admission at participating schools.

Rehnquist then elaborated on the issue of government endorsement of religion by explaining,

We further observed that "[b]y according parents freedom to select a school of their choice, the statute ensures that a government-paid interpreter will be present in a sectarian school only as a result of the private decision of individual parents." Our focus again was on neutrality and the principle of private choice, not on the number of program beneficiaries attending religious schools. Because the program ensured that parents were the ones to select a religious school as the best learning environment for their handicapped child, the circuit between government and religion was broken, and the Establishment Clause was not implicated.

Impact

The *Zelman* decision was the object of a great deal of attention when it was made in 2002, and it reflected the intense feeling related to school vouchers.

Education Reform

Referencing the historic importance of this issue, Justice Clarence Thomas wrote, "If society cannot end racial discrimination at least it can arm minorities with the education to defend themselves from some of discrimination's effects." Justice John Paul Stevens reasoned, "Whenever we remove a brick from the wall that was designed to separate religion and government, we increase the risk of religious strife and weaken the foundation of our democracy."

However, the decision has not had the powerful impact that many voucher advocates had hoped. While the Cleveland program still exists, as do others such as the Opportunity Scholarship Program in Washington, D.C., vouchers have struggled to gain ground. One main reason for this has been the consistent growth of charter schools, which provide parents whose children attend failing schools accessible options that have proven more politically and practically viable than vouchers. In 2009, President Obama and Secretary of Education Arne Duncan expressed their preference for charter schools over vouchers, with Duncan saying that the few voucher programs that do exist usually serve only 1 to 2 percent of the students in a community and that the federal government, local governments, and local school districts must be "more ambitious than that."

CHAPTER 3

CHRONOLOGY

This chapter provides a chronology of important events in the history of education reform. It focuses primarily on events that have occurred since 1920.

360 B.C.

- Plato writes *The Republic*, expressing benefits of state support of an educational system.

First Century A.D.

- Roman educator Quintilian expresses the importance and benefits of a broad public education system.

Late Thirteenth Century

- Dominican monk, philosopher, and scholar Thomas Aquinas establishes the foundation of Roman Catholic education.

1511

- Dutch humanist Desiderius Erasmus writes *Upon the Method of Right Instruction*, proposing the systematic training of teachers.

1516

- Erasmus publishes *Of the First Liberal Education of Children*.

1635

- The Boston Latin School becomes British North America's first secondary school and later the model for similar schools throughout New England.

Education Reform

1642

- The passage of the Massachusetts Law requires that the selectmen of each town determine that parents and masters of apprentices are providing for the education of children.

1647

- The Education Law is passed in Massachusetts ordering every township of 100 or more households to establish a grammar school.

1683

- The Pennsylvania Assembly enacts a law providing that all children be instructed in reading, writing, and a useful trade, yet formal education remains primarily a private or denominational endeavor largely owing to the diversity of religious groups in the colonies.

1690

- *The First New England Primer*, featuring an English-language guide and biblical content, is published and quickly becomes the main instructional text of the pre-Revolutionary period.

1762

- French philosopher Jean-Jacques Rousseau writes the novel *Emile*, providing early description of the benefits of child-centered education.

1776–81

- Many British Colonial schools close or are abandoned due to the Revolutionary War.

1779

- Thomas Jefferson's Bill for the More General Diffusion of Knowledge, proposing tax-supported education for three years to all white children, is defeated in the Virginia legislature.

1783

- Noah Webster publishes the *Elementary Spelling Book*, often referred to as the "Blue-Back Speller," which includes distinctively American spelling, grammar, and content.

Chronology

1787

- *July 13:* The Northwest Ordinance is adopted proclaiming, "religion, morality, and knowledge being necessary to good government and the happiness of mankind, schools and the means of education shall forever be encouraged."
- *September 17:* The U.S. Constitution is adopted making no mention of education.

1812

- New York becomes the first state to appoint a superintendent of education.

1821

- Boston English Classical School, later named Boston English High School, becomes the nation's first high school.

1828

- Catherine Beecher founds the Hartford Female Seminary, a key forerunner in the training of teachers.

1837

- Massachusetts legislator Horace Mann becomes the first secretary of the nation's first state board of education, significantly contributing to increased support for public education.
- Buffalo, New York, becomes the first major city to appoint a local superintendent whose major duty is to develop a uniform course of study.

1846

- Horace Mann's *Tenth Annual Report* asserts that education is the right of every child and that it is the state's responsibility to ensure that every child is provided with an education.

mid-1800s

- Enrollment in private secondary academies reaches more than 250,000 students at more than 6,000 schools throughout the United States.

1852

- The first compulsory school attendance law is approved by the Massachusetts legislature.

Education Reform

1861

- Twenty-eight of 34 states have established state boards of education and have chief state school officers whose responsibilities include distributing school funds and organizing the state's system of common schools.

1865

- More than 50 percent of the nation's children are enrolled in public schools, with the lowest rate of enrollment in the South.

1870

- Massachusetts congressman George Hoar's bill to establish a federal school system in the South is defeated.
- The National Education Association (NEA) is founded.

1873

- The Maine legislature enacts the first law providing state aid for public high schools.

1874

- The Michigan Supreme Court rules in the Kalamazoo School Case *(Stewart et al. v. School District No. 1 of the Village of Kalamazoo)* that the state legislature can tax for the support of both elementary and public schools.

1875

- Sales of Noah Webster's "Blue-Back Speller" reach 75 million copies, making it the most influential book in U.S. schools.

1876

- The U.S. Supreme Court decision in *Plessy v. Ferguson* establishes the legal foundation for racial segregation in education.

1890

- Rapid industrialization and increased immigration lead to the establishment of more than 2,500 high schools, whose enrollment doubles that of private academies.

1892

- The Committee of Ten is formed by the National Education Association and recommends uniform subject matter and instruction for all high school students.

Chronology

- New York College for the Training of Teachers, later known as Teachers College, becomes part of Columbia University.

1896

- Professor and philosopher John Dewey establishes the University of Chicago Laboratory School as a center of progressive educational practice emphasizing learning through experience and the preparation of children for full participation in democratic society.

1900

- More than 300 normal schools designed to train teachers exist throughout the United States.

1907

- W. E. B. DuBois cofounds the National Association for the Advancement of Colored People (NAACP) and advocates for expanded educational opportunity for blacks.

1909

- The cities of Columbus, Ohio, and Berkeley, California, establish the nation's first junior high schools.

1910

- The illiteracy rate among Americans over age 10 drops to 7.7 percent, compared to 20 percent in 1870.

1916

- John Dewey publishes *Democracy and Education*, which describes his progressive educational philosophy for a generation of educators.
- The measurement movement, featuring the increased use and application of intelligence and aptitude tests, grows in schools following its pervasive use in the World War I–era military.

1917

- Congress passes the Smith-Hughes Act, the first federal program for education of any kind, establishing federal aid for vocational education.

1918

- All states enact laws requiring full-time school attendance until the child reaches a certain age or grade.

- The Commission on the Reorganization of Secondary Education issues *The Cardinal Principles of Secondary Education*, which counters much of the Committee of Ten's recommendations.

1919

- The Progressive Education Association forms, giving organizational strength to the burgeoning progressive movement.

1932

- The Progressive Education Association begins an eight-year study of 3,000 high school students, which results in a report showing the academic and social benefits of progressive education.

1933

- Depression-era New Deal programs, including the Civilian Conservation Corps (CCC) and the National Youth Administration (NYA), provide many out-of-school youth with employment and signify the increase in the federal role for education.

1935

- A liberal wing of progressive educators begins the publication of the journal the *Social Frontier*, which argues in favor of the social reconstruction role of schools and signifies a division within the movement.

1938

- Education professor William Bagley publishes support for the educational theory of essentialism, which criticizes social reconstructionsists and argues in favor of an emphasis on the school's role in developing fundamental knowledge.

1940

- The National Teachers Exam is administered for the first time.

1953

- Professor Arthur Bestor publishes *Educational Wastelands*, criticizing progressive education's influence on U.S. schools.

1954

- The U.S. Supreme Court rules 9-0 in *Brown v. Board of Education* that segregated educational facilities are inherently unequal and orders an end to racial segregation in education.

Chronology

1955

- The motion picture *Blackboard Jungle*, portraying a chaotic urban public high school, is released.
- Rudolf Flesch publishes *Why Johnny Can't Read*, setting off national debate about quality of reading instruction and school curricula.

1957

- President Dwight Eisenhower sends federal troops to ensure the safe passage of black students integrating Little Rock, Arkansas, Central High School.

1958

- Largely in response to the previous year's Soviet launch of the *Sputnik* satellite, President Dwight Eisenhower signs the National Defense Education Act, which increases funding for science, math, and foreign language curricula and significantly raises the federal role in elementary and secondary education.

1959

- Former Harvard president James Conant publishes *The American High School Today.*

1963

- The Vocational Education Act more than quadruples federal funds for vocational education.

1964

- John Holt publishes *How Children Fail*, establishing the foundation for the homeschooling movement.
- Congress passes the Civil Rights Act, including the Title VI provision that prohibits discrimination against students based on race, religion, and national origin and provides federal financial assistance to school districts attempting to desegregate.

1965

- *April 11:* President Lyndon Johnson signs the Elementary and Secondary Education Act (ESEA), providing more than $1 billion in federal funds to education and representing the most significant education contribution of his Great Society legislation.

Education Reform

1966

- Under Title VI, the Elementary and Secondary Education Act (ESEA) expands to include programs for Native American students, children of migrant workers, and the disabled.

1967

- Title VII of the Elementary and Secondary Education Act (ESEA) adds programs for students with limited English-speaking ability.
- President Lyndon Johnson signs the Education Professions Development Act to provide funding for expanded in-service training for teachers.

1969

- Federal funding for education reaches $3 billion, a threefold increase from 1964.

1970s

- The open education movement grows in popularity.

1971

- The U.S. Supreme Court determines in *Lemon v. Kurtzman* that direct government aid to religious schools is unconstitutional.

1972

- Title IX of the Elementary and Secondary Education Act (ESEA) prohibits sex discrimination against students in educational programs receiving federal funds.
- The U.S. Supreme Court strikes down many state compulsory attendance laws as a violation of the Constitution's Free Exercise Clause in *Wisconsin v. Yoder.*

1973

- In *San Antonio School District v. Rodriguez,* the U.S. Supreme Court upholds the use of property taxes in determining school financing.

1974

- U.S. Supreme Court rules in *Lau v. Nichols* that schools must provide special language programs for non-English-speaking students.

Chronology

1975

- The Education for All Handicapped Children Act establishes the right of the disabled to a free and appropriate education.

1979

- President Jimmy Carter establishes the Department of Education as a cabinet-level part of the executive branch.

1981

- President Ronald Reagan signs the National Education Consolidation and Improvement Act, which combines federal education aid into several large block programs.

1983

- *A Nation at Risk*, a report released by the National Commission on Excellence in Education, blasts the "rising tide of mediocrity" in schools and sparks increased focus on education reform.
- Theodore Sizer publishes *Horace's Compromise*, advocating a new wave of progressive education including increased local control, parental involvement, and a de-emphasis on standardized tests. Sizer also starts the Coalition of Essential Schools to help promote his ideas of education reform.

1987

- E. D. Hirsch's book *Cultural Literacy*, which emphasizes the importance of creating a common, explicit curriculum in schools, is published and becomes a best seller.

1988

- The Illinois state legislature approves the Chicago School Reform Act, which shifts significant powers and money to the local schools. Elected local school councils are created with the authority to hire principals and approve local education and spending plans.
- Vice President George H. W. Bush campaigns for (and will win) the presidency promising to be the "Education President."
- Retired teacher Ray Budde writes *Education by Charter: Restructuring School Districts*, proposing charter schools as a method of providing schools with greater flexibility and accountability for student performance.
- American Federation of Teachers president Albert Shanker endorses the idea of charter schools in speeches and editorials.

1989

- President Ronald Reagan concludes his two terms in office with a 17 percent drop in federal funding for elementary and secondary education compared to the beginning of his administration.

1990

- Recent Princeton graduate Wendy Kopp founds Teach For America to attract noneducation majors to teach with alternative certification in areas with persistent teaching shortages.
- The National Governors Association and the Bush administration approve six national educational goals, known as America 2000, to be accomplished by 2000.
- The Milwaukee Parental Choice Program is enacted, allowing up to 1 percent (approximately 1,000) of economically disadvantaged students in the Milwaukee public schools to use their state share of education funds as full payment of tuition at participating nonsectarian private schools.

1991

- Minnesota enacts the nation's first charter school legislation.

1992

- School management company the Edison Project (later named Edison Schools) is founded.

1994

- President Bill Clinton signs the GOALS 2000: Educate America Act.
- The Republican takeover of Congress includes the "Contract with America," featuring prominent support for choice and privatization in education.
- Congress approves creation of the Public Charter Schools Program (PCSP) to help charter schools defray some of the costs associated with school planning and implementation.
- President Clinton signs the bipartisan Safe and Drug-Free Schools Act and the Gun-Free Schools Act.
- National History Standards are released by the University of California, Los Angeles Center for History in the Schools and are immediately met by protest.

1995

- The Milwaukee choice program is expanded to include religious schools among the options. Following a suit on separation of church and state

grounds, the Wisconsin Supreme Court allows nonsectarian expansion of the program but prohibits inclusion of religious schools.
■ The Ohio legislature enacts the Pilot Project Scholarship Program allowing Cleveland students to use tuition scholarships and assistance grants to attend participating private schools within Cleveland or public schools in participating adjacent districts.

1998

■ Congress passes the Charter School Extension Act, which reauthorizes the Public Charter Schools Program (PCSP) and creates grants to operate charter schools.
■ California voters overwhelmingly approve ballot initiative that effectively eliminates that state's bilingual education programs.

1999

■ Ohio Supreme Court overturns Cleveland voucher program on a legal technicality. The Ohio legislature reauthorizes the program, which is then halted under a judicial injunction, during which current students in the program return to their school of choice.
■ Florida enacts the nation's first statewide voucher program as part of the A+ Plan for Education, for students in "chronically failing" schools (defined as failing to meet minimum state standards two out of four years).
■ *April 30:* Two high school students murder 12 students and a teacher at Columbine High School in Littleton, Colorado, leading to increased calls for zero-tolerance policies that will impose mandatory suspensions for a variety of offenses including making verbal threats.

2000

■ Florida's voucher program is ruled unconstitutional by a state circuit judge in *Bush et al. v. Holmes et al.*, but the program is allowed to continue while the decision is appealed to the Florida Supreme Court.
■ The Board of Education of Cincinnati and the district's teachers' union adopt an incentive-based merit pay system, including the use of peer evaluators.
■ *December 11:* Cleveland's voucher program is rejected by a federal appeals panel on the grounds that it violates the separation of church and state. The ruling is later appealed to the U.S. Supreme Court, which accepts the case *Zelman v. Simmons-Harris*.

2001

■ Homeschooled population is estimated at 1 million students.

Education Reform

2002

- *January 8:* President George W. Bush signs the No Child Left Behind Act.
- *June 27:* In a 5-4 decision that provides major support for full school choice advocates, the U.S. Supreme Court rules in *Zelman v. Simmons-Harris* that the Cleveland voucher program does not infringe on the constitutional separation of church and state.
- *August 6:* A Florida circuit court judge rules that the Florida A+ Education Plan's provision allowing children in failing schools to receive vouchers to attend private schools violates the state's constitution. The decision is appealed by voucher supporters.
- *Fall:* The number of charter schools operating reaches 2,699.

2003

- *January 15:* New York City mayor Michael Bloomberg announces major overhaul of nation's largest school system, featuring increased administrative centralization, adoption of unified curriculum for most schools, and expanded parent involvement initiatives.
- *January 27:* First lawsuit filed seeking rights provided by the No Child Left Behind Act of 2001 is filed in New York City, charging that students have been denied transfers and guaranteed supplemental educational services.
- *February 19:* Colorado State House passes first voucher law allowing public funding for private school tuition since the U.S. Supreme Court decision in *Zelman v. Simmons-Harris.*
- *May 19:* The U.S. Supreme Court agrees to hear *Davey v. Locke* to consider Washington's Blaine Amendment prohibiting state scholarship aid for religious instruction.

2006

- The Florida Supreme Court upholds the finding of a lower court judge and strikes down the state's voucher program on the grounds that it is a violation of the uniformity clause, which requires the state to provide an uniform system of free public schools.

2007

- Combined federal, state, and local funding under No Child Left Behind legislation increases more than $100 billion dollars since the law's passage in 2002.

2009

- *March 10:* Newly inaugurated President Barack Obama describes his education reform vision as providing support from "cradle to career," with emphasis on increasing instructional time, boosting early childhood initiatives, expanding performance-based pay programs, and maintaining high state reading and math standards.

- *July 24:* President Obama and Secretary of Education Arne Duncan announce creation of Race to the Top Fund, a school reform project for states funded by money from the economic stimulus package.
- The number of charter schools operating reaches more than 5,000, serving more than 1.5 million students.

2010

- *July 21:* Less than two months after the nation's governors and state school chiefs released their final recommendations for national educational standards, 27 states adopt them and a dozen more are expected to do so shortly thereafter.

CHAPTER 4

BIOGRAPHICAL LISTING

This chapter briefly profiles key individuals in the history of U.S. education reform, including activists, writers, educators, and legal and political leaders.

Mortimer Adler, professor and founder of the Great Books curriculum, which was created in the mid-20th century to counter many progressive education measures seen as inhibiting academic achievement.

Jeanne Allen, president of the Center for Education Reform, a Washington, D.C.–based advocacy organization she founded in 1993. Allen is a frequent contributor to media examinations of education reform issues, speaking out in favor of school choice, charter schools, and the standards movement.

Thomas Aquinas, 13th-century Dominican monk, philosopher, and scholar who established the foundation of Roman Catholic education by explaining reason and faith as complementary sources of truth.

William Chandler Bagley, early 20th-century professor of education, well known for his critique of popular reforms of that era. Bagley emphasized the importance of a general liberal education, which he viewed as crucial in equipping individuals with skills to confront new situations.

Henry Barnard, late 19th-century Connecticut legislator and editor of the *American Journal of Education.* He was famed for his philosophy "schools good enough for the best and cheap enough for the poorest," and is considered the Father of American School Administration.

Roland Barth, a former Massachusetts teacher and principal. His popular and influential book, *Open Education and the American School,* described his enthusiasm and ultimate disillusionment with the open education movement in the United States during the 1960s–1970s.

Catherine Beecher, founder of the Hartford Female Seminary, a leading institution for teacher training in the late 19th century. Her leadership was key in providing support for the role of women as teachers in U.S. schools.

William Bennett, secretary of education 1985–88, during the Reagan administration. He has been an influential conservative critic of the failure of U.S. public schools and prominent supporter of the school choice and standards movements. Bennett became editor of the best-selling Book of Virtues series, designed to provide children with examples of moral behavior.

Arthur Bestor, a history professor and author of the influential 1953 book *Educational Wastelands,* which attacked progressive education's de-emphasis on intellectual disciplines.

John Franklin Bobbitt, author of *The Curriculum,* the earliest and widely used textbook on the theory of curriculum construction. Bobbitt's view that educators could use schools to precisely address deficiencies in the social order was particularly influential in the 1920s.

John Boehner, Republican (Ohio) chairman of the House Committee on Education and the Workforce 2001–06. He was a consistent supporter of President George W. Bush's educational initiatives, including the No Child Left Behind Act and expansion of school choice programs.

Clint Bolick, former litigation director for the Institute for Justice. Bolick was a leading legal advocate in the nationwide effort to defend school choice programs, and he played a key role in voucher victories in Milwaukee, Wisconsin, and Cleveland, Ohio.

Carl Brigham, professor of psychology at Princeton in the first half of the 20th century who is credited with the creation of the Scholastic Aptitude Test (SAT) in the 1920s. Brigham's work was very influential in the spread of intelligence testing throughout U.S. schools.

George H. W. Bush, 41st president of the United States. Bush won the election of 1988 campaigning as "the Education President" and organized the 1989 Education Summit with all 50 governors to establish national education goals.

George W. Bush, 43rd president of the United States. One of the first major legislative accomplishments of his administration was his signing of the No Child Left Behind Act (2001). As governor of Texas in the 1990s, Bush advocated accountability measures for districts, schools, teachers, and students.

Nicholas Butler, a founder of what later became known as Columbia's Teachers College in 1887 and president of Columbia University 1902–45. Butler's leadership in professional teacher training strengthened the progressive movement in education and influenced the formal study of pedagogy and curriculum.

Hollis Caswell, dean of Columbia's Teachers College in the 1930s–40s. Caswell's expertise in curriculum reform emphasized teacher leadership through the creation of in-service trainings.

Bob Chase, president of the National Education Association (NEA) 1996–2002. During his tenure, Chase led union opposition to many controversial proposed education reforms, particularly private school vouchers, and advocated for such measures as class-size reduction.

Lynne Cheney, former chairwoman of the National Endowment for the Humanities (NEH) and frequent conservative critic of U.S. public schooling. Cheney's vocal opposition to the proposed National History Standards in 1994 helped lead to increased debate about the role and composition of academic standards.

Kenneth Clark, influential City College of New York professor and psychologist. Clark's research in the 1940s demonstrating that segregation adversely affected the self-image of African-American children played a pivotal role in the movement to desegregate public schools.

Bill Clinton, 42nd president of the United States. He signed the GOALS 2000 legislation that provided funds for states to develop standards and assessments. Clinton supported the expansion of charter schools and public school choice, though he consistently opposed vouchers that would allow public funds to be used for public education.

James Conant, former president of Harvard and author of the 1959 book *The American High School Today.* The highly praised and popular book supported the elimination of small high schools that could not offer a full array of services, but otherwise supported the common practices of schools and refuted critics who called for widespread strengthening of academic standards.

George Counts, educational sociologist at Columbia's Teachers College 1927–55. His progressive-era journal the *Social Frontier* reflected his view that schools can and should lead the way in creating a new social order.

Elwood Cubberley, teacher, superintendent, and professor of education at Stanford. Cubberley was a major figure in the early 20th-century progressive education movement, advocating for the introduction of vocational education, professional management of public schools, and the use of schools as a tool to assimilate immigrants.

Richard M. Daley, mayor of Chicago since 1989. Daley obtained unprecedented control over the Chicago public schools from the Illinois General Assembly in 1995 and handpicked a management team that pursued academic performance through the reduction of the budget deficit, construction of new schools and building improvements, restriction of social promotion, and expansion of summer and early education programs.

John Dewey, philosopher and professor whose educational theories broke new ground in the first half of the 20th century and remain the foundation for modern advocates of progressive education. Dewey rejected the formalized drill-and-recitation methods of early U.S. public education, arguing in favor of a child-centered education based on experience, reflection, and the world outside the classroom. His creation of the University of Chicago Laboratory School in 1896 emphasized project-based learning that sought to appeal to children's interests and served as a model for the burgeoning progressive education movement.

W. E. B. DuBois, scholar, educator, writer, and leading African-American voice in the late 19th and early 20th centuries. He was a cofounder of the National Association for the Advancement of Colored People (NAACP) and used his position as editor of the organization's newspaper, the *Crisis*, to advocate for increased educational opportunity for African Americans.

Arne Duncan, U.S. secretary of education since 2009. Prior to assuming this position in the Obama administration, Duncan was the CEO of the Chicago Public Schools, the director of an educational nonprofit organization in Chicago, and a professional basketball player in Australia.

Dwight Eisenhower, 34th president of the United States. In 1958, Eisenhower signed the National Defense Education Act in response to Soviet advances in technology. The act sent for the first time massive amounts of federal money to aid public education.

Desiderius Erasmus, Dutch humanist and writer who proposed the systematic training of teachers in *Upon the Method of Right Instruction* (1511). He later advocated for the abolition of corporal punishment and advanced the necessity of understanding individual needs and abilities in education in *Of the First Liberal Education of Children*.

Rudolf Flesch, author of the 1955 book *Why Johnny Can't Read*. Flesch's primary contention that education professors were responsible for the diminished use of phonics in reading instruction touched off a national debate about literacy and intensified the national discussion of curriculum reform.

Milton Friedman, professor and prominent U.S. economist of the 20th century. In 1955, Friedman first proposed vouchers as an education reform.

Lou Gerstner, former CEO of IBM and Nabisco and cochair of the education reform organization Achieve 1996–2002. Gerstner has been the most prominent business executive advocate for school improvement since the early 1990s.

Jay Heubert, professor at Columbia University and a nationally recognized expert in the law of education reform. Much of Heubert's research has assessed the equity and efficiency of standardized testing as well as issues of discrimination.

E. D. Hirsch, English professor at the University of Virginia and author of the 1987 best-selling book *Cultural Literacy*. In it, Hirsch urged schools to emphasize specific knowledge of basic information and adoption of explicit curriculum to promote social justice and help increase opportunities for disadvantaged children.

John Holt, former teacher and author whose book *How Children Fail* (1964) and magazine *Growing Without Schooling* have led many to consider him the Father of Modern Homeschooling.

Education Reform

John Hughes, Catholic archbishop of New York City 1850–64. Hughes led protests against anti-Catholic bias in U.S. public schools and became known as the Father of Parochial Schools following his role in creating a privately funded national system of Catholic schools.

Thomas Jefferson, third president of the United States and author of the Declaration of Independence. Jefferson's opinions linking the health of a democracy to the establishment of education for common people helped provide the foundation for the early formation of the U.S. school system.

Lyndon Johnson, 36th president of the United States. During Johnson's administration upward of 60 education bills were passed, more than in any other administration. A former teacher before becoming involved in politics, Johnson explained the landmark Elementary and Secondary Education Act of 1965 by stating, "No measure I have signed, or will ever sign, means more to the future of America."

Isaac Kandel, prominent critic of the progressive education movement during the 1930s–40s. Kandel's advocacy for common, rigorous standards led to his influential support for the National Teacher Examinations.

Edward Kennedy, Democratic senator from Massachusetts from 1962 until his death in 2007 and former chairman of the Senate's Committee on Health, Education, Labor, and Pensions. Kennedy led the bipartisan congressional support for President George W. Bush's 2001 No Child Left Behind Act but sought more funding for the plan than proposed by the White House.

William Heard Kilpatrick, a key figure in the U.S. progressive education movement in the first quarter of the 20th century. Kilpatrick helped popularize and extend ideas such as project-based learning, curriculum integration, and whole child education.

Joel Klein, chancellor of the New York City Department of Education since 2002. Previously, Klein served as the CEO of the media corporation Bertelsmann and as a lawyer in the U.S. Department of Justice and in private practice.

Wendy Kopp, founder and director of Teach For America (TFA), a national teaching corps created to recruit, train, and place top college graduates in school districts with persistent teaching shortages. Kopp's senior thesis at Princeton University served as the model for TFA, which has been a leader in the drive for alternative certification for new teachers, as well as a target of that movement's critics.

Jonathan Kozol, author of the popular school-themed books *Death at an Early Age* (1967) and *Savage Inequalities* (1991), which reflect on the oppressive educational conditions among urban poor of the United States. Kozol remains a frequent critic of conservative school reforms.

John Locke, 17th-century English philosopher. His explanation of the value of experience and truth's relationship to objective reality helped establish a foundation for early American practical education.

Horace Mann, Father of the Common School, established America's first board of education in Massachusetts and left his position as a state senator to serve as its first secretary. Mann fought for reforms that resulted in the creation of training institutes for teachers and an increase in funding for teacher salaries, books, and school construction.

Thurgood Marshall, lawyer who argued against school segregation in the landmark U.S. Supreme Court case *Brown v. Board of Education* (1954). In 1967, Marshall became the first African-American Supreme Court justice. During his 24-year tenure on the bench, he played a critical role in education reform decisions, including his strong dissent against the property tax system's impact on school financing.

William Henry Maxwell, New York City schools superintendent in the early 20th century. His support of traditional instructional methods, including a general education curriculum, and opposition to many of the progressive movement's ideas, such as vocational education and junior high schools, placed him in the minority of education leaders of the time.

Deborah Meier, founder and former principal of Central Park East School in the Harlem section of New York City and current faculty member at New York University's Steinhardt School of Education. Meier's success in raising student achievement through an emphasis on active learning, parent/community involvement, and teacher autonomy has served as a model for many urban charter schools. She is a prominent opponent of the movement for standards-based reform.

Barack Obama, 44th president of the United States. Among the early priorities of his educational policy were an emphasis on early childhood programs and reform of the No Child Left Behind legislation.

Rod Paige, U.S. secretary of education from 2001 to 2005 in the George W. Bush administration. Paige played a key role in the initial implementation of No Child Left Behind provisions.

Plato, ancient Greek philosopher and author of *The Republic*. He expressed the belief that the state should operate an educational system with the aim to discover and develop abilities of the individual and prepare the individual for a role in society.

Quintilian, first-century A.D. Roman educator who advocated broad instruction with an emphasis on public education's advantages for socialization.

Diane Ravitch, a leading education historian and author of many books related to school reform. Ravitch was an assistant secretary of education during President George H. W. Bush's administration and is currently a senior fellow in education policy at the Brookings Institution.

William Rehnquist, chief justice of the U.S. Supreme Court from 1986 to 2005. Rehnquist wrote the majority decision in the 2002 Cleveland school voucher case and provided key support of other conservative positions on education reform issues.

Michelle Rhee, chancellor of Washington, D.C., public school system since 2007 and a leading figure of urban education reform. Previously, Rhee was a corps member in Teach For America and the cofounder of the New Teacher Project.

Jean-Jacques Rousseau, 18th-century French philosopher and author. Rousseau's ideas about education profoundly influenced supporters of progressive education, particularly his emphasis on learning by experience over book-based, rote memorization practices.

Albert Shanker, president of the American Federation of Teachers, the nation's largest teachers' union, from 1974 until his death in 1997. He was an influential voice in favor of national standards and assessment through his frequent op-ed pieces in the Sunday edition of the *New York Times*, arguing that social promotion offered students few incentives to excel.

Charles Silberman, journalist and author of the 1970s best-selling book *Crisis in the Classroom.* Silberman's book decried the "grim, joyless" conditions in public schools and extolled the advantages of open education, which encouraged increased informality in schools and student freedom in course selection and instructional time.

Theodore (Ted) Sizer, education professor, author, and founder and chairman of the Coalition of Essential Schools, a national network of schools and centers engaged in restructuring and redesigning schools to promote student learning and achievement.

Adam Smith, Scottish economist and author of the 1776 book *Wealth of Nations.* Smith expressed the belief that the state should give parents money for the education of their children, providing a philosophical foundation for supporters of school vouchers.

David Snedden, early 20th-century progressive education advocate. As Massachusetts commissioner of education and later as a Teachers College professor, Snedden helped lead efforts to implement aspects of social efficiency into public high schools.

David Souter, associate justice of the U.S. Supreme Court from 1990 to 2009. Souter wrote the lead dissent in the Cleveland school voucher case, expressing a deep concern for the protection of the separation of church and state.

Paul Vallas, superintendent of the Recovery School District of Louisiana (New Orleans) and former CEO of the Philadelphia school district and the Chicago public schools. In the mid- to late 1990s, Vallas led the effort to implement provisions of the Chicago School Reform Act, and he is often credited with helping turn around that city's struggling schools.

Booker T. Washington, founder of Tuskegee Institute in 1881 and a prominent voice for educational and economic advancement for African Americans in the late 19th and early 20th centuries. Washington supported the application of vocational education to help African Americans gain skills that would raise their status in U.S. society.

Noah Webster, early 19th-century lexicographer and advocate for widespread, systematic, and publicly supported education. Webster's books, *Grammatical Institute of the English Language* and the *Compendious Dictionary*, were enormously successful textbooks that helped define and popularize U.S. education practices.

Randi Weingarten, president of the American Federation of Teachers since 2008. She is a former lawyer and the first openly gay leader of a major American labor union.

Chris Whittle, founder and chairman of Edison Learning, the U.S. leading private, for-profit manager of public schools. Since its creation in 1995 as Edison Schools, the company has grown to operate more than 100 schools serving more than 70,000 students. Whittle's prominence has led to increased debate over the privatization of schools, school choice, and school financing.

Ella Flagg Young, teacher, principal, superintendent, and professor of pedagogy at the University of Chicago in the early 20th century. Flagg was the first female superintendent of schools, in Chicago 1907–15. In 1910, she became the first female president of the National Education Association.

CHAPTER 5

GLOSSARY

This chapter presents definitions of the most significant terms related to education reform and provides descriptions of their significance.

achievement gap The difference in academic success, particularly as measured by standardized assessment, that often exists between economically disadvantaged students and students of color from less disadvantaged backgrounds.

accountability A policy that holds districts, schools, and/or students responsible for performance. School and district accountability systems generally include public reporting and apply rewards or sanctions according to performance or improvement on assessment exams over time. Student accountability typically requires students to pass a test to be promoted from grade to grade or to graduate from high school.

adequate yearly progress (AYP) The measure that determines whether schools are meeting the required goal of No Child Left Behind legislation of bringing 100 percent of its students to academic proficiency by the end of the 2013–14 school year. Performance on reading and math assessments is the main indicator of whether AYP is being met, but graduation rates and at least one additional indicator for elementary schools (decided on by the state) also must be included.

alternative assessment Any form other than traditional standardized tests of measuring what students know and are able to do. Popular types include portfolios and performance-based assessments.

alternative certification The effort to expand entries into the teaching profession beyond the traditional path of taking pedagogy courses before entering the classroom. Programs require a bachelor's degree and a demonstration of knowledge in the subject area but allow intensive or compressed training while practice teaching or teaching students.

alternative school A public school that is set up by a state or school district to serve populations of students who are not succeeding in the traditional public school environment. While there are many different kinds of alternative schools, they are often characterized by their flexible schedules, smaller teacher-student ratios, and modified curricula.

assessment　An exercise, such as a standardized exam, written test, portfolio, or experiment, that seeks to measure a student's knowledge or skills in a subject area.

at risk　Term used to describe a student facing socioeconomic challenges, such as high poverty or teen pregnancy rates and exposure to violence, that may place him or her at a greater risk of failing, dropping out, or not achieving academic, social, and career goals.

bilingual education　An instructional program for students whose native language is not English in which students are taught for some portion of the day in their native language to allow them to keep up academically while they learn English.

Blaine amendments　Provisions of state constitutions restricting government aid to religious schools beyond those noted in the U.S. Constitution. They are named for late 19th-century Speaker of the House and proponent James Blaine and they are currently a key focus of legal challenge by advocates of school vouchers.

business-education partnership　A school-reform coalition formed by private businesses and schools or school districts. Such partnerships include resource support for individual schools, the introduction of management principles into public schools, and often advocacy of school choice and performance standards reforms.

character education　A national movement advocating specific instruction in basic virtues or morals as a means of combating concerns about the values and behavior of students.

charter school　A school that receives public funding but is run independently of the traditional public school system. Charter schools are often organized and established by groups made up of teachers, parents, or foundations, are free of many district regulations, and are often tailored to community needs.

Chicago School Reform Act　Sweeping legislation passed by the Illinois legislature in 1993 (with amendments in 1995) that includes a wide range of measures to improve public school performance, including **reconstitution, local control,** and opposition to **social promotion.**

child-centered curriculum　Pedagogical approach designed with the child's interests and needs at the center of the learning process, with an emphasis on experiential and problem-solving activities. Popular among educational progressives, it is also known as student-centered curriculum.

class-size reduction initiatives　A series of measures designed to improve the quality of classroom instruction by allowing teachers to focus on fewer students. The broad popularity of such laws has recently been undercut by concerns over cost and teacher availability.

Commission of the Reorganization of Secondary Education (CRSE) A 1918 group composed mainly of professors of education that redefined curricula in high schools to reflect notions of social efficiency, including providing different curricula for different groups of students based on their interests and likely future occupation. The CRSE's published plan, which shaped comprehensive high school instructional practice, was lauded by progressives for its inclusive nature and criticized by others for its lack of academic rigor.

Committee of Ten A panel dominated by college presidents that published a report in 1893 expressing the belief that every high school student should have a solid liberal education regardless of the student's ultimate occupation. The committee's findings were very influential in shaping the academically oriented nature of secondary education through the early 1900s.

common school A publicly supported school started during the mid-1800s that was open to all students.

compensatory education Programs established to overcome the academic deficiencies associated with the socioeconomic, cultural, or minority group disadvantages of students.

core curriculum A curriculum that stresses the required minimum subjects and topics that all students are expected to learn.

criterion-referenced test A standardized test that is aligned with a state's academic standards and intended primarily to measure students' performance related to those standards rather than to the performance of their peers nationally.

dame school Colonial and early national period low-level primary school usually conducted by an untrained woman in her own home. Instructors taught only basic fundamentals for which they were paid small fees.

decentralization The breakup and distribution of power from a central governing authority, most frequently applied in education to describe the transfer of school policymaking authority from the federal to the state level, or the transfer of decision-making authority from the state level to districts or schools (*see also* **local control**).

desegregation The reduction of racial isolation in schools and improvement of racial balance by eliminating the separation of groups of people along racial lines.

dress code School or district policy that requires school uniforms or restrictions on the color and type of clothing allowed in school in an effort to curb the presence of gangs and to reduce disciplinary conflicts.

drug-free and gun-free school zone An area around a school in which people caught or convicted of possession or use of illegal drugs or guns are subject to increased penalties under the law.

Glossary

Edison Learning The United States' largest private manager of public schools. Founded in 1992 as the Edison Project by Christopher Whittle and renamed Edition Schools in 2008, Edison has implemented its school design in 150 public schools, including many charter schools, operating under management contracts with local school districts and charter boards.

educational management organization (EMO) A company that provides curriculum, facility, financial, special education, technological, and other services to schools. Most EMOs are privately run and contract with charter schools.

Eight-Year Study An evaluation undertaken by progressive educators in the 1930s designed to demonstrate that students educated according to progressive philosophies were capable, adaptable learners who could excel even in postsecondary settings.

Elementary and Secondary Education Act (ESEA) Legislation of 1965 representing the federal government's single largest investment in elementary and secondary education. The ESEA focuses on children from high-poverty communities and students at risk of educational failure and authorizes several well-known federal education programs including Title I, Safe and Drug-Free Schools, and Bilingual Education.

English-only movement Advocates English as the official and only language used in the United States. Proponents generally view bilingual education as detrimental to the social mobility and economic advancement of immigrants.

Establishment Clause The Constitution's First Amendment prohibition against government regulation or endorsement of religion. The U.S. Supreme Court requires that public schools never give students the impression that their school officially sanctions religion in general or prefers a specific faith in particular. This has been a common battleground in education as groups argue over the meaning of this requirement

experiential education Curriculum and instruction that stresses hands-on experience through such activities as field trips, internships, and service learning projects as opposed to traditional classroom learning.

extended day programs After-school opportunities for students that provide a variety of activities, such as child care, tutoring, academic enrichment, and sports teams, and are often offered in conjunction with public facilities such as libraries and recreation centers. Such programs have increased dramatically in recent decades in response to the desires and needs of families where adults are not at home when students are dismissed from school.

Florida A+ Plan An education reform law passed in 1999 that includes the United States' first statewide voucher program allowing public funds to be used at private and religious schools, provisions for special education vouchers, and corporate tax incentives to support vouchers. The law was overturned by the Florida Supreme Court in 2006.

gifted and talented   Term applied to students who demonstrate high degrees of academic aptitude and achievement. There is no federal mandate requiring states to educate such students, and major provisions of No Child Left Behind legislation do not address their educational needs.

GOALS 2000: Educate America Act   A federal program signed by President Bill Clinton in 1994 that provides grants to states and school districts in exchange for the establishment of challenging academic content standards and accompanying assessments.

Head Start   A federal program established in 1965 that provides economically deprived preschoolers with education, nutrition, health, and social services at special centers based in schools and community settings throughout the country.

high-stakes testing   Assessments, typically standardized exams, that carry serious consequences for students or for educators. Schools gain public praise or financial rewards for high scores, and low scores may bring public embarrassment or heavy sanctions. For individual students, high scores may bring recognition of exceptional academic accomplishment and low scores may result in students being held back a grade or denied a high school diploma.

homeschooling   The educating of a student at home instead of in a public or private school setting. Legal in all 50 states, with regulations, the movement grew in the 1990s following parents' dissatisfaction with the quality of curricula, moral instruction, and school safety.

inclusion   The practice of educating children with disabilities alongside their nondisabled peers, often in a regular education classroom. Inclusion has become more prominent since the 1975 passage of the Individuals with Disabilities Education Act (IDEA) and subsequent amendments.

Kalamazoo School Case   An 1874 legal decision by the Michigan Supreme Court that supported public financial support for high schools in Michigan, influencing similar decisions and legislation across the United States.

in-service training   The lectures and workshops (often referred to as professional development) designed to keep teachers informed of the latest developments in their field. The training is called "in-service" to distinguish it from "pre-service" training, which means undergraduate coursework taken by those intending to teach.

local control   District or school flexibility and decision-making authority in the use of federal education funds for the unique needs of that community's students.

magnet school   A school that places special emphasis on academic achievement or on a particular field such as science, math, or performance arts. Such schools are designed to attract students from any part of a school district.

Massachusetts Act of 1642 and Massachusetts Law of 1647 Laws that established government influence on education. The 1642 law stated that parents and masters of those children apprenticed to them were responsible for their basic education and literacy. The 1647 law required the establishment of elementary schools in all towns of 50 or more families and the establishment of secondary schools in towns of more than 100 families.

merit pay A plan to pay teachers on the basis of their demonstrated competence in teaching and academic achievement of their students. Difficulty in objectively identifying good teaching and concern about how such a plan would be fairly administered have slowed its progress.

Milwaukee Parental Choice Program The first voucher legislation in the United States, passed in 1990, that allows students to attend private, nonreligious schools at taxpayer expense. The program originally allowed up to 1 percent of economically disadvantaged pupils in the Milwaukee, Wisconsin, public schools to use their state share of education funds as full payment of tuition in participating private schools.

multicultural education A curriculum that seeks to highlight subjects from diverse cultural, ethnic, racial, and gender perspectives beyond the traditional white, western European tradition.

National Assessment of Educational Progress (NAEP) Known as "the nation's report card," the NAEP is a national testing program administered by the U.S. Department of Education. Since 1969, NAEP tests have been conducted periodically in reading, math, science, writing, history, and geography and have provided comparable data over time on the achievement of fifth, eighth, and 10th graders across the nation.

National Defense Education Act Legislation of 1958 from the Eisenhower administration that responded to the fear of Soviet technological gains with a major federal influx of money for school construction, improved math and science curricula, and calls for higher academic standards.

A Nation at Risk This 1983 Reagan administration report has played a key role in initiating education reform efforts in the late 20th century. It warned that U.S. schools were lagging dangerously behind changes in society and the economy and that lax academic and behavioral standards needed to be dramatically improved.

No Child Left Behind Act The reauthorization of the **Elementary and Secondary Education Act** signed in 2001 by President George W. Bush. The act contains many education reform–related measures reflecting an emphasis on **accountability,** state flexibility and **local control,** public school choice, and teaching methods.

norm-referenced test   A standardized test designed primarily to compare the performance of students with that of their peers nationally. Such tests do not generally measure how students perform in relation to a state's own academic standards.

Ohio Pilot Project Scholarship Program (Cleveland voucher program)   A law adopted in 1995 that provides school vouchers for public school students to attend private and religious schools and to receive tutorial aid for students who chose to remain in public school. Legal challenges to the program led to the U.S. Supreme Court's 2002 decision *Zelman v. Simmons-Harris*, which upheld the legality of the program.

open education   A popular movement in the late 1960s and 1970s that emphasized student initiative to pursue their own interests in learning, teachers as facilitators rather than transmitters of knowledge, and large learning environments without walls. The movement faded, but its effects remained including increased course electives and reductions in graduation requirements.

outcome-based education   An education theory that guides curriculum by setting goals for students to accomplish rather than establishing subject content that students must master.

parochial school   A school that is affiliated with a religious denomination, most commonly associated with Roman Catholicism.

pay equity   The common form of teacher compensation, which pays teachers based on a single-salary schedule according to how many years they have been teaching and how many educational credits or degrees they have accumulated.

private scholarship program   A funding source from foundations or individuals intended to provide low-income families with money to pursue educational opportunities. Such programs are popular among supporters of school choice.

privatization   The transfer of the management of public schools of private or for-profit education organizations that emphasize common business-oriented concepts such as cost-effectiveness and customer satisfaction in running schools.

progressive education movement   An influential period in the history of U.S. schools that sought to make schools an instrument of social reform by focusing on instruction becoming more practical and centered on the interests of students. Supporters also increased the professionalization of teaching and school administration. It grew in prominence in the late 19th century and the first half of the 20th century largely due to the leadership of philosopher and professor John Dewey.

Race to the Top Fund   A $5 billion grant program administered by the U.S. Department of Education, created as part of the American Recovery and Reinvestment Act of 2009 (the stimulus package). The fund is designed to create or strengthen standards and assessments, data systems that track progress and foster continuous improvement, improvements in teacher effectiveness and in the equitable distribution of qualified teachers for all students, and providing intensive support and effective interventions for the lowest-performing schools.

reconstitution   School accountability measure in which a governing authority can disband a low-performing school's faculty following an intervention process and reopen the building with a new staff, structure, and curriculum.

school-based management   A form of decentralization, also known as site-based management, in which decision-making authority shifts from school districts to individual schools. Such proposals usually give control of a school's operation to a school council composed of parents, teachers, and local administrators.

school choice   A broad term that refers to proposals that allow students to attend schools outside their local district boundaries, with public funding for all or some of the tuition costs. The controversy over school choice largely revolves around the concern with using public funds for private or parochial schools.

school financing   A term broadly used to describe the mechanisms that fund the construction and maintenance of schools as well as the expenses associated with personnel, instruction, and student services. Typically, local property taxes make up the most significant portion of school financing, leading many to argue for a more equitable system.

school reform   The variety of efforts to improve schools. Reform encompasses issues of curriculum, instruction, financing, governance, discipline, and other factors in education.

school survey movement   The period between 1911 and 1930 in which nearly 200 cities and states were surveyed by experts from the major schools of education to determine school efficiency. The findings usually included recommendations for more curricular differentiation, increased intelligence testing to properly place students in programs, new vocational programs, and more power to administrators.

separation of church and state   *See* **Establishment Clause.**

service learning   Programs that incorporate citizenship values into education by requiring students to perform community service, which in some districts is a mandatory requirement for graduation.

Smith-Hughes Act   A 1917 act passed by the U.S. Congress that established federal aid for vocational education. It was the first federal program of any kind for public education.

social efficiency   The popular early 20th-century progressive education movement that emphasized curriculum and instruction that served purposes outside the classroom. Many supporters of this movement believed that many academic subjects, or at least the traditional approaches to them, lacked relevance for the great majority of students.

social promotion   The practice of schools and districts allowing students to proceed to the next grade, even if they are not performing at grade level. Opposition to social promotion grew with the popularity rise in the standards movement.

special education   Programs designed to serve children with mental and physical disabilities. Special education students are entitled to individualized education plans that detail the services needed to reach their educational goals. Traditionally, special education has taken place in separate classrooms, though increasingly, the services may also be offered in regular schools and classrooms (*see* **inclusion**).

special populations   Student subgroups by race/ethnicity, socioeconomic status, English language proficiency, and disability, whose performance on standardized assessment is disaggregated, reported, and factored into adequate yearly progress (AYP) results by requirement of No Child Left Behind (NCLB) legislation.

standardized curriculum   Instructional content that specifies in detail the carefully selected topics that will be covered in every subject area at every grade level at the school, district, state, or national level. Strict adherence to such curricula suggests that teachers should not have the option of disregarding or replacing that content.

standards   Subject-matter benchmarks that measure students' academic achievement. Although most agree that public schools' academic standards need to be raised, there is national debate over the construction and content of such standards and whether they should be national or local, voluntary or mandated.

state board of education   A state agency charged with adopting regulations and monitoring local school districts to ensure implementation of the constitutional and statutory mandates related to the operation of the state system of schools.

supplemental services   Academic assistance and educational interventions, such as tutoring and remediation, that must be provided outside of the regular school day by No Child Left Behind provisions to students attending schools that fail to meet adequate yearly progress for three or more consecutive years.

Teachers College   The leading education institution in the nation during the progressive education movement, located at Columbia University in New York City. Its professors and graduates have been among the most influential voices in school reform since its founding in 1887.

Title I   Also known as Chapter I, this is the nation's largest federal education program, with a 1995 funding level of $7.2 billion. Created in 1965 as part of President Lyndon Johnson's War on Poverty, Title

Glossary

I of the **Elementary and Secondary Education Act** serves remedial education programs to poor and disadvantaged children in nearly every school district in the country. Amendments to the law in 1994 have linked the program to schoolwide and districtwide reforms based on academic standards.

tuition tax credits   A mechanism that refunds expenses made toward education, including tutoring, texts, and computers, and, in the states that have them so far, private school tuition, up to a fixed figure. State legislation determines the amount of credit and what can be included in the deductions.

vocational education   Instruction that prepares a student for employment immediately after the completion of high school. Traditionally, the curriculum has focused on manufacturing industries, though in recent decades it has expanded to include computer-related fields.

voucher   A document that can be used by parents to pay tuition at an out-of-district public school, a private school, and/or a religious school. The term is also used to describe school choice proposals in which states would help pay tuition for children attending private or religious schools (*see* **school choice**).

year-round education   A modified school calendar that offers short breaks throughout the year, rather than the traditional summer vacation. Reasons for switching to a year-round schedule include to relieve crowding and to prevent students from forgetting much of the material covered in the previous year.

zero tolerance   School discipline policies that specify mandatory and strict punishment for breaking rules, usually relating to guns, drugs, or violence. These policies are designed to serve as a deterrent and protect the school population, but critics suggest they are often illogically applied.

PART II

GUIDE TO FURTHER RESEARCH

CHAPTER 6

HOW TO RESEARCH EDUCATION REFORM ISSUES

The explosive growth of the Internet, particularly the World Wide Web, has allowed students, teachers, and advocates of education reform to gain research access to relevant and specific information more efficiently than ever before. Despite the Internet's expansive reach, good old-fashioned library research remains an essential component to finding information on education reform. This chapter explains what is available to the education reform researcher via the Internet, bibliographical resources, and in the area of legal research. It also describes strategies for their effective use.

ONLINE RESOURCES

The Internet provides a kind of library that never closes and can serve as an excellent starting point for education reform researchers, particularly those seeking the most recent articles and developments. The ability to explore the vast expanse of information found on the Internet is a critical skill needed to conduct efficient research projects. Understanding how to navigate online can help the researcher find the information he or she is seeking and lead to many other useful Web sites that contain even more relevant information.

APPROACHING THE WEB

Searching for information online can be an exhilarating and exasperating experience. In order to avoid the frustrations that can accompany online searching, a few approaches are helpful. First, understand that the specific research being sought may be found quickly or may be uncovered only after investigating other usually related and often interesting links. When conducted with discipline and focus, the initial search will usually prove fruitful, if longer than anticipated, and may very well yield additional rewarding information.

During the course of Web searching, one can easily get distracted and lose track of a particularly useful site previously encountered. In these situations, there are two critical routes back to the intended site. The "Back" button directly retraces all the sites previously viewed all the way to the beginning of the search, allowing the researcher to view any of the sites along the way. The "History" button provides a similar function. It allows the researcher to review all of the sites previously viewed and can track these by order visited on that particular day, the previous day, the previous week, and even as far back as many weeks prior to the current search.

Added to this celebration of the Internet's use for education reform researchers is an important caveat: Some material posted on Web sites may be inaccurate or unreliable. In conducting research, one will likely encounter sites created by credible and well-known individuals and groups as well as those created by unknown origin. The material on such sites may be valuable but should be checked scrupulously. Exposure to the variety of Web sites will allow the researcher to sharpen his or her instincts regarding the quality of information presented, and it will also help the researcher to properly interpret and use it.

RESEARCH ORGANIZATIONAL TOOLS

The greatest benefit of conducting online research, access to the volume of diverse information, can also be its greatest pitfall. Strategies and tools to keep this research organized are critical.

A Web browser's "Favorites" menu (sometimes called "Bookmarks") allows the education reform researcher to create a folder (and subfolders) for key topics. A Web browser also provides the user with the option of creating links that can be organized in a conspicuous space on the user's computer screen, allowing even quicker access to commonly viewed sites.

Utilizing the Favorites or Bookmarks links is often more efficient than downloading a copy of an entire Web page or Web site because of the large amount of disk space that downloading can require. If during the course of research, it is discovered that a Web site is no longer active, it may still be found by using the Internet Archive Wayback Machine. This whimsically named site is a collaboration among the Internet Archive, the Library of Congress, and the California Digital Library. As of late 2009, the Internet Archive Wayback Machine had archived more than 150 billion Web pages that were published since 1996.

Another online method allowing researchers to stay informed of recent information is to subscribe to Web sites. This usually does not involve any monetary transaction but rather simply requires providing contact information. The person or group administering the Web site can then send notifications of important information.

WEB DIRECTORIES AND SEARCH ENGINES

The potentially daunting task of searching for information on the Web is made manageable thanks to Web directories and search engines. A Web directory is similar to a library's subject catalog. Web directories attempt to organize the seemingly limitless amount of information on the Web into topics and subtopics, such as News, Health, Business, Entertainment, Sports, and Education. A Web directory such as Yahoo! (http://www.yahoo.com) is an excellent site to start a search if one has a good sense of how to find the intended subjects within a hierarchy of larger subjects.

For instance, the education reform researcher can go to Yahoo! and find the topic heading Education. A click on the Education link leads to multiple categories including Reform. Clicking "Reform" leads the researcher to more category links including Books, Organizations, and School Choice, as well as a direct link to many of the most popular sites about education reform on the World Wide Web.

This top-down organization of Web content allows the researcher to search for a particular subject while simultaneously reviewing other related issues and links. In addition, Yahoo! employs indexers who evaluate sites for quality, which for many raises confidence that the information retrieved is accurate.

In addition to Yahoo!, other top Web directories include

- About.com (http://www.about.com)
- Open Directory Project (http://www.dmoz.org)

A search engine, like a library's card catalog, serves as an index enabling the researcher to seek out specific words or phrases. With the assistance of a search engine, one can locate individual appearances of such words in all documents throughout the Web, allowing the researcher to scan quickly the millions of sites and billions of words on the Web for the precise information desired.

Directions for using search engines are usually straightforward and reliant on the use of keywords. Those wishing for more specific instruction may investigate the many Web tutorials available online. To find one, simply type in "Web search tutorial" into the keyword section of any of the search engines listed at the conclusion of this section.

Following are some tips for the effective use of search engines:

- When searching for a broad topic, simply enter keywords that are as descriptive as possible (for example, "zero tolerance policies in schools"). Most search engines will then return a list of Web sites that match those terms.

- To narrow a search, use "AND" in the keyword box. For example, "charter schools AND Michigan" will match only links that include both terms.

- To broaden a search, use "OR" in the keyword listing. For example, "bilingual programs OR limited English proficiency" will match any page that has either term.

- To exclude unwanted results, use "NOT" as part of the keyword instruction. For example, "school voucher cases NOT Zelman" finds sites that include information about school voucher cases but not the *Zelman v. Simmons-Harris* case.

Many search engines now have built large subject catalogs, minimizing the difference between them and Web directories. There are scores of commonly used search engines, but among the most popular and efficient are the following:

All the Web (http://www.alltheweb.com)
AltaVista (http://www.altavista.com)
Ask (http://www.ask.com/)
Excite (http://www.excite.com)
Google (http://www.google.com)
HotBot (http://www.hotbot.com)
Lycos (http://www.lycos.com)
MSN (http://www.msn.com/)
WebCrawler (http://www.webcrawler.com)

Because search engines and Web directories have different orientations and strengths, one may wish to use a metasearch site, which automatically processes the query to multiple search engines. Among the top metasearch sites are the following:

Clusty (http://clusty.com/)
Dogpile (http://www.dogpile.com)

EDUCATION REFORM SITES

While Web directories and search engines will lead the education reform researcher to useful sites, there are many sites that are particularly helpful because of their thorough organization, detailed information, and numerous links to other resources. Such sites have become so rich in information and user-friendly that they are the most valuable tool to research education reform issues. They allow the researcher to simply type in a desired term and within seconds become connected to hundreds or more articles and publications that typically reach back several years.

Among these especially content-rich sites are the following:

- The Education Resources Information Center (ERIC) (http://www. askeric.org) is a personalized Internet-based service providing education information through subject-specific clearinghouses, including assessment and evaluation and teacher education. This site also includes a link to the ERIC database, the world's largest source of education information, with more than 1.3 million abstracts of documents and journal articles on education research and practice.

- Yahoo! has an education issues page (http://news.yahoo.com/us/education) that comprises links to a variety of sources and includes featured daily articles on a wide range of education reform issues.

- The Center for Education Reform (http://www.cer.org) offers thorough sets of links relating to issues, analysis, and resources of education reform. This advocacy organization is a strong supporter of school vouchers and charter schools.

- The American Federation of Teachers Web site (http://www.aft.org) features positions of the nation's largest teachers' union on many of the key education reform issues. The site also includes archives of more than 1,000 articles from the organization's Where We Stand series.

- *Education Week's* Web site (http://edweek.com) offers links to current and archived articles, daily news, special reports, and a Hot Topics section featuring a wealth of information on education reform issues, including accountability, charter schools, homeschooling, school finance, standards, violence and safety, and vouchers.

- CNN's Web site has an Education Policy page (http://topics.cnn.com/ topics/education_policy) that features updated articles and videos related to educational policy issues.

- The *New York Times* Web site (http://www.nytimes.com/pages/education/ index.html) provides easy links to current and recent education-related articles as well as archived articles.

- The Public Education Network Web site (http://www.publiceducation. org/index.asp) features a wealth of informative links, including current and recent publications on a variety of education reform topics, such as No Child Left Behind, standards and accountability, and teacher quality.

- The Education Commission of the States Web site (http://www.ecs.org) includes links on nearly 100 key topics in education reform, with free downloadable links.
- The Mid-Continent Regional Educational Laboratory, a provider of research-based expertise for educators and policy makers, has a site (http://www.mcrel.org) that includes links to policy issues and sources of research with guidelines for its interpretation and application.
- The U.S. Department of Education's Web site (http://www.ed.gov) provides a remarkably extensive range of links related to the federal role in public education, including policy and research statistics. It also includes links to the complete text of key federal education legislation.

In addition to all the news and education-related sites where one can find myriad useful articles, a researcher may also discover a wealth of information by accessing publication databases, which are typically offered free at public libraries. With one of these services, such as ProQuest, finding articles from newspapers, magazines, and professional journals is straightforward and enormously accessible, allowing searches for specific education reform terms within preferred publication dates, resulting in links to articles.

FINDING ORGANIZATIONS AND INDIVIDUALS

The education reform sites listed and the myriad others that exist on the Web may lead the researcher to seek more information about particular groups or people. The simplest method to finding this additional information is to enter the group's or person's name into a search engine's keyword space. This should lead to Web sites and possibly contact information.

Guessing what an organization's Web address is, though seemingly a shortcut, can often take longer than working through a search engine. For example, one might think that Teach For America's address would be http://www.tfa.org, but it is actually http://www.teachforamerica.org. Conversely, the Committee for Education Funding uses an acronym for its site, http://www.cef.org.

Finally, it is important to note the suffix that is used for particular sites. In general, most advocacy groups use the suffix ".org," government sites employ ".gov," educational institutions use ".edu," and commercial and many personal sites use ".com."

BIBLIOGRAPHIC RESOURCES

Any printed resource that identifies and lists books, periodical articles, and other published works that deal with education reform can also be an enormously useful tool in conducting research. Among these resources are library catalogs, bookstore catalogs, and periodical databases.

LIBRARY CATALOGS

Card catalogs, once ubiquitous at public and academic libraries, have largely been replaced or complemented by online catalogs that often allow researchers remote access via the Internet.

The Library of Congress has the largest library catalog, and online access to it is available (http://catalog.loc.gov/). A subject search at this site for "education reform" leads to almost 3,000 results, which can easily be sorted by title, author, date (ascending or descending), and relevance.

In addition to the Library of Congress's online library catalog, most public and academic libraries now offer online access, which in many cases allows the researcher to check an institution's holdings from any computer with Internet capability. Directions for using the online catalogs at local, school, and university libraries are usually similar to those noted for the Library of Congress.

BOOKSTORE CATALOGS

The impact of the Internet on research is also evident in another bibliographic resource: the bookstore catalog. A growing number of bookstores, such as Borders and Barnes & Noble, have rich online catalogs (http://www.borders.com and http://www.barnesandnoble.com). The prominent bookseller Amazon provides only an online catalog, although it is the world's largest (http://www.amazon.com).

Many researchers find these online bookstore catalogs attractive because of their ease of use and their inclusion of publisher's information, available excerpts, book reviews, and readers' commentary about a particular book. Although the education reform researcher can find great benefits in exploring the online bookstores, visiting "brick-and-mortar" bookstores and personally holding and reviewing a book remains a valuable experience.

PERIODICAL DATABASES

Database services such as InfoTrac are commonly found in most public libraries. Such subscription-based services index articles from hundreds of general interest and some specialized periodicals. The database can be searched by author, words in the title, subject headings, and occasionally words found anywhere in the text. Depending on the database used, "hits" can result in a bibliographical description (featuring author's name, title, pages, periodical name, issue date, etc.), a description plus an abstract (a paragraph summarizing the contents of the article), or the full text of an article.

Most libraries also provide Internet access to their periodical databases as an option in their catalog menu. Licensing restrictions, however, usually mean that only researchers who have a library card for that particular library can access the database. In such cases, the researcher need only type in his or her name and card number.

Another avenue that may lead to useful database information is to find the Web sites for periodicals likely to cover the topic of interest. Some scholarly publications put all or most of their articles online, while the more popular publications tend to offer a more limited selection. Some publications of both types offer archives of several years' back issues that can be searched by author or keyword.

LEGAL RESEARCH

The continuing focus on education reform issues in public debate has led to a growing body of legislation and court cases. Because legal research is so often heavy with specialized terminology, it can be more difficult to conduct than bibliographical or general research.

Again, the Internet has provided a variety of helpful tools to combat this potential research roadblock. The Internet offers a variety of ways to look up local laws and court cases without having to delve into the often-intimidating bound volumes in law libraries, which may not be accessible to the general public.

FINDING LAWS

When federal legislation is approved, it becomes part of a massive legal compendium known as United States Code. Laws in the U.S. Code can be referred to either by their popular name or by a formal citation. The U.S. Code can be searched online (http://uscode.house.gov/) and via Cornell Law School's Web site (http://www4.law.cornell.edu/uscode/).

Many states also have their codes of law online. The Internet Law Library provides a link to state laws that can be accessed (http://www.lawgurv.com/ilawlib/?id=17). Cornell Law School's Web site also provides links to this information (http://www.law.cornell.edu/states).

TRACKING LEGISLATION

Congress and state legislatures regularly debate education reform–related bills. The Library of Congress's catalog site includes files that summarize legislation by the number of the congressional session (every two-year session of Congress is designated a consecutive number; for example, the 111th

Congress was in session in 2009–10). Legislation can be searched for at this site by the name of its sponsor, the bill number, or by keywords.

The Library of Congress's THOMAS site (http://thomas.loc.gov/) provides a clearer and easier resource for keeping up with legislative developments. At THOMAS, the education reform researcher can search for summaries of legislation considered by each Congress by name, bill number, or keyword. For example, the No Child Left Behind Act can be found by its name or under its bill number, H.R. 1. If one has heard about a bill increasing parental choice in where a child attends school but does not know the bill's number, a keyword search for "school choice" may produce useful listings. Clicking on the bill number of a particular listing leads to a screen with links to a summary, legislation text, current status, floor action, and other related information.

FINDING COURT DECISIONS

Legal decisions are also organized using a system of citations. The general form for citation is *Party 1 v. Party 2, volume and court reporter (year)*. An example of this is *Zelman v. Simmons-Harris*, 200 U.S. 321 (2002). Here the parties are Zelman (plaintiff) and Simmons-Harris (defendant), the case is in volume 200 of the U.S. Supreme Court Reports, beginning on page 321, and the case was decided in 2002. (For the Supreme Court, the name of the court may be omitted, though it would be included for other cases.)

Finding federal court decisions involves determining the level of the court involved: District courts are the lowest level and are where trials are normally held, circuit courts are the main courts of appeals, and the Supreme Court is the nation's highest court. Once this is ascertained the education reform researcher can visit sites on the Web to find cases by citation and often the names of the parties. Among the most useful sites for locating court decisions are

- The **Legal Information Institute** Web site (http://supct.law.cornell.edu/supct/), which features all Supreme Court decisions since 1990 as well as more than 600 other influential, earlier decisions. It also provides links to other databases with early court decisions.
- The **Washburn University School of Law** Web site (http://www.washlaw.edu), which provides links to a variety of court decisions, including those from state courts, and includes information about many important topics in legal research.

More information about conducting legal research online can be gained by visiting a reliable search engine and typing "conducting legal research online tutorial" into the keyword bar and then visiting the selected sites listed.

CHAPTER 7

ANNOTATED BIBLIOGRAPHY

This chapter provides bibliographic information and brief content descriptions of books, periodicals articles, Internet articles, and other media relating to education reform issues. This bibliography lists a representative sample of sources, primarily those published since 2001. It also includes some earlier materials that have particular historical relevance. Listings are categorized as books, periodicals (including magazines, newspapers, and journals), Internet articles (some of which also appear in print), and other media (including videos and Web casts). Sources have been selected to present clear and useful research from a variety of viewpoints.

BOOKS

Abernathy, Scott. *No Child Left Behind and the Public Schools.* Ann Arbor: University of Michigan Press, 2007. Analyzes the successes and failures of No Child Left Behind legislation and questions whether any test can properly measure effective education.

Allen, Michael I. *The Two Faces of Education: An Insider's View of School Reform.* Lanham, Md.: Rowman & Littlefield Education, 2006. Focuses on issues students bring to school that impede their learning and explores how teachers can successfully address them.

Anderson, Gary. *Advocacy Leadership: Toward a Post-Reform Agenda in Education.* New York: Routledge, 2009. Criticizes managerial role of educational leaders, particularly in low-income areas, and proposes an advocacy-based form of leadership.

Ayers, William, ed. *Zero Tolerance: Resisting the Drive for Punishment.* New York: New Press, 2001. Criticizes the implementation of zero-tolerance policies in schools, claiming they are ineffective, racially biased, and constitutionally unsound.

Barth, Roland Sawyer. *Open Education and the American School.* New York: Schocken Books, 1974. Analyzes the initial growth and subsequent difficulties of the open education movement in the early 1970s.

Bestor, Arthur. *Educational Wastelands: The Retreat from Learning in Our Public Schools.* Reprint, Champaign: University of Illinois Press, 1988. Criticizes progressive education's anti-intellectual effect on schools and advocates for a rigorous and well-defined curriculum. This influential book was first published in 1953.

Bracey, Gerald W. *The War Against America's Public Schools: Privatizing Schools, Commercializing Education.* Boston: Allyn & Bacon, 2001. Criticizes individuals and organizations that have promoted politically conservative and market approaches to school reform.

Brown, Dan. *The Great Expectations School: A Rookie Year in the New Blackboard Jungle.* New York: Arcade Publishing, 2008. Explores a young teacher's first year teaching at an elementary school in the Bronx and describes the challenges of working within an often unresponsive system as well as the ultimate inspiration derived from the experience.

Buckly, Jack, and Mark Schneider. *Charter Schools: Hope or Hype?* Princeton, N.J.: Princeton University Press, 2009. Uses data on Washington, D.C., charter schools to provide balanced assessment of the movement's effectiveness.

Carini, Patricia F., and Joseph Featherstone. *Starting Strong: A Different Look at Children, Schools, and Standards.* New York: Teachers College Press, 2001. Counters critics of public schools and proponents of high-stakes testing by describing the learning capacity of young students.

Carnoy, Martin, Rebecca Jacobsen, Lawrence Mishel, and Richard Rothstein. *The Charter School Dust-Up: Examining the Evidence on Enrollment and Achievement.* New York: Teachers College Press, 2005. Criticizes many of the claims of educational improvement and effectiveness made by charter school advocates.

Casella, Ronnie. *At Zero Tolerance: Punishment, Prevention, and School Violence.* New York: Peter Lang Publishing, 2001. Argues against the proliferation of "get-tough" policies in schools and offers methods of violence prevention including school restructuring and vocational education.

Chavous, Kevin. *Serving Our Children: Charter Schools and the Reform of American Public Education.* Herndon, Va.: Capital Books, 2004. Uses Washington, D.C., as a model for how charter schools can improve the quality of education in America.

Christensen, Clayton M., Curtis W. Johnson, and Michael B. Horn. *Disrupting Class: How Disruptive Innovation Will Change the Way the World Learns.* New York: McGraw-Hill, 2008. Includes case studies and neuroscience research to explain that the future of effective education requires a greater integration of technology and customized curriculum.

Chubb, John E. *Learning from No Child Left Behind: How and Why the Nation's Most Important but Controversial Education Law Should Be Renewed.* Stanford, Calif.: Hoover Press, 2009. Outlines 10 specific lessons and recommendations that identify the strengths and weaknesses of NCLB and offers suggestions for improving the law, building on its current foundation.

Cohen, David K., and Heather C. Hill. *Learning Policy: When State Education Reform Works.* New Haven, Conn.: Yale University Press, 2001. Argues that effective state reform depends on conditions that most reforms ignore: coherence in practice as well as policy and opportunities for professional learning.

Conant, James. *The American High School Today: A First Report to Interested Citizens.* New York: McGraw-Hill, 1959. Recommends replacing small high schools with larger, comprehensive schools offering broader services and rejects calls for popular school reform strategies of the late 1950s.

Corbett, H. Dickson, and Bruce L. Wilson. *Listening to Urban Kids: School Reform and the Teachers They Want.* Albany: State University of New York Press, 2001. Presents the voices and perspectives of urban middle school students, who explain how to make school more relevant and meaningful.

Corwin, Ronald G. *The School Choice Hoax: Fixing America's Schools.* Lanham, Md.: Rowman & Littlefield Education, 2007. Argues that school choice as typically described and implemented is not effective but can improve education if altered in a more research-based and integrated manner.

Darling-Hammond, Linda. *The Flat World and Education: How America's Commitment to Equity Will Determine Our Future.* New York: Teachers College Press, 2010. Outlines problems that harm the quality and equity of the American educational system and proposes changes to improve it.

———. *The Right to Learn: A Blueprint for Creating Schools That Work.* New York: Jossey-Bass, 2001. Describes learner-centered schools that work for students in all kinds of communities and outlines the policies and practices that are needed to create these schools on a systemwide basis.

Dewey, John. *Democracy and Education: An Introduction to the Philosophy of Education.* Reprint, Washington, D.C.: Freer Gallery of Art, 1997. Describes strategies for training students to become socially responsible adults and conscientious citizens concerned with the rights of others and the common good, while developing the knowledge and technical skills to be productive members of society. This landmark book in the progressive education movement was first published in 1916.

Digiulio, Robert C. *Educate, Medicate, or Litigate? What Teachers, Parents, and Administrators Must Do About Student Behavior.* Thousand Oaks, Calif.: Corwin Press, 2001. Explores bullying and other antisocial behavior in schools, analyzes common myths about school violence and its origins, and prescribes methods of prevention.

Annotated Bibliography

Dingerson, Leigh, ed. *Keeping the Promise? The Debate Over Charter Schools.* Milwaukee: Rethinking Schools Ltd., 2008. This volume includes collection of essays from nationally known educators such as Ted Sizer and Linda Darling-Hammond, interviews with leaders of community-based charter schools, and analyses of how charters have developed in cities such as New Orleans and Washington, D.C.

Dwyer, James G. *Vouchers Within Reason: A Child-Centered Approach to Education Reform.* Ithaca, N.Y.: Cornell University Press, 2001. Advocates vouchers for private schools as a fair, child-centered approach for good schooling and proposes a plan that would restrict vouchers to secular aspects of school programs, sidestepping legal issues relating to the separation of church and state.

Education Week. *Education Week Guide to K–12 Terminology.* New York: Jossey-Bass, 2009. Provides a thorough description and analysis of current vocabulary, jargon, and acronyms in education.

———. *The Obama Education Plan: An Education Week Guide.* New York: Jossey-Bass, 2009. Outlines the educational policy of newly inaugurated president Barack Obama.

Elmore, Richard. *School Reform from the Inside Out: Policy, Practice, and Performance.* Cambridge, Mass.: Harvard Education Press, 2004. A collection of essays that assert successful school reform stems from teachers, administrators, and school staff, not external mandates or standards.

Engel, Michael. *The Struggle for Control of Public Education: Market Ideology vs. Democratic Values.* Philadelphia: Temple University Press, 2000. Argues that the battle of school control is an ideological one and urges increased openness, social awareness, and idealism in community-controlled schools over vouchers, charter schools, and standards.

Evans, Robert. *The Human Side of School Change: Reform, Resistance, and the Real-Life Problems of Innovation.* New York: Jossey-Bass, 2001. Adopts a holistic approach to education reform, concentrating on why substantive innovation has been difficult to achieve.

Flesch, Rudolf. *Why Johnny Can't Read.* Reprint, New York: HarperCollins, 1986. Asserts that reading instruction has suffered due to the abandonment of the phonics method. Originally published in 1955, the best-selling book represented a rejection of much of progressive education's curricular philosophy.

Foote, Donna. *Relentless Pursuit: A Year in the Trenches with Teach For America.* New York: Vintage Books, 2008. Profiles four first-year teachers at an urban Los Angeles high school who are part of the Teach For America program.

Forness, Steven R., and James M. Kaufmann. *Education Deform: Bright People Sometimes Say Stupid Things About Education.* Lanham, Md.: Scarecrow Press, 2002. Rejects the common ideological rhetoric from the left and the right in favor a reasoned focus on improving instruction for the entire spectrum of students.

Fuller, Bruce, ed. *Inside Charter Schools.* Cambridge, Mass.: Harvard University Press, 2001. Provides an analysis of the charter school movement through studies of six diverse charter schools.

Gatto, John Taylor. *Weapons of Mass Instruction: A Schoolteacher's Journey Into the Dark World of Compulsory Schooling.* Gabriola Island, BC, Canada: New Society Publishers, 2008. Focuses on mechanisms of familiar schooling that cripple imagination, discourage critical thinking, and create a false view of learning as a by-product of rote-memorization drills.

Hacsi, Timothy A. *Children As Pawns: The Politics of Educational Reform.* Cambridge, Mass.: Harvard University Press, 2002. Presents stories of five important topics in education reform—Head Start, bilingual education, small class size, social promotion, and school funding—and shows the problems with the design of these popular policies and programs.

Hamilton, Laura S. *Standards-Based Accountability Under No Child Left Behind.* Santa Monica, Calif.: RAND Corporation, 2007. Sheds light on how accountability policies have been translated into actions at the district, school, and classroom levels in three states.

Hawley, Willis D. *The Keys to Effective Schools: Educational Reform as Continuous Improvement.* Thousand Oaks, Calif.: Corwin Press, 2006. Focuses on how to change a school's organizational structure and culture to improve the quality of teaching and learning.

Hayes, William. *No Child Left Behind: Past, Present, and Future.* Lanham, Md.: Rowman & Littlefield Education, 2008. Provides a thorough description of the No Child Left Behind Act, including its history and provisions for accountability, teacher quality, and choice.

Henig, Jeffrey. *Spin Cycle: How Research Is Used in Policy Debates: The Case of Charter Schools.* New York: Russell Sage Foundation Publications, 2008. Explores how controversies over the charter school movement illustrate the use and misuse of research in policy debates.

Henig, Jeffrey, Desiree S. Redescleaux, Marion Orr, and Richard C. Hula. *The Color of School Reform: Race, Politics, and the Challenge of Urban Education.* Princeton, N.J.: Princeton University Press, 2001. Focuses on influence of race in education reform in Atlanta, Baltimore, Detroit, and Washington, D.C., where local governmental authority has passed from white to black leaders, and explains that black administrative control of big-city school systems has not yet translated into broad improvements in the quality of public education.

Hersch, Barton J., and Nancy L. Deutsch. *A Place to Call Home: After School Programs for Urban Youth.* Washington, D.C.: American Psychological Association, 2005. Identifies strengths of increasingly popular after-school programs for students and suggests ways they can become more effective.

Hershberg, Theodore, and Clare Robertson-Kraft. *A Grand Bargain for Education Reform*. Cambridge, Mass.: Harvard Education Press, 2009. Offers an ambitious new system for evaluating, compensating, and providing professional development for school teachers and administrators.

Hess, Frederick M. *Common Sense School Reform*. New York: Palgrave Macmillan, 2006. Criticizes "status quo" reform efforts that focus on such issues as class size reduction and professional development in favor of an approach emphasizing rewarding excellence and punishing failure.

————. *The Future of Educational Entrepreneurship: Possibilities for School Reform*. Cambridge, Mass.: Harvard Education Press, 2006. Supports the case that economic forces can be leveraged to improve educational performance of schools.

Hirsch, E. D., Jr. *Cultural Literacy*. New York: Vintage, 1988. Argues that children are being deprived of the basic knowledge that would enable them to function in contemporary society and includes, in dictionary style, 5,000 essential facts to know.

Howell, William H., and Paul E. Peterson. *The Education Gap: Vouchers and Public Schools*. Washington, D.C.: Brookings Institute, 2002. Analyzes research on various voucher programs and indicates that, while not a panacea for the complex problems facing U.S. schools, vouchers may help close the achievement gap between African-American and white students.

Jacobs, Joanne. *Our School: The Inspiring Story of Two Teachers, One Big Idea, and the School That Beat the Odds*. New York: Palgrave Macmillan, 2007. Describes the successful efforts of two teachers who opened a San Jose charter school.

Johnson, Amanda Walker. *Objectifying Measures: The Dominance of High-Stakes Testing and the Politics of Schooling*. Philadelphia: Temple University Press, 2009. Critiques the increasingly influential industry of high-stakes assessment and warns of its costs in educational quality.

Johnston, Michael. *In the Deep Heart's Core*. New York: Grove Atlantic Press, 2002. Recounts the experience in Greenville, Mississippi, of a member of Teach For America, the nation's largest alternative certification organization.

Knowles, Kaeli T., Barbara S. Plake, and David Z. Robinson, eds. *Testing Teacher Candidates: The Role of Licensure Tests in Improving Teacher Quality*. Washington, D.C.: National Academy Press, 2001. Examines teacher licensure tests, evaluates the merits of using test results to hold states and institutions accountable, and suggests alternatives for developing beginning teacher competence.

Kohn, Alfie. *The Homework Myth: Why Our Kids Get Too Much of a Bad Thing*. Cambridge, Mass.: Da Capo Press, 2207. Argues that the assigning of homework does not improve student understanding or performance and in fact diminishes student success by suppressing enjoyment of learning.

————. *What Does It Mean to Be Well Educated? And More Essays on Standards, Grading, and Other Follies.* Boston: Beacon Press, 2004. Critiques many education policies, including the corporate influence in schools and the heavy reliance on standardized testing, in a vast selection of previous writings.

Kopp, Wendy. *One Day, All Children . . . : The Unlikely Triumph of Teach For America and What I Learned Along the Way.* New York: Public Affairs, 2001. Describes the creation and impact of Teach For America, which recruits, trains, and places top college graduates in districts with persistent teaching shortages, founded by the author as a 21-year-old college senior.

Kornhaber, Mindy, and Gary Orfield, eds. *Raising Standards or Raising Barriers? Inequality and High Stakes Testing in Public Education.* Washington, D.C.: Century Foundation Press, 2001. Examines economic and educational assumptions behind the prominence of high stakes tests and suggests that they may be doing more harm than good.

Kozol, Jonathan. *Letters to a Young Teacher.* New York: Three Rivers Press, 2008. Features correspondence between the author and a young innercity teacher in Boston named Francesca and includes reflections upon the challenges, rewards, and nature of the job.

————. *Savage Inequalities: Children in America's Schools.* New York: Harper-Perennial, 1992. Explores the deplorable conditions of decaying buildings, overcrowded classrooms, understaffed faculty, and deteriorating neighborhoods in which inner-city children are educated.

————. *Shame of the Nation: The Restoration of Apartheid Schooling in America.* New York: Three Rivers Press, 2006. After visiting 60 schools in 11 states, Kozol calls resegregation of schools "a national horror hidden in plain view."

Levin, Henry M., ed. *Privatizing Education: Can the School Marketplace Deliver Freedom of Choice, Efficiency, Equity, and Social Cohesion?* Boulder, Colo.: Westview Press, 2001. A collection of essays about efforts to move education from the public to private sector through such tactics as tuition tax credits and vouchers.

Lipman, Pauline. *High Stakes Education: Inequality, Globalization, and Urban School Reform.* New York: RoutledgeFalmer, 2003. Examines the implications of education accountability reforms, particularly in urban schools, in the context of intensifying globalization and increasing social inequality.

Mathews, Jay. *Work Hard. Be Nice: How Two Inspired Teachers Created the Most Promising Schools in America.* Chapel Hill, N.C.: Algonquin Books, 2009.

Profiles Mike Feinberg and Dave Levin, who founded the Knowledge Is Power Program (KIPP) network of schools, which has gained widespread acclaim and grown to include more than 80 urban schools serving over 20,000 students.

Meier, Deborah, ed. *In Schools We Trust: Creating Communities of Learning in an Era of Testing and Standardization.* Boston: Beacon Press, 2002. Promotes the idea that schools must be smaller, more self-governed places of choice to allow kids and their families to feel part of a genuine learning community.

Meier, Deborah, and George Wood, eds. *Many Children Left Behind: How the No Child Left Behind Act Is Damaging Our Children and Our Schools.* Boston: Beacon Press, 2004. Asserts that underfunding and misguided implementation of the No Child Left Behind Act will likely cause more harm than benefit to the education of American students.

Merseth, Katherine, ed. *Inside Urban Charter Schools: Promising Practices and Strategies in Five High-Performing Schools.* Cambridge, Mass.: Harvard Education Press, 2008. Analyzes successful Massachusetts charter schools and shows how they effectively apply human resource strategies, culture, and clarity of mission.

Moe, Terry M. *Schools, Vouchers, and the American Public.* Washington, D.C.: Brookings Institute, 2001. Offers a description of the voucher movement and explains that though Americans like public school, they, particularly the socially disadvantaged, are also very open to vouchers.

Mondale, Sarah, and Sarah Patton, eds. *School: The Story of American Public Education.* Boston: Beacon Press, 2001. Provides the history of public education in the United States for the layperson, with an emphasis on photos and the perspectives of minorities. The book serves as the companion piece to the PBS television special of the same name.

Murray, Charles. *Real Education: Four Simple Truths for Bringing American Schools Back to Reality.* New York: Three Rivers Press, 2009. Explains that children have different abilities, half of the children are below average, too many children go to college, and America's future depends on the gifted.

Neal, Richard. *The Alliance Against Education Reform.* Bloomington, Ind.: AuthorHouse, 2006. Asserts that school choice is needed because school board members, administrators, professors, bureaucrats, and teachers' unions have worked against real education reform.

Nehring, James. *Upstart Startup: Creating and Sustaining a Public Charter School.* New York: Teachers College Press, 2002. Takes the reader on a tour of one charter school, describing daily challenges and ultimate achievements.

Ouchi, William. *The Secret of TSL: The Revolutionary Discovery That Raises School Performance.* New York: Simon & Schuster, 2009. Explains that

151

when principals are able to control their school's budget, they typically hire more teachers, which leads to a reduction in total student load (TSL) for each teacher and dramatic improvement for students.

Peterson, Paul E., ed. *The Future of School Choice*. Stanford, Calif.: Hoover Press, 2003. Consists of essays from leading education reform experts, describing the post–Cleveland school vouchers decision landscape.

Peterson, Paul E., and Martin R. West, eds. *No Child Left Behind?: The Politics and Practice of School Accountability*. Washington, D.C.: Brookings Institution Press, 2003. Early treatment of then newly passed NCLB law examines its origins, the political and social forces that gave it shape, and predicts its potential issues and consequences.

Plato. *The Republic*. Rev. ed. Translated by Desmond Lee. New York: Viking Press, 1955. Includes first written expression of value of organized education system. The work was originally written in the fourth century B.C.

Pope, Denise. *Doing School*. New Haven, Conn.: Yale University Press, 2001. Offers a view of the ways today's high school students pursue high grades and success and raises questions about the ability of schools to provide an engaging and positive culture of growth.

Price, Todd Alan. *The Myth and Reality of No Child Left Behind: Public Education and High Stakes Assessment*. Lanham, Md.: University Press of America, 2008. Provides an examination of No Child Left Behind's early effects on K–12 education.

Proefriedt, William A. *High Expectations: The Cultural Roots of Standards Reform in American Education*. New York: Teachers College Press, 2008. Explores how standards-based education reform is rooted in American cultural beliefs about individual possibility and responsibility, about opportunity and merit, and about the role of schooling in creating social change.

Ravitch, Diane. *The Death and Life of the Great American School System: How Testing and Choice Are Undermining Education*. New York: Basic Books, 2009. Argues that the increasing reliance on standardized assessments are negatively affecting the quality of instruction and learning in American classrooms.

Reed, Douglas S. *On Equal Terms: The Constitutional Politics of Educational Opportunity*. Princeton, N.J.: Princeton University Press, 2001. Focuses on evolution of "resource segregation" of U.S. schools and describes efforts to improve poorly funded schools.

Richin, Roberta, Rita Prager Stein, Francine Banyon, and Richard Banyon. *Induction: Connecting Teacher Recruitment to Retention*. Thousand Oaks, Calif.: Corwin Press, 2003. Explores the most effective ways to successfully attract teaching candidates and strategies to keep them engaged in the profession.

Annotated Bibliography

Rousseau, Jean-Jacques. *Emile*. Reprint, New York: Everyman's Library, 1993. Describes an ideal child-centered education focused on the child's natural abilities. The book was originally published in France in 1762.

Sacks, Peter. *Standardized Minds: The High Price of America's Testing Culture and What We Can Do to Change It*. Cambridge, Mass.: Perseus, 2001. Explains how standardized tests sustain the privileged and punish the poor and includes a plan for alternative means of assessment.

Sarason, Seymour Bernard. *Questions You Should Ask About Charter Schools and Vouchers*. New York: Heinemann, 2002. Warns of the danger of moving ahead in these key and complex reform areas without scrutinizing the important issues that affect the ultimate success or failure of efforts to improve public education.

Schlecty, Phillip. *Leading for Learning: How to Transform Schools Into Learning Organizations*. New York: Jossey-Bass, 2009. Explains how technology and strategic thinking can transform schools from bureaucracies into dynamic, responsive institutions.

Senge, Peter. *Schools That Learn: A Fifth Discipline Fieldbook for Educators, Parents, and Everyone Who Cares About Education*. New York: Doubleday, 2000. Features articles, case studies, and anecdotes from prominent educators to provide examples of successful school improvement techniques.

Silberman, Charles. *Crisis in the Classroom*. New York: Random House, 1971. Decries the "grim, joyless" conditions in public schools and extols the advantages of open education, which encourages increased informality in schools and student freedom in course selection and instructional time.

Sirotnik, Kenneth. *Holding Accountability Accountable: What Ought to Matter in Public Education*. New York: Teachers College Press, 2004. Asserts that however well-intentioned, past and current accountability practices in public education are "miseducative, misdirected, and misanthropic."

Sizer, Ted. *Horace's Compromise*. New York: Mariner Books, 2004. A classic in the field, this book calls for significant reform of schools burdened by unresponsive leadership, rushed classes, and excessive testing that does not meaningfully assess students.

Springer, Matthew G. *Performance Incentives: Their Growing Impact on American K–12 Education*. Washington, D.C.: Brookings Institution Press, 2009. Identifies and examines the potential strengths and weaknesses of performance-based pay for teachers and addresses key conceptual and implementation issues that have dominated this growing debate.

Sunderman, Gail, James S. Kin, and Gary Orfield. *NCLB Meets School Realities: Lessons from the Field*. Thousand Oaks, Calif.: Corwin Press, 2005. Helps educators understand the issues raised by NCLB and its implications for educating students based on data from six states and 11 districts.

Education Reform

Taubman, Peter. *Teaching by Numbers: Deconstructing the Discourse of Standards and Accountability in Education*. New York: Routledge, 2009. Offers interdisciplinary ways to understand both the educational reforms in urban education, teaching, and teacher education and their impact on what it means to teach.

Temes, Peter S. *Against School Reform (and in Praise of Great Teaching)*. Chicago: Ivan R. Dee, Inc., 2002. Argues the need to provide greater support for individual teachers rather than the more commonly proposed solutions for education reform.

Tough, Paul. *What It Takes: Geoffrey Canada's Quest to Change Harlem and America*. New York: Mariner Books, 2009. Examines the efforts of community activist Canada, who seeks to improve the lives of Harlem's most at-risk children through the use of an interlocking web of services collectively known as the Children's Zone.

United States Department of Education. *A Nation At Risk: The Imperative for Education Reform*. Washington, D.C.: Government Printing Office, 1983. Influential report commissioned by the Reagan administration's Department of Education. The report warns of the weaknesses of the U.S. education system, stating, "If an unfriendly foreign power had attempted to impose on America the mediocre educational performance that exists today, we might well have viewed it as an act of war."

Vander Ark, Thomas, Tony Wagner, and Joseph P. Viteritti. *Choosing Equality: School Choice, the Constitution, and Civil Society*. Washington, D.C.: Brookings Institute, 2001. Argues that critics of school choice have been proven wrong and suggests a policy designed to benefit the poor rather than a pure market approach to education reform.

Wagner, Tony. *The Global Achievement Gap: Why Even Our Best Schools Don't Teach the New Survival Skills Our Children Need—And What We Can Do About It*. New York: Basic Books, 2008. Explores how other nations such as China and India are gaining advantage by teaching critical thinking skills, creativity, and effective communication, while American schools provide passive learning environments and uninspired lesson plans that focus on test preparation and reward memorization.

———. *Making the Grade: Reinventing America's Schools*. New York: Routledge, 2001. Describes the need for accountability systems that focus on what students can do with their knowledge and smaller schools where teachers and students know one another and the children feel valued.

Webster, Noah. *The American Spelling Book: Containing the Rudiments of the English Language for the Use of Schools in the United States*. Reprint, Bedford, Mass.: Applewood Books, 1999. Emphasizes distinctively American spelling, grammar, and content. Originally published in 1783, it became the most influential textbook of the 19th century, eventually selling more than 75 million copies.

Williams, Joe. *Cheating Our Kids: How Politics and Greed Ruin Education.* New York: Palgrave Macmillan, 2005. Explains how unions, politicians, vendors, and consultants waste and mismanage funds meant to improve education.

Wise, Bob. *Raising the Grade: How High School Reform Can Save Our Youth and Our Nation.* New York: Jossey-Bass, 2008. The former governor of West Virginia explains the danger of continuing to ignore problems, such as the achievement gap and high dropout rates, in secondary education.

Witte, John F., Jr. *The Market Approach to Education: An Analysis of America's First Voucher Program.* Princeton, N.J.: Princeton University Press, 2001. Analyzes the Milwaukee, Wisconsin, school choice experiment and explains that although it seems to be working, it may not promote equal education when applied on a broader scale.

PERIODICALS

Agnew-Tally, J. C. "The Paradoxes of High Stakes Testing: How They Affect Students, Their Parents, Teachers, Principals, Schools, and Society." *Choice,* October 2009, p. 365. Provides an overview of the significant consequences of high-stakes testing in the context of contemporary school reform policy.

Allen, Mike. "For Lynne Cheney, the Children's Hour: Ex-NEA Leader Plays Teacher in Toned-Down Role." *Washington Post,* September 18, 2002, p. A27. Explains how Lynne Cheney, wife of former vice president Dick Cheney and a leading conservative voice for education reform, lowered her profile on controversial issues while becoming a best-selling author of a children's book.

Alter, Jonathan. "Peanut-Butter Politics: Education Is a Sticky Issue." *Newsweek,* June 15, 2009, p. 37. Referencing a study showing that more than 99 percent of teachers are rated satisfactory, Alterman asserts that teacher quality will not improve until entrenched "educrats and politicians who claim to support reform but remain fiercely committed to the status quo" are required to adhere to enforceable teacher effectiveness standards.

———. "Stop Pandering on Education: It's time to move from identifying failing schools to identifying failing teachers." *Newsweek,* February 12, 2007, p. 55. Advocate attacking what New York City schools chief Joel Klein calls the "culture of excuses" by instituting robust accountability measures for teachers.

Ambrosino, John. "No Child Left Behind: The Case of Roosevelt High School." *Phi Delta Kappan* 85, no. 9 (May 2004): 709. Focuses on a low-income high school in Portland, Oregon, to describe how the punitive effects of No Child Left Behind requirements are adversely influencing education reform.

Annig, Greg. "An Idea Whose Time Has Gone." *Washington Monthly,* April 2008, p. 29. Describes the significant drop in influence among advocates of school voucher programs, which have been increasingly replaced by other educational reform strategies.

Archer, Jeff. "Foundation Stirs Debate with Report Questioning Research on Licensure." *Education Week* 21, no. 7 (October 17, 2001): 17. Examines reaction to a report by the Abell Foundation saying that there is little evidence that students benefit when teacher candidates are required to complete coursework in education.

Arey, Kelly. "When Standardization Replaces Innovation." *Education Week* 21, no. 34 (May 8, 2002): 32–33. Decries efforts in many urban schools that require teachers to follow instructional and classroom management techniques prescribed by outside authorities.

"Are Zero-Tolerance Policies Effective in the Schools? An Evidentiary Review and Recommendations." *The American Psychologist* 63, no. 9 (December 2008): 857. Explores the controversial zero-tolerance procedures and applies research data to measure their effectiveness, finding that they largely fail to achieve improvements in school discipline and safety.

Arguelles, Lourdes, and Susan L. Flynn. "The Story of a Charter School Closure." *Paths of Learning: Options for Families and Communities,* Summer 2001, p. 44. Tells the story of a charter school closing from the perspectives of students, parents, teachers, and community members who feel that the sponsoring district revoked the charter for political reasons, despite broad local support.

Banchero, Stephanie, and Ana Beatriz Cholo. "Only 7% Seek to Transfer to a Better School." *Chicago Tribune,* August 20, 2002, p. A1. Sheds light on why parents are not transferring students despite federal law allowing transfers for students in underperforming schools.

Banchero, Stephanie, and Michael Martinez. "Federal School Reform Stumbles." *Chicago Tribune,* August 28, 2002, p. A1. Explains that the initial implementation of the No Child Left Behind Act was marked by widespread confusion, infighting among local authorities, and circumventing of the law's requirements.

Banchero, Stephanie, and Diane Rado. "Chicago Restricts Transfer Options." *Chicago Tribune,* July 30, 2002, p. B1. Portrays the difficulties that big cities such as Chicago faced in complying with new federal education law, mainly because of enrollment pressures and high rates of student failure.

Banks, Ann. "Is Zero Tolerance a Good Idea for School Discipline and Safety?" *NEA Today* 20, no. 5 (February 2002): 11. Presents a point-counterpoint-style examination of the effectiveness of zero-tolerance policies in schools.

Barlow, Dudley. "Objectifying Measures: The Dominance of High-Stakes Testing and the Politics of Schooling." *The Education Digest* 74, no. 8 (April 2009): 71. Reviews a book of the same title by Amanda Walker Johnson and concludes that reliance on high-stakes testing is largely fueled by oversimplified and widespread myths of their ability to foster success for students.

Barrett, Wayne. "Ticket to Nowhere." *Village Voice*, July 9, 2002, p. 23. Criticizes the school funding formula used in New York State as insufficient for the poor and middle class.

Berends, Mark, Sheila Natraj Kirby, and Susan Bodilly. "Looking Back over a Decade of Whole School Reform: The Experience of New American Schools." *Phi Delta Kappan* 84, no. 2 (October 2002): 168. Warns that policy makers may be overreaching by seeking reforms that are not well integrated and analyzes the experience of the New American Schools initiative.

Berger, Joseph. "A Post-Katrina Charter School in New Orleans Gets a Second Chance." *New York Times*, October 17, 2007, p. B6. Describes how a charter school devastated by Hurricane Katrina in 2005 has rebounded through new legislation, funding, and leadership.

Berliner, David C. "Our Impoverished View of Educational Research." *Teachers College Record* 108, no. 6 (June 2006): 949–995. Analyzes the role of poverty in school reform, particularly as it relates to its persistent effect on poor academic performance.

Berry, Barnett. "No Shortcuts for Preparing Good Teachers." *Educational Leadership* 58, no. 8 (May 2001): 32. Criticizes alternative teacher certification programs that fail to produce qualified educators and shortchange students.

Blair, Julie. "Teacher-Trainers Fear a Backfire from New ESEA." *Education Week* 21, no. 25 (March 6, 2002): 1, 38–39. Explains concerns that the federal requirement that all K–12 teachers who serve poor children be "highly qualified" may actually lower standards for educators by dumbing down measures such as licensure tests and preservice exams that are supposed to bar easy entry into the field.

Bolick, Clint. "Choice Struggles On." *National Review*, October 11, 2004, p. 40. Examines the state of the school choice movement, which remains a favorite of many education reform advocates despite a seemingly lagging influence.

Boss, Shira J. "Virtual Charters: Public Schooling at Home." *Christian Science Monitor*, January 8, 2002, p. 14. Explains both sides of the argument over "cyber charters," public schools with classes held via computer and teleconference by real-time teachers, and examines their legality.

Bracey, Gerald W. "Who's Pushing Privatization?" *Principal Leadership*, May 2008, p. 56. Examines the several pro-privatization organizations, such as the Center for Education Reform and Black Alliance for Educational Options, that have received millions of dollars in funding.

Breslau, Karen. "Edison's Report Card." *Newsweek*, July 2, 2001, p. 48. Details the controversial experience of the for-profit school management company Edison Schools in the San Francisco public school system.

Brooks, David. "The Quiet Revolution." *New York Times*, October 23, 2009, p. A35. Praises early efforts of President Obama's education policies and notes the widespread approval of it across the political spectrum.

Burroughs, Robert. "Composing Standards and Composing Teachers: The Problem of National Board Certification." *Journal of Teacher Education* 52, no. 3 (2001): 223. Considers whether the National Board for Professional Teaching Standards Certification is more an evaluation of a teacher's writing about teaching than an evaluation of teaching itself.

Caillier, Stacey L., and Robert C. Riordan. "Teacher Education for the Schools We Need." *Journal of Teacher Education* 60, no. 59 (November/December 2009): 489–496. Discusses trends that are influencing teacher education and suggests ways to make it more relevant and likely to ensure instructional excellence and retention.

Casse, Daniel. "Schoolyard Brawl." *The Weekly Standard*, May 17, 2008, p. 17. Describes widespread problems in the Milwaukee school district, 15 years after implementation of most expansive school choice program in any urban school district in the United States.

Cavanaugh, Cathy. "Effectiveness of Cyber Charter Schools: A Review of Research on Learnings." *TechTrends* 53, no. 4 (July/August 2009): 28–31. Examines studies of increasingly popular models of distance education programs, which allow students to gain instruction via the Internet.

Cech, Scott J. "Charter Laws Rated." *Education Week* 27, no. 37 (May 14, 2008): 4. Compares the legislation governing charter schools across the United States.

Chaker, Anne Marie. "Expanding the Charter Option." *Wall Street Journal*, August 13, 2009, p. D1. Explores some of the opportunities and controversies accompanying charter school creation.

"A Charter for Innovation." *Christian Science Monitor*, July 23, 2002, p. 8. Op-ed piece describing varied views of charter school effectiveness but proposing their role in seeking positive change in public education reform.

Chi, Wendy C., and Kevin G. Welner. "Charter Ranking Roulette: An Analysis of Reports That Grade States' Charter School Laws." *American Journal of Education* 114, no. 2 (February 2008): 273. Analyzes various ranking systems of charter school laws, beyond the most often referenced ranking published by the Center for Education Reform.

Annotated Bibliography

Cloud, John, and Jodie Morse. "Home Sweet School." *Time*, August 27, 2001, p. 47. Details the growth of homeschooling and notes how well-publicized academic success has improved its image nationwide.

Cochran-Smith, Marilyn. "Ten Promising Trends (and Three Big Worries)." *Educational Leadership* 63, no. 6 (May 2006): 20–25. Forecasts 10 trends in teacher education and lists the potential pitfalls, including defining quality by test scores, viewing teachers as saviors, and treating education as a workforce supply.

Coeyman, Marjorie. "Just When You Thought You Knew the Rules." *Christian Science Monitor*, July 9, 2002, p. 11. Explores ways the No Child Left Behind Act has turned the status quo "upside down."

———. "Summer School—Despite Rising Role—Faces Major Cuts." *Christian Science Monitor*, May 22, 2002, p. 1. Explains how the economic downturn of the early 2000s has diminished options for a highly touted education reform.

Conley, David T. "The 'Goldilocks' Phenomenon." *Education Week* 21, no. 29 (April 3, 2002): 40, 43. Examines how states determine whether assessment standards are too high, too low, or "just right" and suggests ways to fix the inconsistencies.

Cordova, Kathryn M. "Buenos Dmas, Ahem, Good Morning!" *Hispanic* 14, no. 5 (May 2001): 34. Describes the dismantling of bilingual programs throughout the country and decries the effect this has on serving Latino students.

Crawford, James R. "Teacher Autonomy and Accountability in Charter Schools." *Education and Urban Society* 33, no. 2 (2001): 186. Compares charter schools in Michigan and Colorado and finds that teachers in charter schools may have less autonomy than their traditional school counterparts.

Cruz, Gilbert. "Can Arne Duncan (And $5 Billion) Fix America's Schools?" *Time*, September 14, 2009, p. 26. Examines many prominent issues facing the new secretary of education, including the possibility that he may oppose teachers' unions over issue of whether teachers should be held accountable for the success or failure of their students.

———. "Summer School for Everyone." *Time*, July 23, 2009, p. 53. Explores the growing call for expanding the school day and school year, including the possibility of requiring students to attend school during much of the summer.

Darling-Hammond, Linda. "No Child Left Behind and High School Reform." *Harvard Educational Review* 76, no. 4 (Winter 2006): 642–667. Focuses on the effect that the sweeping education reform law has specifically on American high schools.

Dillon, Sam. "As More Charter Schools Unionize, Educators Debate the Effect." *New York Times*, July 27, 2009, p. A1. Examines the impact of the growing movement to introduce unionization to charter schools, which typically operate outside of certain rules that govern traditional public schools.

———. "Dangling $4.3 Billion, Obama Pushes State to Shift on Education." *New York Times*, August 17, 2009, p. A1. Provides an overview of Race to the Top funding, which requires states to foster innovation, raise standards, recruit effective teachers, turn around failing schools, and build data systems.

———. "'No Child' Law Is Not Closing a Racial Gap." *New York Times*, April 29, 2009, p. A1. Explores the continuing gap in standardized assessment scores among various racial groups.

———. "Report Envisions Shortage of Teachers as Retirements Escalate." *New York Times*, April 7, 2009, p. A16. Examines the issue of teacher quantity in the context of expected retirements and high attrition rate among rookie teachers.

———. "U.S. Eases 'No Child' Law as Applied to Some States." *New York Times*, March 19, 2008, p. A11. Describes how the U.S. Department of Education is permitting some states to focus reform efforts on schools that are drastically underperforming but is intervening less forcefully in schools that are raising the test scores of most students but struggling with one group.

Durbin, Dick. "Voucher Program Flops." *USA Today*, May 19, 2009, p. A10. The U.S. Senator from Illinois expresses his belief that research has determined that vouchers have not provided any meaningful improvement in educational achievement.

"Education as a Civil Rights Issue." *New York Times*, August 1, 2008, p. A18. This editorial applauds stance of civil rights groups that oppose efforts in the House of Representatives and by teachers' unions to exempt states from certain accountability measures in the No Child Left Behind legislation.

Ferguson, J. M. "Vouchers—An Illusion of Choice: Results to Date Show Voucher Programs Aren't Working." *American School Board Journal* 189 (2002): 42. Criticizes the philosophy behind the implementation of voucher programs as well as their effectiveness.

Finn, Chester E., Jr. "Fixing Schools Without a Voucher Fight." *New York Times*, January 13, 2001, p. A13. Claims that the federal government should allow states to set their own rules and limits on the use of federal dollars in education spending.

———. "Removing the Barriers for Teacher Candidates." *Educational Leadership* 58, no. 8 (May 2001): 29. Explains how traditional routes to teacher certification may deter potentially strong teachers from entering the classroom and describes how alternative certification programs may help open the door.

————. "Twenty-Five Years Later, A Nation Still at Risk." *Wall Street Journal*. April 26, 2008, p. A7. Marks the anniversary of the seminal report *A Nation At Risk* and finds many glaring weaknesses in the American educational system.

Fisher, Marc. "Charter Schools: To Each Its Own." *Current*, October 2001, p. 3. Tours five charter schools in Washington, D.C., and evaluates their impact and potential future role in strengthening the public education system.

Fiske, Edward B., and Helen F. Ladd. "When Schools Compete: A Cautionary Tale." *Teachers College Record* 103, no. 1 (February 2001): 77. Provides quantitative and qualitative analysis of reform efforts in New Zealand, whose school system is similar to that of a U.S. state.

Fitz, John, Chris Taylor, and Stephen Gorard, "School Choice Impacts: What Do We Know?" *Educational Researcher* 30, no. 7 (2001): 18. Depicts a positive portrayal of school choice programs, noting their positive impact on standards and socioeconomic stratification.

Fletcher, Michael A. "Big Gift to Schools Brings Small Gains: Study Says $1.1 Billion Donation Could Not Overcome Serious Problems." *Washington Post*, June 12, 2002, p. A2. Details the findings of a report released by the Annenberg Challenge, which has sought to improve the academic performance in beleaguered schools through more than $1 billion in grants.

————. "Panel Supports Special Ed Vouchers." *Washington Post*, July 6, 2002, p. A4. Describes the federal push to allow special education funds to pay for the cost of private services or private schools attended by the disabled.

"Florida Judge Throws Out School Vouchers." *Chicago Tribune*, August 6, 2002, p. 9. Reports state court ruling throwing out wide-ranging school voucher program, saying it violates a constitutional ban on giving tax dollars to religious institutions.

Foote, Donna. "Lessons from Locke." *Newsweek*, August 11, 2008. Profiles recruits and alumni of Teach For America, highlighting Washington, D.C., schools chief Michelle Rhee and the founders of the Knowledge Is Power Program (KIPP) to explain the impact the organization is having and may continue to have in the future.

Ford, Harold E., Jr., Louis V. Gerstner, Jr., and Eli Broad. "Race to the Top in Education." *Wall Street Journal*, November 25, 2009, p. A17. This op-ed piece calls for support of education reform from former congressman Ford and business leaders Gerstner and Broad.

Fox, Margalit. "Theodore R. Sizer Dies at 77: Helped Shape Discourse on Education." *New York Times*, October 23, 2009, p. A26. Describes the life and impact of education reform leader Ted Sizer.

Education Reform

Fraser, James W. "Education Schools Need a Gold Standard." *The Chronicle of Higher Education* 55, no. 31 (April 10, 2009): A27. Calls for the establishment of a national board of certification for education schools.

———. "Time to Cut the Link Between Teacher Preparation and Certification?" *Education Week* 20, no. 20 (January 31, 2001): 40, 56. Op-ed piece by an education professor proposing acceptance of an increased role for state and local governments in deciding who is qualified and hired to teach.

Freedman, Samuel G. "School Officials and Backers of Bilingual Education Are on Different Pages." *New York Times*, February 14, 2007, p. B7. Describes the status of bilingual education and its dwindling influence in recent education reform efforts.

Futrell, Mary Harwood, and Joel Gomez. "How Tracking Creates a Poverty of Learning." *Educational Leadership* 65, no. 8 (May 2008): 74. Discusses education policy makers' efforts to raise standards and close achievement gaps and suggests that the common practice of ability tracking is a significant barrier to achieving these important goals.

Gatlin, Davida. "A Pluralistic Approach to the Revitalization of Teacher Education." *Journal of Teacher Education* 60, no. 5 (November/December 2009): 469–477. Argues that teacher education has floundered in recent years and proposes ways to infuse it with challenging and meaningful changes.

Gehring, John. "Voucher Battles Head to State Capitals." *Education Week* 21, no. 42 (July 10, 2002): 1, 24–25. Explains how lawmakers in many states are seeking to ride momentum of the Supreme Court's decision in the Cleveland voucher case to advance school choice.

Gerstner, Louis V. Jr. "Lessons from 40 Years of Education Reform." *Wall Street Journal*, December 1, 2008, p. A23. Explains that difficult economic times can and should be leveraged to address some of society's longstanding problems, including substandard public schools.

Gewertz, Catherine. "A Great Day, or Dark One, for Schools?" *Education Week* 21, no. 42 (July 10, 2002): 19, 21. Profiles how families and educators affected by the Supreme Court decision in the Cleveland voucher case have reacted.

———. "More Chicago Pupils Flunk Grade." *Education Week* 22, no. 6 (October 9, 2002): 1, 13. Points out trends relating to the Chicago public schools' policy designed to end the social promotion of students.

———. "N.Y.C. Mayor Gains Control over Schools." *Education Week* 21, no. 41 (June 19, 2002): 1, 20. Examines a New York State law giving near total control of schools to New York City's mayor, as previously done in Chicago, Cleveland, Detroit, and Boston.

———. "Philadelphia Lines Up Outside Groups to Run Schools." *Education Week* 21, no. 41 (August 7, 2002): 1, 18–19. Portrays significant activity in Philadelphia school reform, including the hiring of former Chicago public schools CEO Paul Vallas and the possible movement toward privatization.

Gibbon, Peter H. "A Hero of Education." *Education Week* 21, no. 38 (May 29, 2002): 33, 36. Features an excerpted essay profiling the vision and accomplishments of early U.S. education pioneer Horace Mann.

Gilroy, Marilyn. "Bilingual Education on the Edge." *Education Digest* 67, no. 5 (January 2002): 50. Explores the political ramifications of bilingual education programs, which have been lauded by supporters as great successes or by critics as dismal failures.

Goben, Jan. "It Takes a Neighborhood: A Case Study in Turning a School Around." *San Francisco Chronicle*, August 11, 2002, p. E4. Describes one Bay Area community's effort to enact school reform.

Godwin, R. Kenneth, and Frank R. Kemerer. "School Choice Trade-offs." *Education Week* 21, no. 36 (May 15, 2002): 39, 52. Analyzes how school choice programs force education policy makers to confront core values of resource allocation and local control.

Goetz, William W. "Ravitch and Reform: Should Left Back Be Left Back?" *Teachers College Record* 104, no. 6, September 2002, pp. 1,204–1,228. Examines the trend against social promotion through the perspective of noted education reformer Diane Ravitch.

Goodnough, Abby. "Policy Eases the Way Out of Bad Schools." *New York Times*, December 9, 2002, p. B1. Describes how New York City will grant students in the system's more than 300 failing schools preferential transfer treatment in compliance with mandates from the No Child Left Behind Act.

Gootman, Elissa. "Death of Bronx Charter School Holds Mirror to Wider Problem." *New York Times*, April 3, 2006, p. A1. Explores the challenges that financial operations and organizational sustainability present to charter schools.

Graves, Lucia. "An Education Evolution." *U.S. News & World Report*, October 27, 2008, p. 62. Examines the influence of Washington, D.C., education chancellor Michelle Rhee and other alumni of Teach For America who are increasingly holding positions of authority in public education and politics.

Green, Christa, and Kathleen V. Hoover-Dempsey. "Why Do Parents Home School?" *Education and Urban Society* 39, no. 2 (February 2007): 264. Features a systemic study of 136 sets of parents who homeschool their children, investigating the reason why they do so.

Greve, Michael S. "The End of Education Reform." *Weekly Standard* 6, no. 34 (May 21, 2001): 16. Argues that without strong provisions for parental choice, hopes for genuine accountability and public school improvement are dim.

Education Reform

Griffin, Noelle C., and Priscilla Wohlstetter. "Building a Plane While Flying It: Early Lessons from Developing Charter Schools." *Teachers College Record* 103, no. 2 (April 2001): 336–365. Investigates 17 charter schools, with a focus on the key instructional and organizational practices that they established in the start-up phase and the many logistical difficulties encountered.

Guthrie, Stan. "Conservatives Vow to Revive Vouchers." *Christianity Today* 45, no. 10 (August 6, 2001): 20. Describes efforts by conservatives in Congress to allow parents to use taxpayer money to attend religious and private schools.

Hall, Joshua. "The Dilemma of School Finance Reform." *The Journal of Social, Political, and Economic Studies* 31, no. 2 (Summer 2006): 175. Profiles Ohio school districts to analyze persistent educational funding problems and examines possible solutions to them.

Hayasaki, Erika. "Class-Size Reduction Initiatives Faltering." *Los Angeles Times*, May 18, 2002, p. A1. Explains that school districts and states across the country are abandoning the once-popular reform of class-size reduction due to severe budget cuts and mixed findings of the reform's effectiveness.

Helfand, Duke. "Schools Challenge Mandatory Testing." *Los Angeles Times*, May 29, 2002, p. B1. Reports on Los Angeles and San Francisco school districts' efforts to change or abandon the controversial Stanford 9 test and California's new high school exit exam.

Hernandez, Alex, and Matthew Mahoney. "Is the Private Sector Qualified to Reform Schools." *Education Week* 22, no. 3 (September 18, 2002): p. 34. Claims that the private sector has struggled to manage school systems in the same way professional educators have.

Herzenhorn, David M. "Bucking Tide of School Reform, A Superintendent Gets Results." *New York Times*, December 4, 2006, p. A1. Profiles the influential chief of New York City schools, Joel Klein, who advocates reinvention of school administration to overcome generations of failure.

———. "In a Sweeping New Vision for Schools, Big Risks for the Mayor." *New York Times*, January 18, 2007, p. B1. Examines the state of education reform efforts of Mayor Michael Bloomberg in New York City, the nation's largest school system.

Hess, Frederick M. "Whaddya Mean You Want to Close My School? The Politics of Regulatory Accountability in Charter Schooling." *Education and Urban Society* 33, no. 2 (February 2001): 141. Observes that less that 1 percent of charter schools have ever been closed or not had their charters renewed due to poor performance, suggesting that charter school accountability is mainly political rhetoric.

Hoff, David J. "Bush Impact on Schools to Outlive Term." *Education Week* 28, no. 15 (December 10, 2008): 1. Analyzes how the No Child Left Behind Act was a key part of outgoing president George W. Bush's domestic legacy.

———. "School Choice Programs Growing More Rapidly Outside the U.S." *Education Week* 20, no. 41 (June 20, 2001): 5. Notes the trend of school choice methods, such as charter schools and vouchers, in foreign countries including Great Britain, Belgium, the Netherlands, and Spain.

———. "To Know NCLB Is to Like It, ETS Poll Finds." *Education Week* 26, no. 42 (June 20, 2007): 29, 31. Explains that opinions among Americans of the No Child Left Behind legislation is higher among people who know more details of what it actually features.

Holmes, Barbara J. "Understanding the Pros and Cons of Alternative Routes to Teacher Certification." *Teaching and Change* 8, no. 4 (2001): 317. Summarizes the main arguments in the teacher certification debate.

Honawar, Vaishali. "AFT No Longer a Major Player in Reform Arena." *Education Week* 26, no. 21 (January 31, 2007): 1, 16–17. Describes the diminishing influence of the American Federation of Teachers in the education reform movement due to leadership changes within the organization and the federal government.

———. "Performance-Pay Studies Show Few Achievement Gains." *Education Week* 27, no. 27 (March 12, 2008): 7. Counters claims that paying teachers more money based on student achievement is an effective approach to school reform.

Hornbeck, Mark. "Charter Schools Lack Oversight." *Detroit News*, June 14, 2002, p. G1. Reports Michigan's auditor general's charge that the state's education department has failed to monitor the state's charter schools responsibly.

Hough, Lory. "Whither High School?" *Ed.: The Magazine of the Harvard Graduate School of Education* 53, no. 2 (Winter 2010): 28. Describes the opinions of those who believe that today's high schools are obsolete and in need of a complete overhaul.

Hu, Winnie. "Seeing No Progress, Some Schools Drop Laptops." *New York Times*, May 4, 2007, p. A1. Describes how schools are abandoning efforts to provide laptops to students because research has shown little to no meaningful impact of the machines on student achievement.

Isaacson, Walter. "How to Raise Standards in American Schools." *Time*, April 27, 2009, p. 32. Advocates for the creation of rigorous and clear national standards to prevent many of the problems caused by patchwork approach.

Jackson, Derrick Z. "The Big Lie: No Child Left Behind." *Boston Globe*, August 2, 2002, p. A19. Op-ed piece that criticizes the philosophy, approach, and implementation of the No Child Left Behind Act.

Jacobs, Joanne. "Threatened by Success: One Charter School's Fight Against the Education Establishment." *Reason* 33, part 9 (2002): 38. Depicts opposition from teachers' unions and many school administrators to largely successful management of a San Francisco elementary school by Edison Schools.

Jacobson, Linda. "Long-Term Impact of Pre-K Examined." *Education Week* 26, no. 24 (February 21, 2007): 13. Explores the commonly held conception that increased exposure to educational programs before the beginning of kindergarten has an extended beneficial impact on students.

Jeffords, Jim. "Back to School." *New York Times*, December 13, 2001, p. 39. Op-ed article by the senator whose departure from the Republican Party gave Senate majority to Democrats decries President George W. Bush's failure to adequately support education reform plans and warns that this lack of fiscal support may lead the bill to cause more harm than good.

Jerald, Craig. "Aligned by Design." *Education Digest* vol. 75, no. 6 (January 2010): 9. Explores ways to integrate teacher compensation reform with other education reforms, including increased pay for student output, skills acquisition, high workloads, and filling hard-to-staff positions.

Jonsson, Patrik. "When the Tests Fail." *Christian Science Monitor*, August 20, 2002, p. 11. Explains the difficulty states have had establishing effective and reliable assessment programs to hold schools and districts accountable for academic success.

Kahlenberg, Richard D. "All Together Now: Creating Middle-Class Schools Through Public School Choice." *Harvard Educational Review* 71, no. 4 (2001): 756. Argues that economically integrated schools will do more to promote achievement and equity than private school vouchers, standards, or other leading education reform proposals.

Kahlenberg, Richard D., and Lowell P. Weicker. "The New Education Divide." *Christian Science Monitor*, October 9, 2002, p. 9. Argues that efforts must intensify to break down socioeconomic segregation in schools, citing studies demonstrating concentrated poverty's relationship to poor student academic performance.

Kennedy, Mary M. "Against Boldness." *Journal of Teacher Education* 61, no 1/2 (January–April 2010): 16. Argues that strong education reform measures, while maybe well-intentioned, are often misguided and ultimately should not be implemented.

Kennedy, Sheila Suess. "Privatizing Education: The Politics of Vouchers." *Phi Delta Kappan* 82, no. 6 (February 2001): 450. Questions whether vouchers improve anything other than parental attitudes about education and expresses worry about their practical, constitutional, and fiscal effects.

Annotated Bibliography

King, Neil, Jr. "Schools Push Hits the Road—Duncan Enlists Odd Allies in Multi-billion Bid to Shake Up U.S. Education." *Wall Street Journal*, September 30, 2009, p. A3. Explains how new U.S. secretary of education Arne Duncan is seeking to forge strong coalitions to advance school reform.

Klagholz, Leo. "State Policy and Effective Alternative Teacher Certification." *Education Digest* 67, no. 1 (September 2001): 33. Explores ways states such as New Jersey have been able to implement high standards for teachers without causing a teaching shortage by creating an alternative certification program.

Klein, Alyson. "HBO Film Examines School in NCLB Era." *Education Week* 27, no. 42 (June 18, 2008): 23. Reviews the documentary film *Hard Times at Douglass High*, in which filmmakers follow the 2004–05 school year at a high school in the struggling Baltimore school system.

Klein, Joel. "Charter Schools Can Close the Education Gap." *Wall Street Journal*, January 12, 2009, p. A13. Highlights high-performing charter schools, such as those in the Knowledge Is Power Program (KIPP), to explain how charter schools can serve as an effective tool of education reform.

Kronholz, June. "Education Plan Falling Short." *Wall Street Journal*, September 17, 2003, p. A4. Describes states' struggles to meet the standards established by the No Child Left Behind Act.

———. "For Florida Schools Size Is a Big Deal." *Wall Street Journal*, October 10, 2002, p. A4. Examines how proposed amendments to limit class size are causing political problems for Governor Jeb Bush, who opposes the measures.

"Kudos for KIPP." *Wall Street Journal*, March 26, 2007, p. A14. An editorial extolling the virtues of the Knowledge Is Power Program, a charter school leader.

Lankford, Hamilton, and James Wyckoff. "Who Would Be Left Behind by Enhanced Private School Choice?" *Journal of Urban Economics* 50, no. 2 (2001): 288. Looks at who will leave public schools and who will be left behind, an issue known as "skimming."

Lapham, Lewis H. "School on a Hill." *Harper's*, September 2001, p. 49. Presents conversations between the magazine's editor and four leading education experts about the past, present, and future of U.S. public schools.

Levin, Henry M. "Privatizing Education: Can the Marketplace Deliver Choice, Efficiency, Equity, and Social Cohesion?" *Educational Administration Abstracts* 36, no. 4 (2001): 411. Uses a collection of essays by leading education scholars to look at the initiative to move education from the public sector to the private sector.

LeVine, Steve. "Moving Beyond No Child Left Behind." *Business Week*, June 8, 2009, p. 52. Addresses the shortcomings of the No Child Left

Behind legislation from the perspective of businesspeople and projects potential changes to it in the Obama administration.

Lewin, Tamar. "For Mayoral Control of Schools, Chicago Has a Working Blueprint." *New York Times,* June 15, 2002, p. B1. Describes how Chicago reformed its public schools and how New York City mayor Michael Bloomberg may apply that model in the nation's largest school system.

———. "Leaders from Other Professions Reshape America's Schools, from Top to Bottom." *New York Times,* June 8, 2000, p. 18. Describes how many urban districts are turning to law, business, government, and the military for new leadership and outside perspective.

"A Long Road to the Court." *Education Week* 21, no. 42 (July 10, 2002): 18–21. Offers extensive and detailed chronology of school voucher movement.

Lord, Mary. "The New School Choice." *U.S. News & World Report,* August 5, 2002, p. 38. Illustrates one family's experience with the failing school provisions of recent federal education law.

Lytle, James H. "Whole School Reform from the Inside." *Phi Delta Kappan* 84, no. 2 (October 2002): 164. Discusses how urban superintendents with experience collaborating with other school system leaders have worked to improve schools and minority student achievement.

"Making 'No Child' Better." *New York Times,* February 4, 2010, p. A24. An editorial prescribing ways to strengthen the No Child Left Behind law, including provisions to address teacher quality and the achievement gap.

Manno, Bruno V. "The Case Against Charter Schools." *School Administrator* 58, no. 5 (May 2001): 28. Debunks the 10 most common complaints about the charter school movement, including charges that charters rob funds from traditional public schools and that they are too risky and unproven.

Manzo, Kathleen Kennedy. "America Scouts Overseas to Boost Education Skills." *Education Week* 27, no. 34 (April 23, 2008): 1, 14–16. Explains how many American education reform leaders are looking to other countries to learn about successful approaches to improve schools.

Marantz Cohen, Rosetta. "The Key to School Reform: Becoming Teacher-Centered." *Current,* September 2002, p. 3. Calls for school reforms to focus on boosting the training and work conditions of teachers.

Mathews, Jay. "How to Build a Better High School." *Newsweek,* May 16, 2005, p. 52. Examines how advanced placement courses and international baccalaureate curricula increase the rigor of high school and lead to improved school performance.

———. "Success for Some." *Washington Post,* July 21, 2002, p. W30. Examines a controversial method for teaching reading in underachieving schools that focuses on a highly structured and monitored form of instruction.

Maxwell, Lesli. "Districts Shun Stimulus Bid; Some Refuse to Sign States' Plans." *Education Week* 29, no. 18 (January 20, 2010): 1. Explains how and why hundreds of school districts across the United States have rejected the chance at a share of more than $4 billion in Race to the Top funds for a variety of reasons, including concern over federal intrusion and fear that the government would not cover program mandates.

————. "Obama Team's Advocacy Boosts Charter Momentum." *Education Week* 28, no. 35 (June 17, 2009): 1, 24–25. Describes the pro-charter orientation and plans of the Obama administration's education leaders.

McArdle, Elaine. "Right on the Money." *Ed.: The Magazine of the Harvard Graduate School of Education* 50, no. 2 (Winter 2010): 22. Examines opinions of those who claim that rewarding teachers and their students based on classroom performance fails to improve education.

McCombs, Barbara L. "What Makes a Comprehensive School Reform Model Learner Centered?" *Urban Education* 37, no. 4 (September 2002): 476–496. Focuses on improving schools by prioritizing effective instructional approaches for students.

McDonald, Sister Dale. "A Chronology of Parental Choice in Education." *Momentum* 32, no. 2 (April–May 2001): 10. Provides historical overview of parental choice with an emphasis on its relation to Catholic education.

McNeil, Michele. "Duncan Carving Deep Mark on Policy." *Education Week* 29, no. 18 (January 20, 2010): 1. Profiles Arne Duncan's first year as secretary of education and explains that his energy and focus on innovation could make him among the most influential leaders of the Department of Education.

————. "Leaner Class Sizes Add Fiscal Stress to Florida Districts." *Education Week* 27, no. 24 (February 20, 2008): 1, 18. Explains the difficulty Florida and other states are experiencing in implementing the relatively costly reform of lowering class sizes.

————. "Starting Gun Sounds for 'Race to the Top.'" *Education Week* 29, no. 12 (November 18, 2009): 1, 18–19. Describes final rules for program designed to provide states with $4 billion in education stimulus aid.

McPherson, Stephanie Sammartino. "*Lau v. Nichols:* Bilingual Education in Public Schools." *School Library Journal* 47, no. 2 (February 2001): 136. Explains the history of education for non-English speakers in the United States and details the landmark Supreme Court case that helped establish bilingual education programs.

McQuaid, John. "Will Obama's Choice Change Education in America?" *Ed.: The Magazine of the Harvard Graduate School of Education* 53, no. 1 (Fall 2009): 16. Profiles President Obama's choice for secretary of education, Arne Duncan, and examines how his goals may affect education reform efforts.

Meade, Katie. "Mayors' Education Advisors Discuss School Reform, Education Priorities." *Nation's Cities Weekly*, December 15, 2008, p. 1. Describes a meeting of the Education Policy Advisors' Network, a group of representatives from the nation's 75 largest cities, where attendees shared strategies and learned about the education priorities of the incoming Obama administration.

Medina, Jennifer. "Smaller-Is-Better Theory of Class Size Faces New Test in a Time of Pinched Budgets." *New York Times*, February 22, 2009, p. A29. Examines how economic crisis and the restricted funds available to schools are affecting the popular but costly reform of class-size reduction.

Miller, Matthew. "A New Deal for Teachers." *Atlantic Monthly*, July/August 2003, p. 32. Argues in favor of paying better teachers more money based on the performance of students and allowing districts to fire bad teachers quickly in an effort to improve troubled urban schools.

Miniter, Brendan. "School Choice Is the New Civil Rights Struggle." *Wall Street Journal*, May 30, 2009, p. A11. Focuses on South Carolina to explain that black and white school-choice candidates have replaced anti-choice lawmakers in the state legislature and examines the ramifications that this change may have in the creation of school reform policy in the state.

Mintrom, Michael. "The Market Approach to Education: An Analysis of America's First Voucher Program." *American Political Science Review* 95, no. 1 (March 2001): 227. Provides framework for understanding Milwaukee, Wisconsin's school choice program, arguing that although it seems to be working in Milwaukee, such programs, if applied more broadly, may harm the poor.

Morse, Jodie. "Do Charter Schools Pass the Test?" *Time*, June 4, 2001, p. 60. Analyzes the mixed results charter schools have had on education reform in Arizona and nationwide.

———. "A Victory for Vouchers." *Time*, July 8, 2002, p. 32. Reviews the Supreme Court decision in the Cleveland school voucher case and previews other potential legal skirmishes over school choice.

Murray, Joseph, Hunter N. Moorman, and Martha McCarthy. "A Framework for Rebuilding Initial Certification and Preparation Programs in Educational Leadership: Lessons From Whole-State Reform Initiatives." *Teachers College Record* 110, no. 10 (October 2008): 2,172–2,203. Examines the extent of reform in preparation programs in school leadership in six states.

"Nine Shared Strengths of Reform-Minded Districts." *What Works in Teaching and Learning* 34, no. 19 (September 18, 2002): 6. Comprises a report by the Council of Great City School, identifying characteristics exhibited by four districts that have helped spur successful changes in student achievement, instructional quality, and system accountability.

Nossiter, Adam. "A Tamer of Troubled Schools Offers a Plan for New Orleans." *New York Times*, September 24, 2007, p. A1. A feature profile of Paul Vallas, superintendant of the New Orleans Recovery School District, who had previously presided over major education reform efforts in Chicago and Philadelphia.

———. "Changes at New Orleans Schools Bring Gains in Test Scores." *New York Times*, May 7, 2008, p. A23. Describes how Louisiana's recent Recovery School District Law has helped strengthen education reform in New Orleans.

Obama, Barack. "Remarks on Education Reform." *Daily Compilation of Presidential Documents*, April 24, 2009, p. 1. Features the complete record of President Obama's first major speech on education policy.

O'Connor, Lona. "More and More Parents Opt for Home-Schooling, Census Study Finds." *South Florida Sun Sentinel*, July 15, 2002, p. 1A. Relates information from a U.S. Census Bureau study recording homeschooled population of more than 670,000 compared to about 500,000 enrolled in charter schools.

Olson, Lynn. "Prospective Principals Groomed Through Teach For America, District Partnerships." *Education Week* 27, no. 6 (October 3, 2007): 12. Describes new program in districts across the United States in which partnership with Teach For America develops an increased pool of principal candidates in areas of high socioeconomic need.

———. "Testing Rules Would Grant States Leeway." *Education Week* 21, no. 25 (March 6, 2002): 1, 36–37. Describes new federal regulations for standardized assessments that have been generally welcomed by state officials while criticized by others as creating a patchwork system.

Opfer, V. Darleen. "Charter Schools and the Panoptic Effect of Accountability." *Education and Urban Society* 33, no. 2 (2001): 201. Analyzes Georgia's charter school policy and points out that the centralizing effect of accountability laws can prevent the autonomy promised by charter school advocates.

Oplinger, Doug, and Dennis J. Willar. "School Overhaul Ordered." *Akron Beacon Journal*, December 12, 2002, p. A1. Explains the Ohio Supreme Court ruling that requires the state to reduce its reliance on property tax funding.

Osborne, Evan. "Education Reform as Economic Reform." *Cato Journal* 25, no. 2 (Spring 2005): 297–316. Applies findings of research studies on economic reform to draw lessons about repairing American education.

"Over-Punishment in Schools." *New York Times*, November 29, 2009, p. WK7. Editorial analyzing the draft of a bill that would require police and education officials to file regular reports to show how suspensions affect minority students and those with disabilities.

Patashnik, Josh. "Reform School." *New Republic,* March 28, 2008, p. 12. Examines the education reform–related positions of candidate Barack Obama and what they might mean if he becomes elected to the presidency.

Paulson, Amanda. "A Plan to Trust Schools—Not Just Tests." *Christian Science Monitor,* September 17, 2002, p. 14. Features an interview with prominent education reform advocate Deborah Meier, who states that testing lowers standards by emphasizing breadth over depth and makes schools accountable for the wrong things.

———. "True Believer." *Christian Science Monitor,* September 10, 2002, p. 15. Profiles the background, educational philosophy, and current impact of Secretary of Education Rod Paige.

Pestritto, Ronald J. "Home School Backlash." *Orange County Register,* September 2, 2002. Op-ed piece defending homeschooling from attacks by state bureaucracies and teachers' unions.

Ponnuru, Ramesh. "Bush's Centerpiece." *National Review,* October 9, 2006. Examines the impact of one of President George W. Bush's most significant domestic achievements, the passage of the No Child Left Behind law.

Popescu, Roxana. "No Child Outside the Classroom." *Newsweek,* February 11, 2008, p. 12. Explores the severe decrease in the number of field trips in U.S. classrooms and explains that a large part of the reason is the intense emphasis on test preparation and curriculum mandates.

Rasheed, Aesha. "Mayoral Takeovers of Schools Show Promise: Expert Recommends Multifaceted Plan." *New Orleans Times-Picayune,* October 8, 2002, p. 1. Details meeting between Vanderbilt University professor and education reform expert Kenneth Wong and Louisiana's Local Education Governance and Administration Task Force, which is evaluating various approaches to school improvement.

Rauch, Jonathan. "Now for Tonight's Assignment." *Atlantic Monthly,* November 2004, p. 54. Advocates for increased assignment of homework to improve student learning and performance.

Ravitch, Diane. "National Standards." *Education Week* 25, no. 17 (January 5, 2006): 54, 56, 58. Asserts that "50 standards for 50 states is a formula for incoherence and obfuscation."

Reid, Karla Scoon. "Black Alliance Weighs in with Pro-Voucher Campaign." *Education Week* 20, no. 38 (May 30, 2001): 8. Describes efforts of the Black Alliance for Educational Options, organized by the former Milwaukee, Wisconsin, schools superintendent.

———. "Minority Parents Quietly Embrace School Choice." *Education Week* 21, no. 14 (December 5, 2001): 1, 20–21. Explains emergence of minority parents as visible and vocal leaders in cities with voucher programs.

Renner-Ariev, Peter. "The Hidden Curriculum of Performance-Based Teacher Education." *Teachers College Record* 110, no. 1 (2008): 105–138. Describes and analyzes the student and faculty experiences of a performance-based preservice teacher education program at a large university in the mid-Atlantic region.

"Revise Teacher Certification." *Detroit News*, July 16, 2002, p. A6. Op-ed piece that calls for significant changes in the way teachers become certified, including a loosening of the emphasis on pedagogy popular in schools of education.

Rickert, Cynda S. "The Secret of Safe, Civil Schools." *Education Digest* 71, no. 3 (November 2005) 29. Discusses a school discipline model that has had success in improving schoolwide atmosphere by emphasizing proactive, positive, and instructional measures.

Rimer, Sara. "More Chaotic Start, More Orderly Students." *New York Times*, September 27, 2002, p. 22. Presents the ups and downs of Edison, Inc.'s management of some Philadelphia schools.

Ripley, Amanda. "Can She Save Our Schools?" *Time*, December 8, 2008, p. 36. Profiles the new chief of Washington, D.C., schools, Michelle Rhee, and examines various controversies surrounding her leadership.

————. "Inside the Revolt Over Bush's School Rules." *Time*, May 9, 2005, p. 30. Describes how some states, including the featured Utah, have opposed certain implementation of penalties from the No Child Left Behind law.

Robelen, Erik W. "An ESEA Primer." *Education Week* 21, no. 16 (January 9, 2002): 28–29. Provides a thorough explanation of the No Child Left Behind Act.

————. "ESEA to Boost Federal Role in Education." *Education Week* 21, no. 16 (January 9, 2002): 1, 28–29, 31. Previews the reauthorization of the Elementary and Secondary Education Act by President George W. Bush, emphasizing the increased prominence of the federal government, particularly in school accountability and assessment.

————. "Few Choosing Public School Choice for This Fall." *Education Week* 21, no. 43 (August 7, 2002): 1, 38–39. Examines reasons why, despite new federal regulations allowing transfers from underperforming schools, very few students have switched schools and explains that some districts do not have available slots.

————. "Kennedy Put Imprint on K–12, Social Issues With Fierce Advocacy." *Education Week* 29, no. 2 (September 2, 2009): 18–19. Explores the significant impact on education reform of recently deceased U.S. Senator Ted Kennedy.

————. "New Tethers Eyed for Milwaukee Vouchers." *Education Week* 28, no. 35 (June 17, 2009): 20. Explains a new Wisconsin law on school accountability that has some voucher supporters concerned because it could restrict the scope and influence of choice programs.

——. "Obama Echoes Bush on Education Ideas." *Education Week* 28, no. 28 (April 8, 2009): 1, 18–19. Describes how, despite their many policy differences, President Barack Obama shares similar positions on some education reform topics, such as accountability and teacher quality.

——. "Ruling Gives Second Wind to Capitol Hill Voucher Advocates." *Education Week* 21, no. 42 (July 10, 2002): 27. Depicts how the Cleveland voucher case has spurred legislative activity within the U.S. Congress.

——. "Senate Deal Would Allow Vouchers for Tutors." *Education Week* 20, no. 30 (April 11, 2001): 29, 31. Reports agreement between key senators and the Bush administration that would allow students in persistently failing schools to use federal dollars for private tutoring but not for private schools.

Romanowski, Michael H. "Common Arguments About the Strengths and Limitations of Home Schooling." *Clearing House* 75, no. 2 (November–December 2001): 79. Details various aspects of the homeschooling debate, including socialization and public school quality.

——. "Undoing the 'Us vs. Them' of Public and Home Schooling." *Education Digest* 66, no. 9 (May 2001): 41. Discusses the lack of understanding among public school educators regarding parental motivation to homeschool children and presents strategies to strengthen dialogue between these groups.

Rothstein, Richard. "Raising School Standards and Cutting Budget: Huh?" *New York Times*, July 10, 2002, p. B8. Points out conflict between pursuing higher academic standards and cutting of programs due to likely drops in fiscal support for education.

Ruenzel, David. "Tortuous Routes." *Education Next* 2, no. 1 (Spring 2002): 42. Criticizes roadblocks preventing nontraditional teaching candidates, usually recent college graduates and career changers who have not attended standard teacher certification programs, from teaching in the classroom.

Sandham, Jessica L. "Challenges to Charter Laws Mount." *Education Week* 20, no. 33 (May 2, 2001): 1, 24–25. Notes serious legal opposition to existing charter school laws in states such as Pennsylvania and Texas that have traditionally been friendly to publicly financed but administratively independent schools.

Sansbury, Jen. "School Reform Guidelines Come Late." *Atlanta Journal-Constitution*, August 3, 2002, p. H1. Explains how the No Child Left Behind regulations were released too late for school systems to comply.

Sawchuk, Stephen. "Spellings Highlights Performance Pay." *Education Week* 28, no. 8 (October 15, 2008): 25. Describes Secretary of Education Margaret Spellings's support for the idea of rewarding teachers for improved achievement of students.

Schemo, Diana Jean. "Failing Schools See a Solution in Longer Day." *New York Times*, March 26, 2007, p. A1. Examines possible benefits to educational quality and achievement of having students attend school for more time each day.

———. "Failing Schools Strain to Meet U.S. Standard." *New York Times*, October 16, 2007, p. A1. Explores the difficulty many schools are having in meeting No Child Left Behind requirements.

"School Reform Retreat?" *Wall Street Journal*, November 27, 2009, p. A20. Editorial criticizing the U.S. Department of Education for easing rules on states to receive Race to the Top funding designed to improve innovation and effectiveness of public schools.

Schroth, S. T. "A Grand Bargain for Education Reform: New Rewards and Supports for New Accountability." *Choice*, February 2010, p. 1,128. Analyzes a model for assessment-driven system of school improvement proposed by two professors.

Shellenbarger, Sue. "Extreme Juggling: Parents Homeschool the Kids While Holding Full Time Jobs." *Wall Street Journal*, September 14, 2006, p. D1. Explains the challenges faced by parents who work outside the home who also seek to homeschool their children, noting the particular need for commitment and flexibility.

Simpson, Michael D. "Dress Codes Are Back in Style." *NEA Today* 19, no. 7 (April 2001): 18. Reports on three court rulings that rejected student free speech claims and reaffirmed broad authority of school officials to tell students how to dress.

Smith, Thomas M. "How Do State-Level Induction and Standards-Based Reform Policies Affect Induction Experiences and Turnover among New Teachers?" *American Journal of Education* 113, no. 2 (February 2007): 273–311. Assesses data to examine the impact of state policy on the turnover rates of beginning teachers.

Staples, Brent. "School Vouchers: A Small Tool for a Very Big Problem." *New York Times*, August 5, 2002, p. A14. Op-ed piece describing weaknesses in arguments of school voucher advocates.

Stengel, Richard. "Arne Duncan: The Apostle of Reform." *Time*, April 27, 2009, p. 16. Profiles new U.S. Secretary of Education Arne Duncan.

Stotsky, Snadra. "Who Should Be Accountable for What Beginning Teachers Need to Know?" *Journal of Teacher Education* 57, no. 3 (May/June 2006): 256–268. Describes institutional problems in teacher education programs and offers suggestions for restructuring these programs.

Stricherz, Mark. "Nonprofit Group Forms to Challenge 'Monopoly.'" *Education Week* 20, no. 30 (April 11, 2001): 4. Describes efforts of philanthropist and financier Theodore Forstman, as well as a bipartisan board of prominent leaders including Martin Luther King II and Senator John McCain, to form Parents in Charge, an organization designed to help strengthen parental voice in choosing schools for their children.

Sugarman, Stephen D. "Approving Charter Schools: The Gate-Keeper Function." *Administrative Law Review* 53, no. 3 (Summer 2001): 869. Examines the charter-granting administrative powers of local school districts and state boards of education and recommends new arrangements to improve the quality of charter schools.

Sunderman, Gail L., and Gary Orfield. "Do States Have the Capacity to Meet the NCLB Mandates?" *Phi Delta Kappan* 89, no. 2 (October 2007): 137–139. Analyzes the obstacles and difficulties states face in implementing the requirements of the No Child Left Behind legislation.

"Teachable Moment." *New Republic.* December 31, 2007, p. 2. Editorial praising the appointment of Michelle Rhee as head of Washington, D.C., schools because it will likely serve as strong challenge to the city's failing system.

Thomas, M. Donald. "No Child Left Behind: Facts and Fallacies." *Phi Delta Kappan* 83, no. 10 (June 2002): 781. Details the commonly held beliefs and misconceptions of recent federal education law.

Thornburgh, Nathan. "Dropout Nation." *Time,* April 17, 2006, p. 30. Examines the persistent problem of high school dropouts and investigates reasons for this situation and ways to address it.

Tomsho, Robert. "California Home Schoolers to Need Credentials." *Wall Street Journal,* March 10, 2008, p. B2. Explains California law requirements and opposition to the legislation from largely conservative groups.

———. "No Child Left Behind Lacks Bite: Worst-Performing Schools Rarely Adopt Radical Remedies." *Wall Street Journal,* May 13, 2008, p. A11. Details how penalties imposed in the No Child Left Behind legislation are often ignored, weakening the overall effect of the law.

Tonn, Jessica L. "Houston in Uproar Over Teachers' Bonuses." *Education Week* 26, no. 22 (February 7, 2007): 5. Describes the controversial merit pay program in Houston and analyzes the issues that have arisen as a result of awarding bonuses to teachers based exclusively on student improvement on standardized assessments.

Toppo, Greg. "Study: Charter School Students Score Lower." *Washington Post,* September 3, 2002, p. A7. Cites information for a study by the Brookings Institute that indicates weaker reading and math scores by charter school students compared to students in regular public schools, noting how many charter schools are designed to attract underachieving students.

Traub, James. "The Test Mess." *New York Times Magazine,* April 7, 2002, p. 46. Expresses the opposition among many educators, parents, and students to the prominence of state-administered tests and how these tests are used to judge students, schools, and teachers.

Trotter, Andrew. "Poll Finds Rise in Unfavorable Views of NCLB." *Education Week* 27, no. 1 (August 29, 2007): 10–11. Analyzes data indicating that opinions on the sweeping education law have been dropping among Americans.

Tumulty, Karen, and Douglass Waller. "The President Who Used to Care About Education." *Time*, April 16, 2001, p. 18. Explains the view that President George W. Bush has abandoned educational initiatives expressed during his 2000 campaign and how this inattention has weakened conservative efforts for federal education reform.

Tyre, Peg. "The Blackboard Bungles: Three Authors Take Us Inside Today's Classroom." *Newsweek*, September 3, 2007 p. 44. Profiles three books on teaching and education: Dan Brown's memoir *The Great Expectations School*, Bel Kaufman's *Up the Down Staircase*, and Jonathan Kozol's *Letters to a Young Teacher.*

———. "A Just Reward." *One Day: Teach For America Alumni Magazine*, Fall 2009, p. 12. Analyzes the effectiveness of current performance-pay methods for teachers.

———. "The New First Grade: Too Much Too Soon." *Newsweek*, September 11, 2006, p. 34. Reports that kids as young as six years old are repeatedly tested and have greater amounts of homework than in generations past, particularly in upper-middle-class areas with high percentages of college-educated parents.

"Unions v. Race to the Top." *Wall Street Journal*, January 7, 2010, p. A16. Editorial describing the concerns of many teachers' union leaders with the Obama administration's Race to the Top funding, including its provision that instructors' effectiveness be measure in part by student performance.

Urbina, Ian. "It's a Fork, It's a Spoon, It's a . . . Weapon?" *New York Times*, October 12, 2009, p. A1. Reports the case of a six-year-old boy in Delaware who was suspended from school under a zero-tolerance weapons policy when he used his Boy Scout utensil to eat his food at lunch. The article examines problems that administrators of such polices have encountered when seeking to apply common sense to minor or technical infractions.

Vaishnav, Anand. "Bilingual Edition Advocates Marshal Forces: Statehouse Rally Sparks War of Words." *Boston Globe*, October 1, 2002, p. B2. Recounts a demonstration by bilingual education supporters against a Massachusetts ballot initiative, led by California businessman Ron Unz, that would replace bilingual programs with English immersion.

———. "MCAS Divides Voters, Poll Finds English Immersion Has Strong Support." *Boston Globe*, September 2, 2002, p. B1. Reports steady approval among Massachusetts citizens for English immersion strategies for teaching English as opposed to bilingual programs.

Vergari, Sandra. "The Politics of Charter Schools." *Educational Policy* 21, no. 1 (January/March 2007): 15. Asserts that charter schools and other market-based reforms such as vouchers are steeped in politics largely because they challenge the legitimacy of traditional power and funding arrangements in public education.

Viadero, Debra. ".5 Million Homeschooled Students in the United States in 2007." *Education Week* 28, no. 18 (January 21, 2009): 15. Describes the rise in the population of homeschooled students and analyzes reasons for this increase, including parental dissatisfaction with the quality of instruction, religious and moral instruction, and the security of the school environment.

———. "Increased Choice Found to Have Modest Impact on School Improvement." *Education Week* vol. 21, no. 14 (December 5, 2001): 11. Cites findings of competition on education by Columbia University's Teachers College National Center for the Study of Privatization of Education, showing a slight improvement in education achievement.

"Walking the Walk on School Reform." *New York Times*, January 17, 2010, p. WK. 7. Editorial arguing that the American Federation of Teachers has been far more reasonable in working toward sensible education reform measures than their larger counterpart, the National Education Association.

Wallis, Claudia. "How to Make Great Teachers." *Time*, February 25, 2008, p. 28. Examines methods to attract and retain excellent teachers, including some of most popular education reform methods currently applied.

Wallis, Claudia, and Sonja Steptoe. "How to Fix No Child Left Behind." *Time*, June 4, 2007, p. 34. Notes the successes of the landmark education reform law and suggests ways to remedy its shortcomings.

Walsh, Mark. "Advocates' Post-Ruling Choice: Bubbly" *Education Week* 21, no. 42 (July 10, 2002): 25. Examines the reaction and strategies of pro-voucher advocates following the Supreme Court's decision in the Cleveland voucher case.

———. "Justices Settle Case, Nettle Policy Debate." *Education Week* 21, no. 42 (July 10, 2002): 1, 18–21. Analyzes the U.S. Supreme Court's landmark ruling upholding the Cleveland voucher program and its implications on the debate over how best to improve public education.

Wasley, Paula. "Home-Schooled Students Rise in Supply and Demand." *The Chronicle of Higher Education* 54, no. 7 (October 12, 2007): A1. Notes how many homeschooled students are seen by college and university officials as an increasingly attractive niche market due to their typically high rates of successful achievement in higher education settings.

Annotated Bibliography

Weiher, Gregory R. "Does Choice Lead to Racially Distinctive Schools? Charter Schools and Household Preferences." *Journal of Policy Analysis and Management* 21, no. 1 (Winter 2002): 79–92. Analyzes survey of families who chose charter schools and finds that whites, Latinos, and African Americans typically transfer into charter schools where their groups comprise 11–14 percent more of the student body than the traditional public schools they are leaving.

Whitford, David. "Big Idea Capitalism." *Esquire*, August 2002, p. 50. Examines the difficulties Edison Schools and CEO Chris Whittle have experienced in Philadelphia.

"Why the Achievement Gap Persists." *New York Times*, December 8, 2006, p. A34. Editorial critiquing the failure of No Child Left Behind legislation to meet the goal of significantly closing the achievement gap and pinning the blame largely on groups such as teachers unions that have stood in the way of successful reforms.

Wildavsky, Ben. "A Blow to Bilingual Education English Immersion May Raise Test Scores." *U.S. News & World Report*, September 4, 2000, p. 20. Cites evidence from studies in California demonstrating a possible link between growth in academic achievement and intensive English instruction to non-English-speaking students.

Wilgoren, Jodi. "Chief Executive of Chicago Schools Resigns." *New York Times*, June 7, 2001, p. 26. Reports the resignation of Paul Vallas, who led the turnaround of Chicago's troubled school system and became national role model for urban school reform.

———. "The New Administration: The Education Issue." *New York Times*, January 23, 2001, p. A1. Summarizes important aspects of President George W. Bush's policies for education reform, including accountability measures such as standardized tests, school report cards, and pay incentives for teachers.

Will, George F. "Calling the Baby Ugly." *Newsweek*, March 23, 2009, p. 49. A look at new U.S. secretary of education Arne Duncan, who said that under No Child Left Behind "we have been lying to students and their parents" by severely diluting the standards of proficiency.

Winans, Dave. "School Funding Adequacy—What It Costs to Do the Job Right." *NEA Today* 21, no. 1 (September 2002): 18. Describes the concept of adequacy, in which components of quality education required by law, standards, or court decisions, are costed out and funded by the state on an ongoing basis with adjustments for inflation, enrollment changes, and evolving student needs.

Winters, Rebecca. "Trouble for School Inc." *Time*, May 27, 2002, p. 53. Describes the problems experienced by Edison Schools, including dissolution of contracts and accusations of accounting irregularities.

179

Yu, Ting. "A New Beginning for American Education?" *One Day: Teach For America Alumni Magazine*, Summer 2009, p. 14. Features an interview with Jon Schnur, the founder and CEO of New Leaders for New Schools and focuses on the future of education reform.

Zehr, Mary Ann. "Bush Plan Could Alter Bilingual Education." *Education Week* 20, no. 23 (February 21, 2001): 17, 19. Details President George W. Bush's proposed education plan seeking the elimination of a federal government stipulation that gives preference to bilingual education programs over English-only programs.

———. "Catholics Laud Voucher Decision, See Potential for Growth." *Education Week* 21, no. 42 (July 10, 2002): 26. Chronicles how religiously affiliated schools view the prospects of increased private school choice.

———. "Elementary Foreign Language Instruction on Descent; Cutbacks Expected to Continue in Recession." *Education Week* 28, no. 23 (March 4, 2009): 8. Describes how the economic downturn has led to decreased funding in programs dedicated to bilingual education.

———. "Nurturing School Minds." *Education Week* 29, no. 6 (October 7, 2009): 24. Profiles UNO, a Chicago-based charter school network that aims to serve primarily Latino students through a strong structure and English immersion instruction.

———. "Poll: Immigrants Value Speaking English." *Education Week* 22, no. 19 (January 22, 2003): 3. Reports findings of survey by Public Agenda that indicates that immigrants are no more likely than the general public to support bilingual education in public schools.

Zernike, Kate. "Crackdown on Threats in School Fails a Test." *New York Times*, May 17, 2001, p. A1. Describes the application of a zero-tolerance policy in suburban Manalapan, New Jersey, where more than 50 elementary students were suspended in less than two months for what were deemed verbal threats, and notes the increasing frustration of parents to this policy.

———. "Decisions That Have Shaped U.S. Education." *Educational Leadership* 59, no. 4 (December 2001–January 2002): 6. Analyzes the most critical legal decisions in education over the past six decades, including decisions affecting freedom of expression, school safety, and equality.

INTERNET DOCUMENTS

American Federation of Teachers, AFL-CIO. "Key Issues." AFT.org. Available online. URL: http://www.aft.org/issues/. Downloaded February 15, 2010. Includes links to several articles about individual education reform issues ranging from adequate yearly progress to vouchers, as well as more than 50 others.

Annotated Bibliography

American Federation of Teachers, AFL-CIO. "News and Publications."
AFT.org. Available online. URL: http://www.aft.org/newspubs/. Downloaded February 15, 2010. Provides links to wealth of information on a
diverse collection of education reform issues.

Center for Education Reform. "Daily Headlines." Available online. URL:
http://edreform.com/Press_Box/Daily_Headlines/. Downloaded December 18, 2009. Provides daily updates and links to the stories that are most
relevant to education reform from a vast array of publications.

Center for Education Reform. "Newswire Library." Available online. URL:
http://www.edreform.com/Press_Box/Newswire_Library/. Downloaded
December 18, 2009. Includes links to hundreds of articles related to education reform from various sources dating back 10 years.

Center for Education Reform. "Press Releases." Available online. URL:
http://www.edreform.com/Press_Box/Press_Releases/. Downloaded
December 18, 2009. Features descriptions of this leading education
reform organization's publications and provides links for downloading
them.

CharlieRose.com. "A Conversation with Arne Duncan, United States Secretary of Education." Available online. URL: http://www.charlierose.
com/view/interview/10140. Posted March 11, 2009. A discussion with
the education secretary at the beginning of the Obama administration.

CharlieRose.com. "A Conversation with Joel Klein, Chancellor of the New
York City Department of Education." Available online. URL: http://
www.charlierose.com/view/interview/8654. Posted August 22, 2007. Exploration of key issues in education reform in New York City and
throughout the United States.

CharlieRose.com. "A Conversation with Randi Weingarten." Available online. URL: http://www.charlierose.com/view/interview/9080. Posted
May 12, 2008. Analysis of key issues facing American education by the
president of the American Federation of Teachers.

CharlieRose.com. "An Hour on Education with Bob Wise and Wendy
Kopp." Available online. URL: http://www.charlierose.com/view/interview/9155. Posted July 1, 2008. Interviews with Wise, former West Virginia governor and education reform advocate, and Kopp, who founded
and runs Teach For America.

CNN.com. "Education Policy." Available online. URL: http://topics.cnn.
com/topics/education_policy. Last updated November 6, 2009. A collection of news articles and videos related to educational policy issues.

CNN.com. "Obama Wants to Overhaul Education from 'Cradle to Career.'"
Available online. URL: http://www.cnn.com/2009/POLITICS/03/10/
obama.education/. Posted March 10, 2009. Key points from President
Obama's speech outlining his vision for education reform.

Cruz, Gilbert. "Are Teacher Colleges Turning Out Mediocrity?" *Time*. Available online. URL: http://www.time.com/time/nation/article/0,8599,1931810,00.html. Posted on October 23, 2009. Explores the issue of whether teacher training programs are meeting the needs of students in light of recent speech by U.S. secretary of education Arne Duncan that criticized their current effectiveness.

Darby, Seward. "Money Well Spent." *New Republic*. Available online. URL: http://www.tnr.com/article/politics/money-well-spent. Posted February 3, 2010. Analyzes the proposed budget of Secretary of Education Arne Duncan, which is based on a competitive formula emphasizing school progress rather than channeling new funds to states and districts, as has typically been the case with previous models.

Dykema, Ravi. "How Schools Fail Kids and How They Could Be Better: An Interview with Ted Sizer." NEXUS, Colorado's Holistic Journal. Available online. URL: http://www.nexuspub.com/articles/2002/may2002/interview1.htm. Posted May/June 2002. Downloaded December 16, 2009. This interview features the thoughts of the prominent education reform advocate and founder of the Coalition of Essential Schools, who died in 2009.

Education Commission of the States. "K–12 Issues." Available online. URL: http://www.ecs.org/ecsmain.asp?page=/html/newsMedia/ECSNewsroom.asp. Downloaded December 18, 2009. Features links on nearly 100 key topics in education reform, such as at-risk youth, class size, charter schools, and minority/diversity issues.

Education Week. Available online. URL: http://www.edweek.org/ew/index.html. Downloaded December 18, 2009. A rich and varied collection of education reform resources, including links to national and state news, a diverse collection of topics, and commentary, almost all of which is free, archived, and downloadable.

General Accounting Office. "School Vouchers: Characteristics of Privately Funded Programs," General Accounting Office. Available online. URL: http://www.gao.gov/new.items/d02752.pdf. Downloaded December 16, 2009. Article analyzes 78 privately funded voucher programs and praises their role in helping support academic improvement of students and school satisfaction of parents.

Hornick, Ed. "Are States Following Stimulus Plan Rules for Schools?" CNN.com. Available online. URL: http://www.cnn.com/2009/POLITICS/10/20/stimulus.education/index.html?iref=allsearch. Posted October 20, 2009. Examines how education reform might be affected by passage of economic stimulus package of 2009.

Kilgore, Ed. "Sorting Out the Dueling Education Coalitions." Salon.com. Available online. URL: http://www.salon.com/politics/war_room/2008/07/11/education_wars/index.html. Examines the positions of civil rights and labor-oriented groups, both of which are deeply involved in education reform issues, and suggests that President Obama seek the input and support of both.

Lips, Dan, and Evan Feinberg. "Homeschooling: A Growing Option in American Education." The Heritage Foundation. Available online. URL: http://www.heritage.org/Research/education/bg2122.cfm. Posted April 3, 2008. A thorough examination of homeschooling characteristics that positively profiles its effect on academic success, college preparedness, and life outcomes.

Midcontinent Research for Education and Learning. "Policy Briefs." Available online. URL: http://www.mcrel.org/topics/policyBrief.asp. Scores of detailed, free, downloadable resources on key education reform topics, including standards, professional development, and the future of schooling.

Miller, Raegen. "Interactive Graphic: Title I Education Spending." Center for American Progress. Available online. URL: http://www.americanprogress.org/issues/2010/02/title_one_graph.html. A clear set of interactive graphics in several different categories that describes how Title I, Part A of the Elementary and Secondary Education Act apportions education funding to the states.

Mosle, Sara. "How Children Stop Failing: It Takes a Village to Raise a School." Slate.com. Available online. URL: http://www.slate.com/id/2198864/. Posted September 2, 2008. Profiles Paul Tough's book *Whatever It Takes* and the author's efforts to improve education in the toughest parts of New York City's Harlem neighborhood.

———. "The Educational Experiment We Really Need: What the Knowledge Is Power Program Has Yet to Prove." Slate.com. Available online. URL: http://www.slate.com/id/2214253/. Posted March 23, 2009. Examines Jay Mathews's book *Work Hard. Be Nice.* and the Knowledge Is Power Program (KIPP) featured in it.

National Center for Education Statistics. "Expenditures of Educational Institutions, by Level and Control of Institution: Selected Years 1899–1900 through 2006–07." Available online. URL: http://nces.ed.gov/programs/digest/d07/tables/dt07_026.asp?referrer=list. Downloaded December 21, 2009. More than 100 years of statistics on the amount of money spent on elementary and secondary schools in the United States, in current dollars.

New York Times. "Education." Available online. URL: http://www.nytimes.com/pages/education/index.html. Downloaded December 18, 2009. A collection of news articles on education-related issues, updated daily.

PBS.org. "*Frontline:* Testing Our Schools." Available online. URL: http://www.pbs.org/wgbh/pages/frontline/shows/schools/. Posted March 28,

2002. This page includes a rich variety of links on topics addressed in the television program as well as a downloadable transcript of the episode.

PBS.org. "NOW with Bill Moyers: American Schools in Crisis: Debating No Child Left Behind." Available online. URL: http://www.pbs.org/now/society/nclb.html. Posted October 17, 2003. A comprehensive collection of resources related to the television broadcast examining No Child Left Behind legislation and other education reform issues.

PBS.org. "School: The Story of American Public Education." Available online. URL: http://www.pbs.org/kcet/publicschool/. Downloaded July 12, 2002. A companion to the network's history of U.S. public K–12 education, broadcast in 2001, the site discusses a variety of topics, such as innovators and classroom equipment through the years, and includes many historic photos.

PublicAgenda.com. "Public Agenda for Educators." Available online. URL: http://www.publicagenda.org/educators. Downloaded December 19, 2009. Highlights the noteworthy findings of public opinion on education and includes links to graphs.

Public Education Network. "Publications." Available online. URL: http://www.publiceducation.org/publications.asp. Downloaded December 18, 2009. A wealth of current and recent publications on a variety of education reform topics, including No Child Left Behind, standards and accountability, and teacher quality.

Ray, Brian D. "The Harms of Homeschooling? Where Are the Premises?" National Home Education Research Institute. Available online. URL: http://www.nheri.org/Latest/The-Harms-of-Homeschooling-Where-Are-the-Premises.html. Downloaded February 15, 2010. Analyzes claims made by critics of homeschooling and attacks their lack of information and understanding about the nature of homeschooling.

Rossmeier, Vincent. "Obama: OK, Let's Try Education Reform, Then." Salon.com. Available online. URL: http://www.salon.com/news/politics/war_room/2009/07/24/education/index.html. Posted July 24, 2009. Examines the education reform plans of the Obama administration, an initiative called Race to the Top.

Roth, Lauren. "Home-schoolers Raising the Spelling Bee's Buzz." The Virginian Pilot. Available online. URL: http://hamptonroads.com/2009/05/homeschoolers-raising-spelling-bees-buzz. Posted May 26, 2009. Explores the disproportionately high rate of success among homeschoolers in national spelling bee competitions.

Russo, Alexander. "Chicago School Days: Obama's Lackluster Record on Education." Slate.com. Available online. URL: http://www.slate.com/id/2188010/. Posted April 2, 2008. Critiques presidential candidate Barack Obama's record regarding education reform while a Illinois state legislator and U.S. senator.

Ryan, Jim. "Education: Fixing Education Policy." Slate.com. Available online. URL: http://www.slate.com/id/2187680/. Posted April 1, 2008. Offers detailed policy prescriptions for the next president to address the weaknesses in the education system.

Streitfeld, Rachel. "Education Chief Favors Longer School Year." CNN.com. Available online. URL: http://www.cnn.com/2009/POLITICS/02/27/education.school.year/index.html. Posted February 27, 2009. Reports the suggestion of U.S. education secretary Arne Duncan that students attend school for an increased number of days each year.

U.S. Department of Education. "Improving Basic Programs Operated by Local Educational Agencies (Title I, Part A)." Available online. URL: http://www2.ed.gov/programs/titleiparta/funding.html. Downloaded February 15, 2010. Details the funding status from 2000 to 2008 of a key portion of the Elementary and Secondary Education Act, including average award and range of awards.

———. "Policy Documents: Elementary and Secondary Education." Available online. URL: http://www.ed.gov/policy/elsec/guid/states/index.html. Downloaded December 18, 2009. Links to scores of free, downloadable U.S. Department of Education documents, such as most the recent legislation and current research.

Walker, Kenly. "Schools Boost Focus on Math and Reading." CBS News. Available online. URL: http://www.cbsnews.com/stories/2007/07/25/national/main3096192.shtml?source=RSSattr=U. S._3096192. Posted July 25, 2007. Reports that No Child Left Behind mandates have led many schools to increase emphasis on most scrutinized subjects of math and reading at the expense of other subjects.

"Yahoo! News: Education News." Yahoo! Available online. URL: http://news.yahoo.com/us/education. Downloaded December 18, 2009. Comprises links to a variety of sources, including the *New York Times, Time,* and *Education Week,* and includes featured daily articles on a wide range of reform issues.

OTHER MEDIA

The Cartel (2008). Heartland Institute: DVD, 2008. Documentary emphasizes the inefficiency and corruption of public schools in New Jersey and argues in favor of school choice.

A Day in the Life (2002). PBS/WGBH/Boston: VHS, 2002. Documentary video presents personal moments of students, their teachers, and their families at a struggling Boston high school to illustrate the impact of education reform.

Hard Times at Douglass High: A No Child Left Behind Report Card (2008). HBO: DVD, 2008. Documentary provides a yearlong glimpse into the workings of a Baltimore high school seeking to thrive under No Child Left Behind requirements.

Lehrer, Tom. *That Was the Year That Was* (1965). Warner Brothers/Reprise Records: CD, 1990. Recording includes collection of satirical songs covering important events of 1964 and features the progressive education–themed song "New Math."

Nightline: Public Schools (2003). ABC News: DVD, 2003. Television broadcast examines the slowing of momentum and the difficulties faced by public school reform efforts in wake of war and economic downturn.

The Principal Story (2009). Ethno Pictures and Nomadic Pictures: DVD, 2009. Originally aired on PBS, this documentary examines the challenges facing America's public schools through the perspective of two principals in low-income schools in Chicago and Springfield, Illinois.

REBORN New Orleans Schools (2008). CreateSpace: DVD, 2008. Documentary chronicles the first year after the devastation of Hurricane Katrina in a New Orleans charter school.

School (2001). Stone Lantern Films/PBS/KCET: DVD, 2001. Originally aired as a PBS series in four episodes, video covers the development of public education in the United States from the late 1770s to the 21st century, focusing on the system's origins, its role in Americanizing immigrants and as a catalyst for and site of social change, and recent challenges and trends.

Soling, Cevin. *The War on Kids* (2009). Spectacle Films: DVD, 2009. Documentary depicts the public school system as dysfunctional and oppressive, due to misguided efforts to control students, such as zero-tolerance policies.

CHAPTER 8

ORGANIZATIONS AND AGENCIES

The following entries include current and active public, private, and academic groups involved in the debate about education reform. The list features organizations dedicated to examining and/or advocating positions on school choice, homeschooling, school financing, standards, teacher certification and quality, and legal issues.

Achieve, Inc.
URL: http://www.achieve.org
E-mail: webform
Phone: (202) 419-1540
Fax: (202) 828-0911
1775 Eye Street NW
Suite 410
Washington, DC 20006
Founded by a nonpartisan group of governors and CEOs. Achieve focuses on advocacy of academic standards and school accountability measures.

Alliance for Excellent Education
URL: http://www.all4ed.org/
E-mail: webform
Phone: (202) 828-0828
Fax: (202) 828-0821
1201 Connecticut Avenue
Suite 901
Washington, DC 20036
Advocacy group that promotes increased education funding and reform for middle and high schools

to help students, particularly those considered at risk, become prepared for college and success in the work world.

Alliance for the Separation of School & State
URL: http://www.schoodand state.org
E-mail: contact@schoolandstate. org
Phone: (559) 292-1776
Fax: (559) 292-7582
1071 North Fulton Street
Fresno, CA 93728
Seeks to influence educational policy debate by attracting public leaders and private citizens to sign a proclamation stating, "I proclaim publicly that I favor ending government involvement in education."

American Civil Liberties Union (ACLU)
URL: http://www.aclu.org

E-mail: web form
Phone: (212) 549-2500
125 Broad Street
18th Floor
New York, NY 10004-2400
Prominent national organization seeking to preserve and defend individual rights. The ACLU is active in support of students' rights issues.

American Educational Research Association
URL: http://www.aera.net
Phone: (202) 238-3200
Fax: (202) 238-3250
1430 K Street NW
Washington, DC 20005
A professional organization consisting of more than 25,000 educators, assessment evaluators, behavioral scientists, and state and federal education administrators concerned with improving the educational process by encouraging scholarly inquiry and by promoting the dissemination and practical application of research results.

American Federation of Teachers (AFT)
URL: http://www.aft.org
E-mail: web form
Phone: (202) 879-4400
555 New Jersey Avenue NW
Washington, DC 20001
Trade union with more than 1.4 million members, active in wide range of labor and educational issues.

Americans United for Separation of Church and State
URL: http://www.au.org
E-mail: americansunited@au.org
Phone: (202) 466-3234
Fax: (202) 466-2587
518 C Street NE
Washington, DC 20002
Organization that promotes litigation, advocacy, and education to protect the constitutional principle of church-state separation, including the opposition to school prayer and the use of tax-supported vouchers for use in parochial schools.

Annenberg Institute for School Reform
URL: http://www.annenberg institute.org
E-mail: AISRInfo@brown.edu
Phone: (401) 863-7990
Fax: (401) 863-1290
Brown University
Box 1985
Providence, RI 02912
Develops and shares information that seeks to improve the condition and outcomes of schooling in the United States, especially in urban communities and in schools serving disadvantaged children.

ASCD
URL: http://www.ascd.org/
Phone: (800) 933-2723
Fax: (703) 575-5400
1703 North Beauregard Street
Alexandria, VA 22311
Formerly called the Association for Supervision and Curriculum Development, an educational leadership organization made up of more than 175,000 professional educators, including superintendents, supervisors, principals, teachers, professors of education, and school board

188

members. ASCD is dedicated to advancing student success through professional development, capacity building, and educational leadership programs.

Building Excellent Schools
URL: http://bes.squarespace. com/
E-mail: bes@buildingexcellent schools.org
Phone: (617) 227-4545
Fax: (617) 227-4551
262 Washington Street
7th Floor
Boston, MA 02108
Provides one year of paid training, extended residency in a high-performing urban school and ongoing support to fellows who develop urban charter schools.

Carnegie Foundation for the Advancement of Teaching
URL: http://www.carnegie foundation.org
E-mail: web form
Phone: (650) 566-5100
Fax: (650) 326-0278
51 Vista Lane
Stanford, CA 94305
National center for research and policy studies about teaching since 1905.

Center for Education Reform
URL: http://www.edreform.com
E-mail: cer@edreform.com
Phone: (800) 521-2118
Fax: (301) 986-1826
910 Seventeenth Street NW
Suite 1120
Washington, DC 20006

Thorough network of information resources and reform advocacy that provides updated reporting of key developments in education reform and includes many links to local groups.

Center for Equal Opportunity (CEO)
URL: http://www.ceousa.org
Phone: (703) 442-0066
Fax: (703) 442-0449
1700 Leesburg Pike
Suite 231
Falls Church, VA 22043
Led by conservative activist Linda Chavez, the CEO is in opposition to bilingual education and in support of school choice initiatives.

Center on Education Policy
URL: http://www.cep-dc.org
E-mail: cep-dc@cep-dc.org
Phone: (202) 822-8065
Fax: (202) 822-6008
1001 Connecticut Avenue NW
Suite 522
Washington, DC 20036
Produces publications and convenes meetings to help citizens "make sense of conflicting opinions and perceptions about public education." The center is sponsored by Phi Delta Kappa and several private foundations.

Coalition of Essential Schools
URL: http://www.essential schools.org
E-mail: staff directory
Phone: (510) 433-1451
Fax: (510) 433-1455
1330 Broadway

Suite 600
Oakland, CA 94612
Network committed to increasing student achievement by improving school design, leadership, classroom practice, and community connections.

Committee for Education Funding
URL: http://www.cef.org
E-mail: web form
Phone: (202) 383-0083
Fax: (202) 383-0097
122 C Street NW
Suite 280
Washington, DC 20001
Coalition of more than 100 education organizations seeking adequate federal financial support for schools.

Core Knowledge Foundation
URL: http://www.coreknowledge. org
E-mail: coreknow@coreknowl edge.org
Phone: (800) 238-3233
Fax: (434) 977-0021
801 East High Street
Charlottesville, VA 22902
Organization founded by professor and best-selling author E. D. Hirsch, promoting a specific, shared curriculum for schools.

Council of Great City Schools
URL: http://www.cgcs.org
Phone: (202) 393-2427
Fax: (202) 393-2400
1301 Pennsylvania Avenue NW
Suite 702
Washington, DC 20004

The only national organization exclusively dedicated to representing the needs of urban public schools, it works to promote urban education through legislation, research, media relations, instruction, management, technology, and other special projects.

Education Commission of the States
URL: http://www.ecs.org
E-mail: ecs@ecs.org
Phone: (303) 299-3600
Fax: (303) 296-8332
700 Broadway
Suite 810
Denver, CO 80203-3460
An interstate compact created in 1965 on the recommendation of James Conant to improve public knowledge about current and emerging issues, trends, and innovations in state education policy.

Education Law Association
URL: http:/educationlaw.org
E-mail: ela@educationlaw.org
Phone: (937) 229-3589
Fax: (937) 229-3845
300 College Park
Dayton, OH 45369
Community of educational and legal scholars and practitioners that supports scholarly research of education law through publications, conferences, seminars, and professional forums.

George Lucas Educational Foundation
URL: http://www.edutopia.org
E-mail: info@edutopia.org

Phone: (415) 507-0399
Fax: (415) 507-0499
P.O. Box 3494
San Rafael, CA 94912
Established by filmmaker George Lucas, the foundation profiles hundreds of successful teaching and learning examples to stimulate education reform.

Home School Legal Defense Association
URL: http://www.hslda.org
E-mail: info@hslda.org
Phone: (540) 538-5600
Fax: (540) 338-2733
P.O. Box 3000
Purcellville, VA 20134
Advocates homeschooling in courtrooms, before government officials, and in the public arena.

KIPP (Knowledge Is Power Program)
URL: http://www.kipp.org
E-mail: info@kipp.org
Phone: 866-345-5477
Fax: (415) 348-0588
135 Main Street
Suite 1700
San Francisco, CA 94105
National nonprofit organization that trains school leaders to open and run schools in underserved areas that emphasize high expectations, an extended school day and school year, and parental and student commitment.

Learning Point Associates
URL: http://www.learningpt.org
Phone: (312) 288-7600
Fax: (312) 288-7601

20 North Wacker Drive
Suite 1231
Chicago, IL 60606
Conducts research and evaluates educational programs, provides states with technical knowledge and research-based best practices, and develops policy recommendations for states, local districts, nonprofits, and private organizations.

Magnet Schools of America
URL: http://www.magnet.edu
E-mail: web form
Phone: (202) 824-0672
Fax: (202) 737-0100
1012 14th Street NW
Suite 203
Washington, DC 20005
Promotes legislation to foster development and improvement of magnet schools.

National Alliance for Public Charter Schools
URL: http://www.publiccharters.org
Phone: (202) 289-2700
1101 15th Street NW
Suite 1010
Washington, DC 20005
The leading national nonprofit organization committed to advancing the charter school movement, particularly in disadvantaged communities, through assistance to state charter school associations and resource centers and policy advocacy.

National Association for Bilingual Education
URL: http://www.nabe.org
E-mail: members@nabe.org

Phone: (202) 898-1829
Fax: (202) 789-2866
1313 L Street NW
Suite 210
Washington, DC 20005
The only national organization exclusively concerned with the education of language minority students in U.S. schools, it promotes educational equity through bilingual education.

National Board for Professional Teaching Standards
URL: http://www.nbpts.org
E-mail: web form
Phone: 800-228-3224
1525 Wilson Boulevard
Suite 500
Arlington, VA 22209
Independent nonpartisan organization created in response to *A Nation At Risk*. Promotes standards for what teachers should know and a voluntary system of assessment and certification for teachers who meet those standards.

National Center for Education Statistics
URL: http://www.nces.ed.gov
Phone: (202) 502-7300
1990 K Street NW
Washington, DC 20006
Primary federal source for collection and analysis of data related to education in the United States and other nations.

National Center for Research on Evaluation, Standards, & Student Testing
URL: http://www.cse.ucla.edu
Phone: (310) 206-1532

Fax: (310) 825-3883
300 Charles E. Young Drive North
GSE & IS Building
3rd Floor
Mailbox 951522
Los Angeles, CA 90095-1522
Partnership of universities addressing issues relating to the design and use of assessment systems that serve multiple purposes.

National Center for the Study of Privatization in Education
URL: http://www.ncspe.org
E-mail: ncspe@columbia.edu
Phone: (212) 678-3259
Fax: (212) 678-3474
Teachers College
Columbia University
Box 181
230 Thompson Hall
525 West 120th Street
New York, NY 10027-6696
Source of analysis on national and international privatization in education issues ranging from preschool to higher education, focusing on research, evaluation, and the dissemination of information.

National Center on Education and the Economy
URL: http://www.ncee.org
E-mail: info@ncee.org
Phone: (202) 379-1800
Fax: (202) 293-1560
2000 Pennsylvania Avenue
Suite 5300
Washington, DC 20006
Emphasizes standards-based reform through policies, technical assistance, and professional development.

National Commission on Teaching and America's Future
URL: http://www.nctaf.org
E-mail: rbrookshire@nctaf.org
Phone: (202) 429-2570
Fax: (202) 429-2571
1420 K Street NW
Washington, DC 20005
Cross section of public officials, business and community leaders, and educators focusing on methods to improve the quality of teaching.

National Council on Teacher Quality (NCTQ)
URL: http://www.nctq.org
E-mail: web form
Phone: (202) 393-0020
Fax: (202) 393-0095
1420 New York Avenue
Suite 800
Washington, DC 20005
Nonpartisan research and advocacy group committed to restructuring the teaching profession.

National Education Association (NEA)
URL: http://www.nea.org
E-mail: web form
Phone: (202) 833-4000
Fax: (202) 822-7974
1201 16th Street NW
Washington, DC 20036
Oldest and largest U.S. organization committed to advancing the cause of public education with a membership of more than 3.2 million.

National Forum to Accelerate Middle-Grades Reform
URL: http://www.mgforum.org
E-mail: debnatforum@gmail.com

Phone: (217) 351-2196
Fax: (217) 351-1068
P.O. Box 224
Savoy, IL 61874
Alliance of educators, researchers, and foundations promoting academic performance and development of young adolescents.

National PTA
URL: http://www.pta.org
E-mail: info@pta.org
Phone: (800) 307-4782
Fax: (312) 670-6783
541 North Fairbanks Court
Suite 1300
Chicago, IL 60611
Supports effective schools through participation of families and educators, with more than 5 million members in 25,000 local units in all 50 states.

New Schools Venture Fund
URL: http://www.newschools.org
E-mail: info@newschools.org
Phone: (415) 615-6860
Fax: (415) 615-6861
49 Stevenson
Suite 575
San Francisco, CA 94105
A national nonprofit venture philanthropy firm that seeks to transform public education—especially for children in underserved communities—by supporting education entrepreneurs and connecting their work to systems change.

Parents in Charge Foundation
URL: http://www.picfoundation. org
E-mail: ray@picfoundation.org

Phone: (703) 383-0908
Fax: (703) 383-5288
9900 Main Street
Suite 303
Fairfax, VA 22031
Coalition that seeks to ensure that all students, regardless of household income, are provided an opportunity to receive a quality education determined by parental choice. The organization's board of advisers includes prominent members of Congress and many former cabinet secretaries.

Project Zero
URL: http://www.pz.harvard.edu
E-mail: info@pz.harvard.edu
Phone: (617) 496-7097
Fax: (617) 495-9709
Harvard Graduate School of Education
124 Mount Auburn Street
Fifth Floor
Cambridge, MA 02138
An educational research group that focuses on the role of the arts in learning, thinking, and creativity, particularly in schools serving disadvantaged populations.

Public Education Network
URL: http://www.publiceducation.org
E-mail: PEN@PublicEducation.org
Phone: (202) 628-7460
Fax: (202) 628-1893
601 13th Street NW
Suite 710 South
Washington, DC 20005
National association of nonprofit community-based organizations advancing school reform in low-income areas across the country. The network focuses on improving funding, assessment, and professional development.

Small Schools Workshop
URL: http://www.smallschoolsworkshop.org
E-mail: smallschoolsworkshop@yahoo.com
Phone: (312) 560-5608
1608 North Milwaukee Avenue
Suite 912
Chicago, IL 60647
Group of educators, organizers, and researchers collaborating with teachers, principals, and parents to create small, innovative public schools.

StandardsWork
URL: http://www.standardswork.org
E-mail: info@standardswork.org
Phone: (202) 835-2000
Fax: (202) 659-4494
1001 Connecticut Avenue NW
Suite 640
Washington, DC 20036
Nonprofit educational consultancy promoting grade-by-grade standards and results-based evaluation systems in communities and schools.

Teach For America (TFA)
URL: http://www.teachforamerica.org
Phone: (800) 832-1230
Fax: (212) 279-2081
315 West 36th Street
7th Floor

New York, NY 10018
National corps of recent college
graduates who commit two years to
teach in low-income communities.

Thomas B. Fordham Institute
URL: http://www.edexcellence.
  net
E-mail: thegadfly@edexcellence.
  net
Phone: (202) 223-5452
Fax: (202) 223-9226
1016 16th Street NW
8th Floor
Washington, DC 20036

A think tank that emphasizes the
promotion of accountability policies and the expansion of education
options.

U.S. Department of Education
URL: http://www.ed.gov
Phone: (800) 872-5327
400 Maryland Avenue SW
Washington, DC 20202-0498
Federal department established in
1980 whose mission includes the
coordination and management of
grant programs, research, and assessment.

PART III

APPENDICES

APPENDIX A

EXCERPTS FROM *CARDINAL PRINCIPLES OF SECONDARY EDUCATION*, 1918

The following extract is taken from the influential 1918 report published by the National Education Association's Commission on the Reorganization of Secondary Education, Department of the Interior, Bureau of Education, which was instrumental in propelling the progressive education movement and shaping comprehensive high school instructional practice throughout much of the 20th century.

I. THE NEED FOR REORGANIZATION

Secondary education should be determined by the needs of the society to be served, the character of the individuals to be educated, and the knowledge of educational theory and practice available. These factors are by no means static. Society is always in process of development; the character of the secondary-school population undergoes modification; and the sciences on which educational theory and practice depend constantly furnish new information. Secondary education, however, like any other established agency of society, is conservative and tends to resist modification. Failure to make adjustments when the need arises leads to the necessity for extensive reorganization at irregular intervals. The evidence is strong that such a comprehensive reorganization of secondary education is imperative at the present time.

1. *Changes in society.*—Within the past few decades changes have taken place in American life profoundly affecting the activities of the individual. As a citizen, he must to a greater extent and in a more direct way cope with problems of community life, State and National Governments, and international relationships. As a worker, he must adjust himself to a more complex economic order. As a relatively independent personality, he has more

leisure. The problems arising from these three dominant phases of life are closely interrelated and call for a degree of intelligence and efficiency on the part of every citizen that cannot be secured through elementary education alone, or even through secondary education unless the scope of that education is broadened.

The responsibility of the secondary school is still further increased because many social agencies other than the school afford less stimulus for education than heretofore. In many vocations there have come such significant changes as the substitution of the factory system for the domestic system of industry; the use of machinery in place of manual labor; the high specialization of processes with a corresponding subdivision of labor; and the breakdown of the apprentice system. In connection with home and family life have frequently come lessened responsibility on the part of the children; the withdrawal of the father and sometimes the mother from home occupations to the factory or store; and increased urbanization, resulting in less unified family life. Similarly, many important changes have taken place in community life, in the church, in the State, and in other institutions. These changes in American life call for extensive modifications in secondary education.

2. *Changes in the secondary-school population.*—In the past 25 years there have been marked changes in the secondary-school population of the United States. The number of pupils has increased, according to Federal returns, from one for every 210 of the total population in 1889–90, to one for every 121 in 1899–1900, to one for every 89 in 1909–10, and to one for every 73 of the estimated total population in 1914–15. The character of the secondary-school population has been modified by the entrance of large numbers of pupils of widely varying capacities, aptitudes, social heredity, and destinies in life. Further, the broadening of the scope of secondary education has brought to the school many pupils who do not complete the full course but leave at various stages of advancement. The needs of these pupils cannot be neglected, nor can we expect in the near future that all pupils will be able to complete the secondary school as fulltime students.

At present only about one-third of the pupils who enter the first year of the elementary school reach the four-year high school, and only about one in nine is graduated. Of those who enter the seventh school year, only one-half to two-thirds reach the first year of the four-year high school. Of those who enter the four-year high school about one-third leave before the beginning of the second year, about one-half are gone before the beginning of the third year, and fewer than one-third are graduated. These facts can no longer be safely ignored.

3. *Changes in educational theory.*—The sciences on which educational theory depends have within recent years made significant contributions. In particular, educational psychology emphasizes the following factors:

200

Appendix A

(a) *Individual differences in capacities and aptitudes among secondary-school pupils.*—Already recognized to some extent, this factor merits fuller attention.

(b) *The reexamination and reinterpretation of subject values and the teaching methods with reference to "general discipline."*—While the final verdict of modern psychology has not as yet been rendered, it is clear that former conceptions of "general values" must be thoroughly revised.

(c) *Importance of applying knowledge.*—Subject values and teaching methods must be tested in terms of the laws of learning and the application of knowledge to the activities of life, rather than primarily in terms of the demands of any subject as a logically organized science.

(d) *Continuity in the development of children.*—It has long been held that psychological changes at certain stages are so pronounced as to overshadow the continuity of development. On this basis secondary education has been sharply separated from elementary education. Modern psychology, however, goes to show that the development of the individual is in most respects a continuous process and that, therefore, any sudden or abrupt break between the elementary and the secondary school or between any two successive stages of education is undesirable.

The foregoing changes in society, in the character of the secondary school population, and in educational theory, together with many other considerations, call for extensive modifications of secondary education. Such modifications have already begun in part. The present need is for the formulation of a comprehensive program of reorganization, and its adoption, with suitable adjustments, in all the secondary schools of the Nation. Hence it is appropriate for a representative body like the National Education Association to outline such a program. This is the task entrusted by that association to the Commission on the Reorganization of Secondary Education.

II. THE GOAL OF EDUCATION IN A DEMOCRACY

Education in the United States should be guided by a clear conception of the meaning of democracy. It is the ideal of democracy that the individual and society may find fulfillment each in the other. Democracy sanctions neither the exploitation of the individual by society, nor the disregard of the interests of society by the individual. More explicitly—the purpose of democracy is so to organize society that each member may develop his personality primarily through activities designed for the well-being of his fellow members and of society as a whole.

201

This ideal demands that human activities be placed upon a high level of efficiency; that to this efficiency be added an appreciation of the significance of these activities and loyalty to the best ideals involved; and that the individual choose that vocation and those forms of social service in which his personality may develop and become most effective. For the achievement of these ends democracy must place chief reliance upon education.

Consequently, education in a democracy, both within and without the school, should develop in each individual the knowledge, interests, ideals, habits, and powers whereby he will find his place and use that place to shape both himself and society toward ever nobler ends.

III. THE MAIN OBJECTIVES OF EDUCATION

In order to determine the main objectives that should guide education in a democracy, it is necessary to analyze the activities of the individual. Normally he is a member of a family, of a vocational group, and of various civic groups, and by virtue of these relationships he is called upon to engage in activities that enrich the family life, to render important vocational services to his fellows, and to promote the common welfare. It follows, therefore, that worthy home membership, vocation, and citizenship demand attention as three of the leading objectives.

Aside from the immediate discharge of these specific duties, every individual should have a margin of time for the cultivation of personal and social interests. This leisure, if worthily used, will recreate his powers and enlarge and enrich life, thereby making him better able to meet his responsibilities. The unworthy use of leisure impairs health, disrupts home life, lessens vocational efficiency, and destroys civic-mindedness. The tendency in industrial life, aided by legislation, is to decrease the working hours of large groups of people. While shortened hours tend to lessen the harmful reactions that arise from prolonged strain, they increase, if possible, the importance of preparation for leisure. In view of these considerations, education for the worthy use of leisure is of increasing importance as an objective.

To discharge the duties of life and to benefit from leisure, one must have good health. The health of the individual is essential also to the vitality of the race and to the defense of the Nation. Health education is, therefore, fundamental.

There are various processes, such as reading, writing, arithmetical computations, and oral and written expression, that are needed as tools in the affairs of life. Consequently, command of these fundamental processes, while not an end in itself, is nevertheless an indispensable objective.

And, finally, the realization of the objectives already named is dependent upon ethical character, that is, upon conduct founded upon right principles, clearly perceived and loyally adhered to. Good citizenship, vocational excellence, and the worthy use of leisure go hand in hand with ethical character; they are at once the fruits of sterling character and the channels through which such character is developed and made manifest. On the one hand, character is meaningless apart from the will to discharge the duties of life, and, on the other hand, there is no guaranty that these duties will be rightly discharged unless principles are substituted for impulses, however well-intentioned such impulses may be. Consequently, ethical character is at once involved in all the other objectives and at the same time requires specific consideration in any program of national education.

This commission, therefore, regards the following as the main objectives of education: 1. Health. 2. Command of fundamental processes. 3. Worthy home membership. 4. Vocation. 5. Citizenship. 6. Worthy use of leisure. 7. Ethical character.

The naming of the above objectives is not intended to imply that the process of education can be divided into separated fields. This cannot be, since the pupil is indivisible. Nor is the analysis all-inclusive. Nevertheless, we believe that distinguishing and naming these objectives will aid in directing efforts; and we hold that they should constitute the principal aims in education.

IV. THE ROLE OF SECONDARY EDUCATION IN ACHIEVING THESE OBJECTIVES

The objectives outlined above apply to education as a whole—elementary, secondary, and higher. It is the purpose of this section to consider specifically the role of secondary education in achieving each of these objectives.

For reasons stated in Section X, this commission favors such reorganization that secondary education may be defined as applying to all pupils of approximately 12 to 18 years of age.

1. *Health.*—Health needs cannot be neglected during the period of secondary education without serious danger to the individual and the race. The secondary school should therefore provide health instruction, inculcate health habits, organize an effective program of physical activities, regard health needs in planning work and play, and cooperate with home and community in safeguarding and promoting health interests.

To carry out such a program it is necessary to arouse the public to recognize that the health needs of young people are of vital importance to society, to secure teachers competent to ascertain and meet the needs of individual pupils and able to inculcate in the entire student body a love for clean sport; to furnish adequate equipment, for physical activities, and to make the school building, its rooms and surroundings, conform to the best standards of hygiene and sanitation.

2. *Command of fundamental processes.*—Much of the energy of the elementary school is properly devoted to teaching certain fundamental processes, such as reading, writing, arithmetical computations, and the elements of oral and written expression. The facility that a child of 12 or 14 may acquire in the use of these tools is not sufficient for the needs of modern life. This is particularly true of the mother tongue. Proficiency in many of these processes may be increased more effectively by their application to new material than by the formal reviews commonly employed in grades seven and eight. Throughout the secondary school, instruction and practice must go hand in hand, but as indicated in the report of the committee on English, only so much theory should be taught at any one time as will show results in practice.

3. *Worthy home membership.*—Worthy home membership as an objective calls for the development of those qualities that make the individual a worthy member of a family, both contributing to and deriving benefit from that membership. This objective applies to both boys and girls. The social studies should deal with the home as a fundamental social institution and clarify its relation to the wider interests outside. Literature should interpret and idealize the human elements that go to make the home. Music and art should result in more beautiful homes and in greater joy therein. The co-educational school with a faculty of men and women should, in its organization and its activities, exemplify wholesome relations between boys and girls and men and women. Home membership as an objective should not be thought of solely with reference to future duties. These are the better guaranteed if the school helps the pupils to take the right attitude toward present home responsibilities and interprets to them the contribution of the home to their development.

In the education of every high-school girl, the household arts should have a prominent place because of their importance to the girl herself and to others whose welfare will be directly in her keeping. The attention now devoted to this phase of education is inadequate, and especially so for girls preparing for occupations not related to the household arts and for girls planning for higher institutions. The majority of girls who enter wage-earning occupations directly from the high school remain in them for only a few years, after which home making becomes their lifelong occupation. For them the high-school period offers the only assured opportunity to prepare for that lifelong occupation, and it is during this period that they are most likely to form their ideals of life's duties and responsibilities. For girls planning to enter higher institutions—our traditional ideals of preparation for higher institutions are particularly incongruous with the actual needs and future responsibilities of girls. It would seem that such high-school work as is carefully designed to develop capacity for, and interest in, the proper management and conduct of a home should be regarded as of importance at least equal to that of any other work. We do not understand how society can properly continue to sanction for girls high-school curriculums that disregard this fundamental need, even though such curriculums are planned in response to the demands made by some of the colleges for women.

In the education of boys, some opportunity should be found to give them a basis for the intelligent appreciation of the value of the well-appointed home and of the labor and skill required to maintain such a home, to the end that they may cooperate more effectively. For instance, they should understand the essentials of food values, of sanitation, and of household budgets.

4. *Vocation.*—Vocational education should equip the individual to secure a livelihood for himself and those dependent on him, to serve society well through his vocation, to maintain the right relationships toward his fellow workers and society, and, as far as possible, to find in that vocation his own best development. This ideal demands that the pupil explore his own capacities and aptitudes, and make a survey of the world's work, to the end that he may select his vocation wisely. Hence, an effective program of vocational guidance in the secondary school is essential.

Vocational education should aim to develop an appreciation of the significance of the vocation to the community and a clear conception of right relations between the members of the chosen vocation, between different vocational groups, between employer and employee, and between producer and consumer. These aspects of vocational education, heretofore neglected, demand emphatic attention.

The extent to which the secondary school should offer training for a specific vocation depends upon the vocation, the facilities that the school can acquire, and the opportunity that the pupil may have to obtain such training later. To obtain satisfactory results those proficient in that vocation should be employed as instructors and the actual conditions of the vocation should be utilized either within the high school or in cooperation with the home, farm, shop, or office. Much of the pupil's time will be required to produce such efficiency.

5. *Civic education* should develop in the individual those qualities whereby he will act well his part as a member of neighborhood, town or city, State, and Nation, and give him a basis for understanding international problems.

For such citizenship the following are essential: A many-sided interest in the welfare of the communities to which one belongs; loyalty to ideals of civic righteousness; practical knowledge of social agencies and institutions; good judgment as to means and methods that will promote one social end without defeating others . . .

Among the means for developing attitudes and habits important in a democracy are the assignment of projects and problems to groups of pupils for cooperative solution and the socialized recitation whereby the class as a whole develops a sense of collective responsibility. Both of these devices give training in collective thinking. Moreover, the democratic organization and administration of the school itself as well as the cooperative relations of pupil and teacher, pupil and pupil, and teacher and teacher, are indispensable. While all subjects should contribute to good citizenship, the social studies—geography, history, civics, and economics—should have this as their dominant aim. Too frequently, however, does mere information, conventional in value and remote in its bearing, make up the content of the social studies. History should so treat the growth of institutions that their present value may be appreciated. Geography should show the interdependence of men while it shows their common dependence on nature. Civics should concern itself less with constitutional questions and remote governmental functions, and should direct attention to social agencies close at hand and to the informal activities of daily life that regard and seek the common good. Such agencies as child-welfare organizations and consumers' leagues afford specific opportunities for the expression of civic qualities by the older pupils.

The work in English should kindle social ideals and give insight into social conditions and into personal character as related to these conditions. Hence the emphasis by the committee on English on the importance of a knowledge of social activities, social movements, and social needs on the part of the teacher of English.

The comprehension of the ideals of American democracy and loyalty to them should be a prominent aim of civic education. The pupil should feel that he will be responsible, in cooperation with others, for keeping the Nation true to the best inherited conceptions of democracy, and he should also realize that democracy itself is an ideal to be wrought out by his own and succeeding generations.

Civic education should consider other nations also. As a people we should try to understand their aspirations and ideals that we may deal more sympathetically and intelligently with the immigrant coming to our shores, and have a basis for a wiser and more sympathetic approach to international problems. Our pupils should learn that each nation, at least potentially, has something of worth to contribute to civilization and that humanity would be incomplete without that contribution. This means a study of specific nations, their achievements and possibilities, not ignoring their limitations. Such a study of dissimilar contributions in the light of the ideal of human brotherhood should help to establish a genuine internationalism, free from sentimentality, founded on fact, and actually operative in the affairs of nations.

6. *Worthy use of leisure.*—Education should equip the individual to secure from his leisure the recreation of body, mind, and spirit, and the enrichment and enlargement of his personality.

This objective calls for the ability to utilize the common means of enjoyment, such as music, art, literature, drama, and social intercourse, together with the fostering in each individual of one or more special vocational interests.

Heretofore the high school has given little conscious attention to this objective. It has so exclusively sought intellectual discipline that it has seldom treated literature, art, and music so as to evoke right emotional response and produce positive enjoyment. Its presentation of science should aim, in part, to arouse a genuine appreciation of nature.

The school has failed also to organize and direct the social activities of young people as it should. One of the surest ways in which to prepare pupils worthily to utilize leisure in adult life is by guiding and directing their use of leisure in youth. The school should, therefore, see that adequate recreation is provided both within the school and by other proper agencies in the community. The school, however, has a unique opportunity in this field because it includes in its membership representatives from all classes of society and consequently is able through social relationships to establish bonds of friendship and common understanding that can not be furnished by other agencies. Moreover, the school can so organize recreational activities that they will contribute simultaneously to other ends of education, as in the case of the school pageant or festival.

7. *Ethical character.*—In a democratic society ethical character becomes paramount among the objectives of the secondary school. Among the means for developing ethical character may be mentioned the wise selection of content and methods of instruction in all subjects of study, the social contacts of pupils with one another and with their teachers, the opportunities afforded by the organization and administration of the school for the development on the part of pupils of the sense of personal responsibility and initiative and, above all, the spirit of service and the principles of true democracy which should permeate the entire school—principal, teachers, and pupils.

Specific consideration is given to the moral values to be obtained from the organization of the school and the subjects of study in the report of this commission entitled "Moral Values in Secondary Education." That report considers also the conditions under which it may be advisable to supplement the other activities of the school by offering a distinct course in moral instruction . . .

XX. CONCLUSION

. . . It is the firm belief of this commission that secondary education in the United States must aim at nothing less than complete and worthy living for all youth, and that therefore the objectives described herein must find place in the education of every boy and girl.

Finally, in the process of translating into daily practice the cardinal principles herein set forth, the secondary school teachers of the United States must themselves strive to explore the inner meaning of the great democratic movement now struggling for supremacy. The doctrine that each individual has a right to the opportunity to develop the best that is in him is reinforced by the belief in the potential, and perchance unique, worth of the individual. The task of education, as of life, is therefore to call forth that potential worth.

While seeking to evoke the distinctive excellencies of individuals and groups of individuals, the secondary school must be equally zealous to develop those common ideas, common ideals, and common modes of thought, feeling, and action, whereby America, through a rich, unified, common life, may render her truest service to a world seeking for democracy among men and nations.

APPENDIX B

PRESIDENT LYNDON B. JOHNSON'S REMARKS UPON SIGNING THE ELEMENTARY AND SECONDARY EDUCATION BILL (HR 2362), APRIL 11, 1965

President Lyndon B. Johnson made these remarks in Johnson City, Texas.

Ladies and gentlemen:

I want to welcome to this little school of my childhood many of my former school mates and many who went to school with me at Cotulla and Houston and San Marcos, as well as some of my dear friends from the educational institutions of this area.

My Attorney General tells me that it is legal and constitutional to sign this act on Sunday, even on Palm Sunday. My minister assured me that the Lord's day will not be violated by making into law a measure which will bring mental and moral benefits to millions of our young people.

So I have chosen this time and this place for two reasons.

First, I do not wish to delay by a single day the program to strengthen this Nation's elementary and secondary schools. I devoutly hope that my sense of urgency will be communicated to Secretary Celebrezze, Commissioner Keppel, and the other educational officers throughout the country who will be responsible for carrying out this program.

Second, I felt a very strong desire to go back to the beginnings of my own education—to be reminded and to remind others of that magic time when the world of learning began to open before our eyes.

In this one-room schoolhouse Miss Katie Deadrich taught eight grades at one and the same time. Come over here, Miss Katie, and sit by me, will you? Let them see you. I started school when I was 4 years old, and they tell me, Miss Kate [sic], that I recited my first lessons while sitting on your lap.

From our very beginnings as a nation, we have felt a fierce commitment to the ideal of education for everyone. It fixed itself into our democratic creed.

Over a century and a quarter ago, the President of the Republic of Texas, Mirabeau B. Lamar, proclaimed education as "the guardian genius of democracy . . . the only dictator that free men acknowledge and the only security that free men desire."

But President Lamar made the mistaken prophecy that education would be an issue "in which no jarring interests are involved and no acrimonious political feelings excited." For too long, political acrimony held up our progress. For too long, children suffered while jarring interests caused stalemate in the efforts to improve our schools. Since 1946 Congress tried repeatedly, and failed repeatedly, to enact measures for elementary and secondary education.

Now, within the past 3 weeks, the House of Representatives, by a vote of 263 to 153, and the Senate, by a vote of 73 to 18, have passed the most sweeping educational bill ever to come before Congress. It represents a major new commitment of the Federal Government to quality and equality in the schooling that we offer our young people. I predict that all of those of both parties of Congress who supported the enactment of this legislation will be remembered in history as men and women who began a new day of greatness in American society.

We are delighted that Senator McCarthy could be speaking at the University of Texas yesterday, and he came up and had lunch with me today, and is returning to Washington with me at 7:30 in the morning. Senator McCarthy is an old friend of mine from Minnesota. Stand up, Senator, and let them see you. He has been working for this educational bill ever since the first day he came to the House of Representatives, and ever since he has been in the Senate.

I am delighted to have another good friend of mine who spent the weekend in his home district—McAlester, Oklahoma—and who came down here to spend the evening with me, and is returning in the morning, the distinguished majority leader of the House, without whose efforts we would never have passed this bill—Carl Albert of Oklahoma.

By passing this bill, we bridge the gap between helplessness and hope for more than 5 million educationally deprived children.

We put into the hands of our youth more than 30 million new books, and into many of our schools their first libraries.

We reduce the terrible time lag in bringing new teaching techniques into the Nation's classrooms.

We strengthen State and local agencies which bear the burden and the challenge of better education.

And we rekindle the revolution—the revolution of the spirit against the tyranny of ignorance.

As a son of a tenant farmer, I know that education is the only valid passport from poverty.

As a former teacher—and, I hope, a future one—I have great expectations of what this law will mean for all of our young people.

As President of the United States, I believe deeply no law I have signed or will ever sign means more to the future of America.

To each and everyone who contributed to this day, the Nation is indebted.

On Tuesday afternoon we will ask the Members of the House and Senate who were instrumental in guiding this legislation through the Congress to meet with us at a reception in the White House.

So it is not the culmination but only the commencement of this journey. Let me urge, as Thomas Jefferson urged his fellow countrymen one time to, and I quote, "Preach, my dear sir, a crusade against ignorance; establish and improve the law for educating the common people . . ."

We have established the law. Let us not delay in putting it to work.

APPENDIX C

EXCERPTS FROM *A NATION AT RISK*, NATIONAL COMMISSION ON EXCELLENCE IN EDUCATION, APRIL 1983

INTRODUCTION

Secretary of Education T. H. Bell created the National Commission on Excellence in Education on August 26, 1981, directing it to examine the quality of education in the United States and to make a report to the Nation and to him within 18 months of its first meeting. In accordance with the secretary's instructions, this report contains practical recommendations for educational improvement and fulfills the commission's responsibilities under the terms of its charter.

A NATION AT RISK

All, regardless of race or class or economic status, are entitled to a fair chance and to the tools for developing their individual powers of mind and spirit to the utmost. This promise means that all children by virtue of their own efforts, competently guided, can hope to attain the mature and informed judgement needed to secure gainful employment, and to manage their own lives, thereby serving not only their own interests but also the progress of society itself.

Our Nation is at risk. Our once unchallenged preeminence in commerce, industry, science, and technological innovation is being overtaken by competitors throughout the world. This report is concerned with only one of the many causes and dimensions of the problem, but it is the one that undergirds American prosperity, security, and civility. We report to the American people that while we can take justifiable pride in what our schools and colleges have historically accomplished and contributed to the United States and the well-being of its people, the educational foundations of our society are presently being eroded by a rising tide of mediocrity that threatens our very future as a Nation and a people. What was unimaginable a generation ago has begun to occur—others are matching and surpassing our educational attainments.

If an unfriendly foreign power had attempted to impose on America the mediocre educational performance that exists today, we might well have viewed it as an act of war. As it stands, we have allowed this to happen to ourselves. We have even squandered the gains in student achievement made in the wake of the Sputnik challenge. Moreover, we have dismantled essential support systems which helped make those gains possible. We have, in effect, been committing an act of unthinking, unilateral educational disarmament.

Our society and its educational institutions seem to have lost sight of the basic purposes of schooling, and of the high expectations and disciplined effort needed to attain them. This report, the result of 18 months of study, seeks to generate reform of our educational system in fundamental ways and to renew the Nation's commitment to schools and colleges of high quality throughout the length and breadth of our land.

That we have compromised this commitment is, upon reflection, hardly surprising, given the multitude of often conflicting demands we have placed on our Nation's schools and colleges. They are routinely called on to provide solutions to personal, social, and political problems that the home and other institutions either will not or cannot resolve. We must understand that these demands on our schools and colleges often exact an educational cost as well as a financial one.

On the occasion of the Commission's first meeting, President Reagan noted the central importance of education in American life when he said: "Certainly there are few areas of American life as important to our society, to our people, and to our families as our schools and colleges." This report, therefore, is as much an open letter to the American people as it is a report to the Secretary of Education. We are confident that the American people, properly informed, will do what is right for their children and for the generations to come.

THE RISK

History is not kind to idlers. The time is long past when American's [sic] destiny was assured simply by an abundance of natural resources and inexhaustible human enthusiasm, and by our relative isolation from the malignant problems of older civilizations. The world is indeed one global village. We live among determined, well-educated, and strongly motivated competitors. We compete with them for international standing and markets, not only with products but also with the ideas of our laboratories and neighborhood workshops. America's position in the world may once have been reasonably secure with only a few exceptionally well-trained men and women. It is no longer.

The risk is not only that the Japanese make automobiles more efficiently than Americans and have government subsidies for development and export. It is not just that the South Koreans recently built the world's most efficient steel mill, or that American machine tools, once the pride of the world, are being displaced by German products. It is also that these developments signify a redistribution of trained capability throughout the globe. Knowledge, learning, information, and skilled intelligence are the new raw materials of international commerce and are today spreading throughout the world as vigorously as miracle drugs, synthetic fertilizers, and blue jeans did earlier. If only to keep and improve on the slim competitive edge we still retain in world markets, we must dedicate ourselves to the reform of our educational system for the benefit of all—old and young alike, affluent and poor, majority and minority. Learning is the indispensable investment required for success in the "information age" we are entering.

Our concern, however, goes well beyond matters such as industry and commerce. It also includes the intellectual, moral, and spiritual strengths of our people which knit together the very fabric of our society. The people of the United States need to know that individuals in our society who do not possess the levels of skill, literacy, and training essential to this new era will be effectively disenfranchised, not simply from the material rewards that accompany competent performance, but also from the chance to participate fully in our national life. A high level of shared education is essential to a free, democratic society and to the fostering of a common culture, especially in a country that prides itself on pluralism and individual freedom.

For our country to function, citizens must be able to reach some common understandings on complex issues, often on short notice and on the basis of conflicting or incomplete evidence. Education helps form these common understandings, a point Thomas Jefferson made long ago in his justly famous dictum:

I know no safe depository of the ultimate powers of the society but the people themselves; and if we think them not enlightened enough to exercise their control with a wholesome discretion, the remedy is not to take it from them but to inform their discretion.

Appendix C

Part of what is at risk is the promise first made on this continent: All, regardless of race or class or economic status, are entitled to a fair chance and to the tools for developing their individual powers of mind and spirit to the utmost. This promise means that all children by virtue of their own efforts, competently guided, can hope to attain the mature and informed judgment needed to secure gainful employment, and to manage their own lives, thereby serving not only their own interests but also the progress of society itself.

INDICATORS OF THE RISK

The educational dimensions of the risk before us have been amply documented in testimony received by the Commission. For example:

- International comparisons of student achievement, completed a decade ago, reveal that on 19 academic tests American students were never first or second and, in comparison with other industrialized nations, were last seven times.

- Some 23 million American adults are functionally illiterate by the simplest tests of everyday reading, writing, and comprehension.

- About 13 percent of all 17-year-olds in the United States can be considered functionally illiterate. Functional illiteracy among minority youth may run as high as 40 percent.

- Average achievement of high school students on most standardized tests is now lower than 26 years ago when Sputnik was launched.

- Over half the population of gifted students do not match their tested ability with comparable achievement in school.

- The College Board's Scholastic Aptitude Tests (SAT) demonstrate a virtually unbroken decline from 1963 to 1980. Average verbal scores fell over 50 points and average mathematics scores dropped nearly 40 points.

- College Board achievement tests also reveal consistent declines in recent years in such subjects as physics and English.

- Both the number and proportion of students demonstrating superior achievement on the SATs (i.e., those with scores of 650 or higher) have also dramatically declined.

- Many 17-year-olds do not possess the "higher order" intellectual skills we should expect of them. Nearly 40 percent cannot draw inferences from written material; only one-fifth can write a persuasive essay; and only one-third can solve a mathematics problem requiring several steps.

- There was a steady decline in science achievement scores of U.S. 17-year-olds as measured by national assessments of science in 1969, 1973, and 1977.

215

- Between 1975 and 1980, remedial mathematics courses in public 4-year colleges increased by 72 percent and now constitute one-quarter of all mathematics courses taught in those institutions.

- Average tested achievement of students graduating from college is also lower.

- Business and military leaders complain that they are required to spend millions of dollars on costly remedial education and training programs in such basic skills as reading, writing, spelling, and computation. The Department of the Navy, for example, reported to the Commission that one-quarter of its recent recruits cannot read at the ninth grade level, the minimum needed simply to understand written safety instructions. Without remedial work they cannot even begin, much less complete, the sophisticated training essential in much of the modern military.

These deficiencies come at a time when the demand for highly skilled workers in new fields is accelerating rapidly. For example:

- Computers and computer-controlled equipment are penetrating every aspect of our lives—homes, factories, and offices.

- One estimate indicates that by the turn of the century millions of jobs will involve laser technology and robotics.

- Technology is radically transforming a host of other occupations. They include health care, medical science, energy production, food processing, construction, and the building, repair, and maintenance of sophisticated scientific, educational, military, and industrial equipment.

Analysts examining these indicators of student performance and the demands for new skills have made some chilling observations. Educational researcher Paul Hurd concluded at the end of a thorough national survey of student achievement that within the context of the modern scientific revolution, "We are raising a new generation of Americans that is scientifically and technologically illiterate." In a similar vein, John Slaughter, a former Director of the National Science Foundation, warned of "a growing chasm between a small scientific and technological elite and a citizenry ill-informed, indeed uninformed, on issues with a science component."

But the problem does not stop there, nor do all observers see it the same way. Some worry that schools may emphasize such rudiments as reading and computation at the expense of other essential skills such as comprehension, analysis, solving problems, and drawing conclusions. Still others are concerned that an over-emphasis on technical and occupational skills will leave little time for studying the arts and humanities that so enrich daily life, help maintain civility, and develop a sense of community. Knowledge of the humanities, they maintain, must be harnessed to science and technology if the latter are to remain creative and humane, just as the humanities need to be informed by science and technology if they are to remain relevant to the human condition. Another analyst, Paul Copperman, has drawn a sobering conclusion. Until now, he has noted:

> *Each generation of Americans has outstripped its parents in education, in literacy, and in economic attainment. For the first time in the history of our country, the educational skills of one generation will not surpass, will not equal, will not even approach, those of their parents.*

It is important, of course, to recognize that *the average citizen* today is better educated and more knowledgeable than the average citizen of a generation ago—more literate, and exposed to more mathematics, literature, and science. The positive impact of this fact on the well-being of our country and the lives of our people cannot be overstated. Nevertheless, *the average graduate* of our schools and colleges today is not as well-educated as the average graduate of 25 or 35 years ago, when a much smaller proportion of our population completed high school and college. The negative impact of this fact likewise cannot be overstated.

FINDINGS

We conclude that declines in educational performance are in large part the result of disturbing inadequacies in the way the educational process itself is often conducted. The findings that follow, culled from a much more extensive list, reflect four important aspects of the educational process: content, expectations, time, and teaching.

FINDINGS REGARDING CONTENT

By content we mean the very "stuff" of education, the curriculum. Because of our concern about the curriculum, the Commission examined patterns of courses high school students took in 1964–69 compared with course patterns in 1976–81. On the basis of these analyses we conclude:

- Secondary school curricula have been homogenized, diluted, and diffused to the point that they no longer have a central purpose. In effect, we have a cafeteria style curriculum in which the appetizers and desserts can easily be mistaken for the main courses. Students have migrated from vocational and college preparatory programs to "general track" courses in large numbers. The proportion of students taking a general program of study has increased from 12 percent in 1964 to 42 percent in 1979.

- This curricular smorgasbord, combined with extensive student choice, explains a great deal about where we find ourselves today. We offer intermediate algebra, but only 31 percent of our recent high school graduates complete it; we offer French I, but only 13 percent complete it; and we offer geography, but only 16 percent complete it. Calculus is available in schools enrolling about 60 percent of all students, but only 6 percent of all students complete it.

- Twenty-five percent of the credits earned by general track high school students are in physical and health education, work experience outside the school, remedial English and mathematics, and personal service and development courses, such as training for adulthood and marriage.

FINDINGS REGARDING EXPECTATIONS

We define expectations in terms of the level of knowledge, abilities, and skills school and college graduates should possess. They also refer to the time, hard work, behavior, self-discipline, and motivation that are essential for high student achievement. Such expectations are expressed to students in several different ways:

- by grades, which reflect the degree to which students demonstrate their mastery of subject matter;

- through high school and college graduation requirements, which tell students which subjects are most important;

- by the presence or absence of rigorous examinations requiring students to demonstrate their mastery of content and skill before receiving a diploma or a degree;

- by college admissions requirements, which reinforce high school standards; and

- by the difficulty of the subject matter students confront in their texts and assigned readings.

Our analyses in each of these areas indicate notable deficiencies:

- The amount of homework for high school seniors has decreased (two-thirds report less than 1 hour a night) and grades have risen as average student achievement has been declining.

- In many other industrialized nations, courses in mathematics (other than arithmetic or general mathematics), biology, chemistry, physics, and ge-

218

ography start in grade 6 and are required of *all* students. The time spent on these subjects, based on class hours, is about three times that spent by even the most science-oriented U.S. students, i.e., those who select 4 years of science and mathematics in secondary school.

- A 1980 State-by-State survey of high school diploma requirements reveals that only eight States require high schools to offer foreign language instruction, but none requires students to take the courses. Thirty-five States require only 1 year of mathematics, and 36 require only 1 year of science for a diploma.

- In 13 States, 50 percent or more of the units required for high school graduation may be electives chosen by the student. Given this freedom to choose the substance of half or more of their education, many students opt for less demanding personal service courses, such as bachelor living.

- "Minimum competency" examinations (now required in 37 States) fall short of what is needed, as the "minimum" tends to become the "maximum," thus lowering educational standards for all.

- One-fifth of all 4-year public colleges in the United States must accept every high school graduate within the State regardless of the program followed or grades, thereby serving notice to high school students that they can expect to attend college even if they do not follow a demanding course of study in high school or perform well.

- About 23 percent of our more selective colleges and universities reported that their general level of selectivity declined during the 1970s, and 29 percent reported reducing the number of specific high school courses required for admission (usually by dropping foreign language requirements, which are now specified as a condition for admission by only one-fifth of our institutions of higher education).

- Too few experienced teachers and scholars are involved in writing textbooks. During the past decade or so a large number of texts have been "written down" by their publishers to ever-lower reading levels in response to perceived market demands.

- A recent study by Education Products Information Exchange revealed that a majority of students were able to master 80 percent of the material in some of their subject-matter texts before they had even opened the books. Many books do not challenge the students to whom they are assigned.

- Expenditures for textbooks and other instructional materials have declined by 50 percent over the past 17 years. While some recommend a level of spending on texts of between 5 and 10 percent of the operating costs of schools, the budgets for basal texts and related materials have been dropping during the past decade and a half to only 0.7 percent today.

FINDINGS REGARDING TIME

Evidence presented to the Commission demonstrates three disturbing facts about the use that American schools and students make of time: (1) compared to other nations, American students spend much less time on school work; (2) time spent in the classroom and on homework is often used ineffectively; and (3) schools are not doing enough to help students develop either the study skills required to use time well or the willingness to spend more time on school work.

- In England and other industrialized countries, it is not unusual for academic high school students to spend 8 hours a day at school, 220 days per year. In the United States, by contrast, the typical school day lasts 6 hours and the school year is 180 days.

- In many schools, the time spent learning how to cook and drive counts as much toward a high school diploma as the time spent studying mathematics, English, chemistry, U.S. history, or biology.

- A study of the school week in the United States found that some schools provided students only 17 hours of academic instruction during the week, and the average school provided about 22.

- A California study of individual classrooms found that because of poor management of classroom time, some elementary students received only one-fifth of the instruction others received in reading comprehension.

- In most schools, the teaching of study skills is haphazard and unplanned. Consequently, many students complete high school and enter college without disciplined and systematic study habits.

FINDINGS REGARDING TEACHING

The Commission found that not enough of the academically able students are being attracted to teaching; that teacher preparation programs need substantial improvement; that the professional working life of teachers is on the whole unacceptable; and that a serious shortage of teachers exists in key fields.

- Too many teachers are being drawn from the bottom quarter of graduating high school and college students.

- The teacher preparation curriculum is weighted heavily with courses in "educational methods" at the expense of courses in subjects to be taught. A survey of 1,350 institutions training teachers indicated that 41 percent of the time of elementary school teacher candidates is spent in education courses, which reduces the amount of time available for subject matter courses.

- The average salary after 12 years of teaching is only $17,000 per year, and many teachers are required to supplement their income with part-time and summer employment. In addition, individual teachers have little influence in such critical professional decisions as, for example, textbook selection.

- Despite widespread publicity about an overpopulation of teachers, severe shortages of certain kinds of teachers exist: in the fields of mathematics, science, and foreign languages; and among specialists in education for gifted and talented, language minority, and handicapped students.

- The shortage of teachers in mathematics and science is particularly severe. A 1981 survey of 45 States revealed shortages of mathematics teachers in 43 States, critical shortages of earth sciences teachers in 33 States, and of physics teachers everywhere.

Half of the newly employed mathematics, science, and English teachers are not qualified to teach these subjects; fewer than one-third of U.S. high schools offer Physics taught by qualified teachers.

RECOMMENDATIONS

In light of the urgent need for improvement, both immediate and long term, this Commission has agreed on a set of recommendations that the American people can begin to act on now, that can be implemented over the next several years, and that promise lasting reform. The topics are familiar; there is little mystery about what we believe must be done. Many schools, districts, and States are already giving serious and constructive attention to these matters, even though their plans may differ from our recommendations in some details.

We wish to note that we refer to public, private, and parochial schools and colleges alike. All are valuable national resources. Examples of actions similar to those recommended below can be found in each of them.

We must emphasize that the variety of student aspirations, abilities, and preparation requires that appropriate content be available to satisfy diverse needs. Attention must be directed to both the nature of the content available and to the needs of particular learners. The most gifted students, for example, may need a curriculum enriched and accelerated beyond even the needs of other students of high ability. Similarly, educationally disadvantaged students may require special curriculum materials, smaller classes, or individual tutoring to help them master the material presented. Nevertheless, there remains a common expectation: We must demand the best effort and performance from all students, whether they are gifted or less able, affluent or disadvantaged, whether destined for college, the farm, or industry.

Education Reform

Our recommendations are based on the beliefs that everyone can learn, that everyone is born with an urge to learn which can be nurtured, that a solid high school education is within the reach of virtually all, and that life-long learning will equip people with the skills required for new careers and for citizenship.

RECOMMENDATION A: CONTENT

We recommend *that State and local high school graduation requirements be strengthened and that, at a minimum, all students seeking a diploma be required to lay the foundations in the Five New Basics by taking the following curriculum during their 4 years of high school: (a) 4 years of English; (b) 3 years of mathematics; (c) 3 years of science; (d) 3 years of social studies; and (e) one-half year of computer science. For the college-bound, 2 years of foreign language in high school are strongly recommended in addition to those taken earlier.*

RECOMMENDATION B: STANDARDS AND EXPECTATIONS

We recommend *that schools, colleges, and universities adopt more rigorous and measurable standards, and higher expectations, for academic performance and student conduct, and that 4-year colleges and universities raise their requirements for admission. This will help students do their best educationally with challenging materials in an environment that supports learning and authentic accomplishment.*

Implementing Recommendations

1. Grades should be indicators of academic achievement so they can be relied on as evidence of a student's readiness for further study.
2. Four-year colleges and universities should raise their admissions requirements and advise all potential applicants of the standards for admission in terms of specific courses required, performance in these areas, and levels of achievement on standardized achievement tests in each of the five Basics and, where applicable, foreign languages.
3. Standardized tests of achievement (not to be confused with aptitude tests) should be administered at major transition points from one level of schooling to another and particularly from high school to college or work. The purposes of these tests would be to: (a) certify the student's credentials; (b) identify the need for remedial intervention; and (c) identify the opportunity for advanced or accelerated work. The tests should be administered as part of a nationwide (but not Federal) system of State and local standardized tests. This system should include other diagnostic procedures that assist teachers and students to evaluate student progress.

4. Textbooks and other tools of learning and teaching should be upgraded and updated to assure more rigorous content. We call upon university scientists, scholars, and members of professional societies, in collaboration with master teachers, to help in this task, as they did in the post-Sputnik era. They should assist willing publishers in developing the products or publish their own alternatives where there are persistent inadequacies.

5. In considering textbooks for adoption, States and school districts should: (a) evaluate texts and other materials on their ability to present rigorous and challenging material clearly; and (b) require publishers to furnish evaluation data on the material's effectiveness.

6. Because no textbook in any subject can be geared to the needs of all students, funds should be made available to support text development in "thin-market" areas, such as those for disadvantaged students, the learning disabled, and the gifted and talented.

7. To assure quality, all publishers should furnish evidence of the quality and appropriateness of textbooks, based on results from field trials and credible evaluation. In view of the enormous numbers and varieties of texts available, more widespread consumer information services for purchasers are badly needed.

8. New instructional materials should reflect the most current applications of technology in appropriate curriculum areas, the best scholarship in each discipline, and research in learning and teaching.

RECOMMENDATION C: TIME

We recommend *that significantly more time be devoted to learning the New Basics. This will require more effective use of the existing school day, a longer school day, or a lengthened school year.*

Implementing Recommendations

1. Students in high schools should be assigned far more homework than is now the case.

2. Instruction in effective study and work skills, which are essential if school and independent time is to be used efficiently, should be introduced in the early grades and continued throughout the student's schooling.

3. School districts and State legislatures should strongly consider 7-hour school days, as well as a 200- to 220-day school year.

4. The time available for learning should be expanded through better classroom management and organization of the school day. If necessary, additional time should be found to meet the special needs of

slow learners, the gifted, and others who need more instructional diversity than can be accommodated during a conventional school day or school year.

5. The burden on teachers for maintaining discipline should be reduced through the development of firm and fair codes of student conduct that are enforced consistently, and by considering alternative classrooms, programs, and schools to meet the needs of continually disruptive students.

6. Attendance policies with clear incentives and sanctions should be used to reduce the amount of time lost through student absenteeism and tardiness.

7. Administrative burdens on the teacher and related intrusions into the school day should be reduced to add time for teaching and learning.

8. Placement and grouping of students, as well as promotion and graduation policies, should be guided by the academic progress of students and their instructional needs, rather than by rigid adherence to age.

RECOMMENDATION D: TEACHING

This recommendation *consists of seven parts. Each is intended to improve the preparation of teachers or to make teaching a more rewarding and respected profession. Each of the seven stands on its own and should not be considered solely as an implementing recommendation.*

1. Persons preparing to teach should be required to meet high educational standards, to demonstrate an aptitude for teaching, and to demonstrate competence in an academic discipline. Colleges and universities offering teacher preparation programs should be judged by how well their graduates meet these criteria.

2. Salaries for the teaching profession should be increased and should be professionally competitive, market-sensitive, and performance-based. Salary, promotion, tenure, and retention decisions should be tied to an effective evaluation system that includes peer review so that superior teachers can be rewarded, average ones encouraged, and poor ones either improved or terminated.

3. School boards should adopt an 11-month contract for teachers. This would ensure time for curriculum and professional development, programs for students with special needs, and a more adequate level of teacher compensation.

4. School boards, administrators, and teachers should cooperate to develop career ladders for teachers that distinguish among the beginning instructor, the experienced teacher, and the master teacher.

5. Substantial nonschool personnel resources should be employed to help solve the immediate problem of the shortage of mathematics and science teachers. Qualified individuals, including recent graduates with mathematics and science degrees, graduate students, and industrial and retired scientists could, with appropriate preparation, immediately begin teaching in these fields. A number of our leading science centers have the capacity to begin educating and retraining teachers immediately. Other areas of critical teacher need, such as English, must also be addressed.

6. Incentives, such as grants and loans, should be made available to attract outstanding students to the teaching profession, particularly in those areas of critical shortage.

7. Master teachers should be involved in designing teacher preparation programs and in supervising teachers during their probationary years.

RECOMMENDATION E: LEADERSHIP AND FISCAL SUPPORT

We recommend *that citizens across the Nation hold educators and elected officials responsible for providing the leadership necessary to achieve these reforms, and that citizens provide the fiscal support and stability required to bring about the reforms we propose.*

Implementing Recommendations

1. Principals and superintendents must play a crucial leadership role in developing school and community support for the reforms we propose, and school boards must provide them with the professional development and other support required to carry out their leadership role effectively. The Commission stresses the distinction between leadership skills involving persuasion, setting goals and developing community consensus behind them, and managerial and supervisory skills. Although the latter are necessary, we believe that school boards must consciously develop leadership skills at the school and district levels if the reforms we propose are to be achieved.

2. State and local officials, including school board members, governors, and legislators, have *the primary responsibility* for financing and governing the schools, and should incorporate the reforms we propose in their educational policies and fiscal planning.

3. The Federal Government, in cooperation with States and localities, should help meet the needs of key groups of students such as the gifted and talented, the socioeconomically disadvantaged, minority

and language minority students, and the handicapped. In combination these groups include both national resources and the Nation's youth who are most at risk.

4. In addition, we believe the Federal Government's role includes several functions of national consequence that States and localities alone are unlikely to be able to meet: protecting constitutional and civil rights for students and school personnel; collecting data, statistics, and information about education generally; supporting curriculum improvement and research on teaching, learning, and the management of schools; supporting teacher training in areas of critical shortage or key national needs; and providing student financial assistance and research and graduate training. We believe the assistance of the Federal Government should be provided with a minimum of administrative burden and intrusiveness.

5. The Federal Government has *the primary responsibility* to identify the national interest in education. It should also help fund and support efforts to protect and promote that interest. It must provide the national leadership to ensure that the Nation's public and private resources are marshaled to address the issues discussed in this report.

6. This Commission calls upon educators, parents, and public officials at all levels to assist in bringing about the educational reform proposed in this report. We also call upon citizens to provide the financial support necessary to accomplish these purposes. Excellence costs. But in the long run mediocrity costs far more.

A FINAL WORD

This is not the first or only commission on education, and some of our findings are surely not new, but old business that now at last must be done. For no one can doubt that the United States is under challenge from many quarters.

Children born today can expect to graduate from high school in the year 2000. We dedicate our report not only to these children, but also to those now in school and others to come. We firmly believe that a movement of America's schools in the direction called for by our recommendations will prepare these children for far more effective lives in a far stronger America.

APPENDIX D

EXCERPT FROM GOALS 2000: EDUCATE AMERICA ACT, JANUARY 25, 1994

The following is section 102 from National Education Goals of H.R. 1804.

The Congress declares that the National Education Goals are the following:

(1) SCHOOL READINESS.—
  (A) By the year 2000, all children in America will start school ready to learn.
  (B) The objectives for this goal are that —
      (i) all children will have access to high-quality and developmentally appropriate preschool programs that help prepare children for school;
      (ii) every parent in the United States will be a child's first teacher and devote time each day to helping such parent's preschool child learn, and parents will have access to the training and support parents need; and
      (iii) children will receive the nutrition, physical activity experiences, and health care needed to arrive at school with healthy minds and bodies, and to maintain the mental alertness necessary to be prepared to learn, and the number of low-birthweight babies will be significantly reduced through enhanced prenatal health systems.
(2) SCHOOL COMPLETION.—
  (A) By the year 2000, the high school graduation rate will increase to at least 90 percent.
  (B) The objectives for this goal are that—

227

(i) the Nation must dramatically reduce its school dropout rate, and 75 percent of the students who do drop out will successfully complete a high school degree or its equivalent; and

(ii) the gap in high school graduation rates between American students from minority backgrounds and their non-minority counterparts will be eliminated.

(3) STUDENT ACHIEVEMENT AND CITIZENSHIP.—

(A) By the year 2000, all students will leave grades 4, 8, and 12 having demonstrated competency over challenging subject matter including English, mathematics, science, foreign languages, civics and government, economics, arts, history, and geography, and every school in America will ensure that all students learn to use their minds well, so they may be prepared for responsible citizenship, further learning, and productive employment in our Nation's modern economy.

(B) The objectives for this goal are that—

(i) the academic performance of all students at the elementary and secondary level will increase significantly in every quartile, and the distribution of minority students in each quartile will more closely reflect the student population as a whole;

(ii) the percentage of all students who demonstrate the ability to reason, solve problems, apply knowledge, and write and communicate effectively will increase substantially;

(iii) all students will be involved in activities that promote and demonstrate good citizenship, good health, community service, and personal responsibility;

(iv) all students will have access to physical education and health education to ensure they are healthy and fit;

(v) the percentage of all students who are competent in more than one language will substantially increase; and

(vi) all students will be knowledgeable about the diverse cultural heritage of this Nation and about the world community.

(4) TEACHER EDUCATION AND PROFESSIONAL DEVELOPMENT.—

(A) By the year 2000, the Nation's teaching force will have access to programs for the continued improvement of their professional skills and the opportunity to acquire the knowledge and skills needed to instruct and prepare all American students for the next century.

(B) The objectives for this goal are that—

(i) all teachers will have access to preservice teacher education and continuing professional development activities that will provide such teachers with the knowledge and skills needed to teach to an increasingly diverse student population with a variety of educational, social, and health needs;

(ii) all teachers will have continuing opportunities to acquire additional knowledge and skills needed to teach challenging subject matter and to use emerging new methods, forms of assessment, and technologies;

(iii) States and school districts will create integrated strategies to attract, recruit, prepare, retrain, and support the continued professional development of teachers, administrators, and other educators, so that there is a highly talented work force of professional educators to teach challenging subject matter; and

(iv) partnerships will be established, whenever possible, among local educational agencies, institutions of higher education, parents, and local labor, business, and professional associations to provide and support programs for the professional development of educators.

(5) MATHEMATICS AND SCIENCE.—

(A) By the year 2000, United States students will be first in the world in mathematics and science achievement.

(B) The objectives for this goal are that—

(i) mathematics and science education, including the metric system of measurement, will be strengthened throughout the system, especially in the early grades;

(ii) the number of teachers with a substantive background in mathematics and science, including the metric system of measurement, will increase by 50 percent; and

(iii) the number of United States undergraduate and graduate students, especially women and minorities, who complete degrees in mathematics, science, and engineering will increase significantly.

(6) ADULT LITERACY AND LIFELONG LEARNING.—

(A) By the year 2000, every adult American will be literate and will possess the knowledge and skills necessary to compete in a global economy and exercise the rights and responsibilities of citizenship.

(B) The objectives for this goal are that—

(i) every major American business will be involved in strengthening the connection between education and work;

    (ii) all workers will have the opportunity to acquire the knowledge and skills, from basic to highly technical, needed to adapt to emerging new technologies, work methods, and markets through public and private educational, vocational, technical, workplace, or other programs;

   (iii) the number of quality programs, including those at libraries, that are designed to serve more effectively the needs of the growing number of part-time and midcareer students will increase substantially;

   (iv) the proportion of the qualified students, especially minorities,who enter college, who complete at least two years, and who complete their degree programs will increase substantially;

    (v) the proportion of college graduates who demonstrate an advanced ability to think critically, communicate effectively, and solve problems will increase substantially; and

   (vi) schools, in implementing comprehensive parent involvement programs, will offer more adult literacy, parent training and life-long learning opportunities to improve the ties between home and school, and enhance parents' work and home lives.

(7) SAFE, DISCIPLINED, AND ALCOHOL- AND DRUG-FREE SCHOOLS.—

(A) By the year 2000, every school in the United States will be free of drugs, violence, and the unauthorized presence of firearms and alcohol and will offer a disciplined environment conducive to learning.

(B) The objectives for this goal are that—

    (i) every school will implement a firm and fair policy on use, possession, and distribution of drugs and alcohol;

   (ii) parents, businesses, governmental and community organizations will work together to ensure the rights of students to study in a safe and secure environment that is free of drugs and crime, and that schools provide a healthy environment and are a safe haven for all children;

   (iii) every local educational agency will develop and implement a policy to ensure that all schools are free of violence and the unauthorized presence of weapons;

   (iv) every local educational agency will develop a sequential, comprehensive kindergarten through twelfth grade drug and alcohol prevention education program;

    (v) drug and alcohol curriculum should be taught as an integral part of sequential, comprehensive health education;

(vi) community-based teams should be organized to provide students and teachers with needed support; and

(vii) every school should work to eliminate sexual harassment.

(8) PARENTAL PARTICIPATION—

(A) By the year 2000, every school will promote partnerships that will increase parental involvement and participation in promoting the social, emotional, and academic growth of children.

(B) The objectives for this Goal are that—

(i) every State will develop policies to assist local schools and local educational agencies to establish programs for increasing partnerships that respond to the varying needs of parents and the home, including parents of children who are disadvantaged or bilingual, or parents of children with disabilities;

(ii) every school will actively engage parents and families in a partnership which supports the academic work of children at home and shared educational decisionmaking at school; and

(iii) parents and families will help to ensure that schools are adequately supported and will hold schools and teachers to high standards of accountability.

APPENDIX E

EXCERPTS FROM *SUSAN TAVE ZELMAN, SUPERINTENDENT OF PUBLIC INSTRUCTION OF OHIO, ET AL. V. DORIS SIMMONS-HARRIS ET AL.,* JUNE 27, 2002

(Note: footnotes and references have been omitted)

CHIEF JUSTICE [William] REHNQUIST delivered the opinion of the Court.

The State of Ohio has established a pilot program designed to provide educational choices to families with children who reside in the Cleveland City School District. The question presented is whether this program offends the Establishment Clause of the United States Constitution. We hold that it does not.

There are more than 75,000 children enrolled in the Cleveland City School District. The majority of these children are from low-income and minority families. Few of these families enjoy the means to send their children to any school other than an inner-city public school. For more than a generation, however, Cleveland's public schools have been among the worst performing public schools in the Nation. In 1995, a Federal District Court declared a "crisis of magnitude" and placed the entire Cleveland school district under state control. Shortly thereafter, the state auditor found that Cleveland's public schools were in the midst of a "crisis that is perhaps unprecedented in the history of American education." The district had failed to meet any of the 18 state standards for minimal acceptable performance. Only 1 in 10 ninth graders could pass a basic proficiency examination, and students at all levels performed at a dismal rate compared with students in other Ohio public schools. More than two-thirds of high school students either dropped or failed out before graduation. Of those students who managed to reach their senior year, one of every four still failed to graduate. Of those students who did graduate, few could read, write, or compute at levels comparable to their counterparts in other cities.

It is against this backdrop that Ohio enacted, among other initiatives, its Pilot Project Scholarship Program. The program provides financial assistance to families in any Ohio school district that is or has been "under federal court order requiring supervision and operational management of the district by the state superintendent." Cleveland is the only Ohio school district to fall within that category.

The program provides two basic kinds of assistance to parents of children in a covered district. First, the program provides tuition aid for students in kindergarten through third grade, expanding each year through eighth grade, to attend a participating public or private school of their parent's choosing. Second, the program provides tutorial aid for students who choose to remain enrolled in public school.

The tuition aid portion of the program is designed to provide educational choices to parents who reside in a covered district. Any private school, whether religious or nonreligious, may participate in the program and accept program students so long as the school is located within the boundaries of a covered district and meets statewide educational standards. Participating private schools must agree not to discriminate on the basis of race, religion, or ethnic background, or to "advocate or foster unlawful behavior or teach hatred of any person or group on the basis of race, ethnicity, national origin, or religion." Any public school located in a school district adjacent to the covered district may also participate in the program. Adjacent public schools are eligible to receive a $2,250 tuition grant for each program student accepted in addition to the full amount of per-pupil state funding attributable to each additional student. All participating schools, whether public or private, are required to accept students in accordance with rules and procedures established by the state superintendent.

Tuition aid is distributed to parents according to financial need. Families with incomes below 200% of the poverty line are given priority and are eligible to receive 90% of private school tuition up to $2,250. For these lowest-income families, participating private schools may not charge a parental co-payment greater than $250. For all other families, the program pays 75% of tuition costs, up to $1,875, with no co-payment cap. These families receive tuition aid only if the number of available scholarships exceeds the number of low-income children who choose to participate. Where tuition aid is spent depends solely upon where parents who receive tuition aid choose to enroll their child. If parents choose a private school, checks are made payable to the parents who then endorse the checks over to the chosen school.

Education Reform

The tutorial aid portion of the program provides tutorial assistance through grants to any student in a covered district who chooses to remain in public school. Parents arrange for registered tutors to provide assistance to their children and then submit bills for those services to the State for payment. Students from low-income families receive 90% of the amount charged for such assistance up to $360. All other students receive 75% of that amount. The number of tutorial assistance grants offered to students in a covered district must equal the number of tuition aid scholarships provided to students enrolled at participating private or adjacent public schools.

The program has been in operation within the Cleveland City School District since the 1996–1997 school year. In the 1999–2000 school year, 56 private schools participated in the program, 46 (or 82%) of which had a religious affiliation. None of the public schools in districts adjacent to Cleveland have elected to participate. More than 3,700 students participated in the scholarship program, most of whom (96%) enrolled in religiously affiliated schools. Sixty percent of these students were from families at or below the poverty line. In the 1998–1999 school year, approximately 1,400 Cleveland public school students received tutorial aid. This number was expected to double during the 1999–2000 school year.

The program is part of a broader undertaking by the State to enhance the educational options of Cleveland's schoolchildren in response to the 1995 takeover. That undertaking includes programs governing community and magnet schools. Community schools are funded under state law but are run by their own school boards, not by local school districts. These schools enjoy academic independence to hire their own teachers and to determine their own curriculum. They can have no religious affiliation and are required to accept students by lottery. During the 1999–2000 school year, there were 10 start-up community schools in the Cleveland City School District with more than 1,900 students enrolled. For each child enrolled in a community school, the school receives state funding of $4,518, twice the funding a participating program school may receive.

Magnet schools are public schools operated by a local school board that emphasize a particular subject area, teaching method, or service to students. For each student enrolled in a magnet school, the school district receives $7,746, including state funding of $4,167, the same amount received per student enrolled at a traditional public school. As of 1999, parents in Cleveland were able to choose from among 23 magnet schools, which together enrolled more than 13,000 students in kindergarten through eighth grade. These schools provide specialized teaching methods, such as Montessori, or a particularized curriculum focus, such as foreign language, computers, or the arts.

In 1996, respondents, a group of Ohio taxpayers, challenged the Ohio program in state court on state and federal grounds. The Ohio Supreme

Court rejected respondents' federal claims, but held that the enactment of the program violated certain procedural requirements of the Ohio Constitution. The state legislature immediately cured this defect, leaving the basic provisions discussed above intact.

In July 1999, respondents filed this action in United States District Court, seeking to enjoin the reenacted program on the ground that it violated the Establishment Clause of the United States Constitution. In August 1999, the District Court issued a preliminary injunction barring further implementation of the program, which we stayed pending review by the Court of Appeals. In December 1999, the District Court granted summary judgment for respondents. In December 2000, a divided panel of the Court of Appeals affirmed the judgment of the District Court, finding that the program had the "primary effect" of advancing religion in violation of the Establishment Clause. The Court of Appeals stayed its mandate pending disposition in this Court. We granted certiorari, and now reverse the Court of Appeals.

The Establishment Clause of the First Amendment, applied to the States through the Fourteenth Amendment, prevents a State from enacting laws that have the "purpose" or "effect" of advancing or inhibiting religion. There is no dispute that the program challenged here was enacted for the valid secular purpose of providing educational assistance to poor children in a demonstrably failing public school system. Thus, the question presented is whether the Ohio program nonetheless has the forbidden "effect" of advancing or inhibiting religion.

To answer that question, our decisions have drawn a consistent distinction between government programs that provide aid directly to religious schools, *Mitchell* v. *Helms, Agostini, supra; Rosenberger* v. *Rector and Visitors of Univ. of Va.,* and programs of true private choice, in which government aid reaches religious schools only as a result of the genuine and independent choices of private individuals, *Mueller* v. *Allen, Witters* v. *Washington Dept. of Servs. for Blind, Zobrest* v. *Catalina Foothills School Dist.* While our jurisprudence with respect to the constitutionality of direct aid programs has "changed significantly" over the past two decades, *Agostini, supra,* our jurisprudence with respect to true private choice programs has remained consistent and unbroken. Three times we have confronted Establishment Clause challenges to neutral government programs that provide aid directly to a broad class of individuals, who, in turn, direct the aid to religious schools or institutions of their own choosing. Three times we have rejected such challenges.

In *Mueller,* we rejected an Establishment Clause challenge to a Minnesota program authorizing tax deductions for various educational expenses, including private school tuition costs, even though the great majority of the program's beneficiaries (96%) were parents of children in religious schools.

We began by focusing on the class of beneficiaries, finding that because the class included "*all* parents," including parents with "children [who] attend nonsectarian private schools or sectarian private schools," the program was "not readily subject to challenge under the Establishment Clause. Then, viewing the program as a whole, we emphasized the principle of private choice, noting that public funds were made available to religious schools "only as a result of numerous, private choices of individual parents of school-age children." This, we said, ensured that "'no imprimatur of state approval' can be deemed to have been conferred on any particular religion, or on religion generally." We thus found it irrelevant to the constitutional inquiry that the vast majority of beneficiaries were parents of children in religious schools, saying:

> *We would be loath to adopt a rule grounding the constitutionality of a facially neutral law on annual reports reciting the extent to which various classes of private citizens claimed benefits under the law.*

That the program was one of true private choice, with no evidence that the State deliberately skewed incentives toward religious schools, was sufficient for the program to survive scrutiny under the Establishment Clause. In *Witters*, we used identical reasoning to reject an Establishment Clause challenge to a vocational scholarship program that provided tuition aid to a student studying at a religious institution to become a pastor. Looking at the program as a whole, we observed that "[a]ny aid . . . that ultimately flows to religious institutions does so only as a result of the genuinely independent and private choices of aid recipients." We further remarked that, as in *Mueller*, "[the] program is made available generally without regard to the sectarian-nonsectarian, or public-nonpublic nature of the institution benefited." In light of these factors, we held that the program was not inconsistent with the Establishment Clause.

Five Members of the Court, in separate opinions, emphasized the general rule from *Mueller* that the amount of government aid channeled to religious institutions by individual aid recipients was not relevant to the constitutional inquiry. Our holding thus rested not on whether few or many recipients chose to expend government aid at a religious school but, rather, on whether recipients generally were empowered to direct the aid to schools or institutions of their own choosing.

Finally, in *Zobrest*, we applied *Mueller* and *Witters* to reject an Establishment Clause challenge to a federal program that permitted sign-language interpreters to assist deaf children enrolled in religious schools. Reviewing our earlier decisions, we stated that "government programs that neutrally provide benefits to a broad class of citizens defined without reference to religion are not readily subject to an Establishment Clause challenge."

Looking once again to the challenged program as a whole, we observed that the program "distributes benefits neutrally to any child qualifying as 'disabled.'" Its "primary beneficiaries," we said, were "disabled children, not sectarian schools."

We further observed that "[b]y according parents freedom to select a school of their choice, the statute ensures that a government-paid interpreter will be present in a sectarian school only as a result of the private decision of individual parents." Our focus again was on neutrality and the principle of private choice, not on the number of program beneficiaries attending religious schools. Because the program ensured that parents were the ones to select a religious school as the best learning environment for their handicapped child, the circuit between government and religion was broken, and the Establishment Clause was not implicated.

Mueller, Witters, and *Zobrest* thus make clear that where a government aid program is neutral with respect to religion, and provides assistance directly to a broad class of citizens who, in turn, direct government aid to religious schools wholly as a result of their own genuine and independent private choice, the program is not readily subject to challenge under the Establishment Clause. A program that shares these features permits government aid to reach religious institutions only by way of the deliberate choices of numerous individual recipients. The incidental advancement of a religious mission, or the perceived endorsement of a religious message, is reasonably attributable to the individual recipient, not to the government, whose role ends with the disbursement of benefits. As a plurality of this Court recently observed:

> *[I]f numerous private choices, rather than the single choice of a government, determine the distribution of aid, pursuant to neutral eligibility criteria, then a government cannot, or at least cannot easily, grant special favors that might lead to a religious establishment.*

It is precisely for these reasons that we have never found a program of true private choice to offend the Establishment Clause.

We believe that the program challenged here is a program of true private choice, consistent with *Mueller, Witters,* and *Zobrest,* and thus constitutional. As was true in those cases, the Ohio program is neutral in all respects toward religion. It is part of a general and multifaceted undertaking by the State of Ohio to provide educational opportunities to the children of a failed school district. It confers educational assistance directly to a broad class of individuals defined without reference to religion, *i.e.,* any parent of a school-age child who resides in the Cleveland City School District. The program permits the participation of *all* schools within the district, religious or non-religious. Adjacent public schools also may participate and have a financial incentive to do so. Program benefits are available to participating families on neutral terms, with no reference to religion. The only preference stated anywhere in the program is a preference for low-income families, who receive greater assistance and are given priority for admission at participating schools.

There are no "financial incentive[s]" that "ske[w]" the program toward religious schools. Such incentives "[are] not present . . . where the aid is allocated on the basis of neutral, secular criteria that neither favor nor disfavor religion, and is made available to both religious and secular beneficiaries on a nondiscriminatory basis." The program here in fact creates financial *dis*incentives for religious schools, with private schools receiving only half the government assistance given to community schools and one-third the assistance given to magnet schools. Adjacent public schools, should any choose to accept program students, are also eligible to receive two to three times the state funding of a private religious school. Families too have a financial disincentive to choose a private religious school over other schools. Parents that choose to participate in the scholarship program and then to enroll their children in a private school (religious or nonreligious) must copay a portion of the school's tuition. Families that choose a community school, magnet school, or traditional public school pay nothing. Although such features of the program are not necessary to its constitutionality, they clearly dispel the claim that the program "creates . . . financial incentive[s] for parents to choose a sectarian school."

Respondents suggest that even without a financial incentive for parents to choose a religious school, the program creates a "public perception that the State is endorsing religious practices and beliefs." But we have repeatedly recognized that no reasonable observer would think a neutral program of private choice, where state aid reaches religious schools solely as a result of the numerous independent decisions of private individuals, carries with it the *imprimatur* of government endorsement. The argument is particularly misplaced here since "the reasonable observer in the endorsement inquiry must be deemed aware" of the "history and context" underlying a challenged program. Any objective observer familiar with the full history and context of the Ohio program would reasonably view it as one aspect of a broader undertaking to assist poor children in failed schools, not as an endorsement of religious schooling in general.

There also is no evidence that the program fails to provide genuine opportunities for Cleveland parents to select secular educational options for their school-age children. Cleveland schoolchildren enjoy a range of educational choices: They may remain in public school as before, remain in public school with publicly funded tutoring aid, obtain a scholarship and choose a religious school, obtain a scholarship and choose a nonreligious private school, enroll in a community school, or enroll in a magnet school. That 46 of the 56 private schools now participating in the program are religious schools does not condemn it as a violation of the Establishment Clause. The Establishment Clause question is whether Ohio is coercing parents into sending their children to religious schools, and that question must be answered by evaluating *all* options Ohio provides Cleveland schoolchildren, only one of which is to obtain a program scholarship and then choose a religious school.

Justice Souter speculates that because more private religious schools currently participate in the program, the program itself must somehow discourage the participation of private nonreligious schools. But Cleveland's preponderance of religiously affiliated private schools certainly did not arise as a result of the program; it is a phenomenon common to many American cities. Indeed, by all accounts the program has captured a remarkable cross-section of private schools, religious and nonreligious. It is true that 82% of Cleveland's participating private schools are religious schools, but it is also true that 81% of private schools in Ohio are religious schools. To attribute constitutional significance to this figure, moreover, would lead to the absurd result that a neutral school-choice program might be permissible in some parts of Ohio, such as Columbus, where a lower percentage of private schools are religious schools, but not in inner-city Cleveland, where Ohio has deemed such programs most sorely needed, but where the preponderance of religious schools happens to be greater. Likewise, an identical private choice program might be constitutional in some States, such as Maine or Utah, where less than 45% of private schools are religious schools, but not in other States, such as Nebraska or Kansas, where over 90% of private schools are religious schools.

Respondents and Justice Souter claim that even if we do not focus on the number of participating schools that are religious schools, we should attach constitutional significance to the fact that 96% of scholarship recipients have enrolled in religious schools. They claim that this alone proves parents lack genuine choice, even if no parent has ever said so. We need not consider this argument in detail, since it was flatly rejected in *Mueller*, where we found it irrelevant that 96% of parents taking deductions for tuition expenses paid tuition at religious schools. Indeed, we have recently found it irrelevant even to the constitutionality of a direct aid program that a vast majority of program benefits went to religious schools. The constitutionality of a neutral educational aid program simply does not turn on whether and why, in a particular area, at a particular time, most private schools are run by religious organizations, or most recipients choose to use the aid at a religious school. As we said in *Mueller*, "[s]uch an approach would scarcely provide the certainty that this field stands in need of, nor can we perceive principled standards by which such statistical evidence might be evaluated."

This point is aptly illustrated here. The 96% figure upon which respondents and Justice Souter rely discounts entirely (1) the more than 1,900 Cleveland children enrolled in alternative community schools, (2) the more than 13,000 children enrolled in alternative magnet schools, and (3) the more than 1,400 children enrolled in traditional public schools with tutorial assistance. Including some or all of these children in the denominator of children enrolled in nontraditional schools during the 1999–2000 school year drops the percentage enrolled in religious schools from 96% to under 20%. The 96% figure also represents but a snapshot of one particular school year. In the 1997–1998 school year, by contrast, only 78% of scholarship recipients attended religious schools. The difference was attributable to two private nonreligious schools that had accepted 15% of all scholarship students electing instead to register as community schools, in light of larger per-pupil funding for community schools and the uncertain future of the scholarship program generated by this litigation. Many of the students enrolled in these schools as scholarship students remained enrolled as community school students, thus demonstrating the arbitrariness of counting one type of school but not the other to assess primary effect. In spite of repeated questioning from the Court at oral argument, respondents offered no convincing justification for their approach, which relies entirely on such arbitrary classifications.

Respondents finally claim that we should look to *Committee for Public Ed. & Religious Liberty* v. *Nyquist*, to decide these cases. We disagree for two reasons. First, the program in *Nyquist* was quite different from the program challenged here. *Nyquist* involved a New York program that gave a package of benefits exclusively to private schools and the parents of private school enrollees. Although the program was enacted for ostensibly secular purposes, we found that its "function" was "*unmistakably* to provide desired financial support for nonpublic, sectarian institutions," (emphasis added). Its genesis, we said, was that private religious schools faced "increasingly grave fiscal problems." The program thus provided direct money grants to religious schools. It provided tax benefits "unrelated to the amount of money actually expended by any parent on tuition," ensuring a windfall to parents of children in religious schools. It similarly provided tuition reimbursements designed explicitly to "offe[r] . . . an incentive to parents to send their children to sectarian schools."

Indeed, the program flatly prohibited the participation of any public school, or parent of any public school enrollee. Ohio's program shares none of these features. Second, were there any doubt that the program challenged in *Nyquist* is far removed from the program challenged here, we expressly reserved judgment with respect to "a case involving some form of public assistance (*e.g.*, scholarships) made available generally without regard to the sectarian-nonsectarian, or public-nonpublic nature of the institution benefited." That, of course, is the very question now before us, and it has since been answered, first in *Mueller*, "[A] program ... that neutrally provides state assistance to a broad spectrum of citizens is not readily subject to challenge under the Establishment Clause," then in *Witters*, "Washington's program is 'made available generally without regard to the sectarian-non-sectarian, or public-nonpublic nature of the institution benefited'" (quoting *Nyquist, supra,*), and again in *Zobrest*, "[T]he function of the [program] is hardly 'to provide desired financial support for nonpublic, sectarian institutions'" (quoting *Nyquist, supra,*). To the extent the scope of *Nyquist* has remained an open question in light of these later decisions, we now hold that *Nyquist* does not govern neutral educational assistance programs that, like the program here, offer aid directly to a broad class of individual recipients defined without regard to religion.

In sum, the Ohio program is entirely neutral with respect to religion. It provides benefits directly to a wide spectrum of individuals, defined only by financial need and residence in a particular school district. It permits such individuals to exercise genuine choice among options public and private, secular and religious. The program is therefore a program of true private choice. In keeping with an unbroken line of decisions rejecting challenges to similar programs, we hold that the program does not offend the Establishment Clause.

The judgment of the Court of Appeals is reversed.

It is so ordered.

APPENDIX F

U.S. SECRETARY OF EDUCATION'S OVERVIEW OF KEY POLICY PROVISIONS IN NO CHILD LEFT BEHIND ACT, JULY 24, 2002

Dear Colleague:

I would like to thank you for the work you are doing to improve the achievement of all students. The *No Child Left Behind Act* (NCLBA) significantly raises expectations for States, local educational agencies and schools in that all students are expected to meet or exceed State standards in reading and in math within 12 years. It also provides a significant increase in resources to assist States in meeting these new expectations. This bipartisan Act is intended to build upon and enhance accountability systems that States have been developing since, or prior to, the 1994 reauthorization of the Elementary and Secondary Education Act (ESEA). I would like to applaud the efforts States have made to develop and implement high quality accountability systems based on challenging standards and assessments and high expectations for students. Working together, we can ensure that all students succeed and that the achievement gap is closed, once and for all.

Accountability is central to the success of the *No Child Left Behind Act*: States need to set high standards for improving academic achievement in order to improve the quality of education for all students. Under the NCLBA, each State establishes a definition of "adequate yearly progress" (AYP) to use each year to determine the achievement of each school district and school. The new definition of AYP is diagnostic in nature, and intended to highlight where schools need improvement and should focus their resources. The statute gives States and local educational agencies significant flexibility in how they direct resources and tailor interventions to the needs of individual schools identified for improvement. Under the NCLBA, schools are held accountable for the achievement of all students, not just average student performance. Ensuring that schools are held accountable for all students' meeting State standards represents the core of the bipartisan Act's goal of ensuring that no child is left behind.

The purpose of the statute, for both assessments and accountability, is to build on high quality accountability systems that States already have in place, not to require every State to start from scratch. Therefore, I want to assure you that the Department will work with States so that they have the tools they need to implement definitions of AYP that meet the requirements of the statute and maintain high standards.

States are to identify for improvement any Title I school that does not meet the State's definition of adequate yearly progress for two consecutive years. However, it is important to underscore the flexibility granted by the statute to State and local educational agencies to direct resources and tailor interventions to the needs of individual schools. For example, the statute gives States and LEAs flexibility in how they can direct Title I school improvement funds to schools that need the most improvement. It also provides a list of consequences under "school improvement," "corrective action" and "restructuring" that allow States to take a range of actions. For example, under "corrective action" the options range from more limited consequences such as hiring an outside expert to advise a school on how to make adequate yearly progress, to more significant measures such as replacing school staff or restructuring the internal organization of a school.

States are free to build on the statutory requirements and to develop differentiated responses based on the degree to which a school has not made AYP. The law does not prescribe how States must officially designate schools that do not meet AYP requirements.

For example, a State could develop categories based on the number of subgroups that make AYP:

1. All groups of students meet AYP goals.
2. All but one or two subgroups meet AYP goals.
3. All but one or two subgroups, and the school as a whole, do not meet AYP goals.
4. No group of students meets AYP goals.

AYP should be used to target the unique needs of schools to improve student achievement. It does not necessitate a "one size fits all" response without regard to how well a school is doing overall. However, any Title I school in which any group of students fails to meet the AYP goal must be identified as in need of improvement, and all such schools that are identified are subject to the timeline for improvement required under Section 1116. Regardless of the degree to which a school is not making AYP, an LEA must take actions to address the needs of the school and improve achievement, provide public school choice for all students in any school that is identified for improvement, and provide supplemental education services for eligible students in schools that continue to not make AYP, as required under Section 1116.

It should be noted that the statute permits schools that do not meet a statewide proficiency goal to also make AYP if, in the subgroup that does not meet this bar, there was at least a ten percent reduction from the previous year in the percentage of students who are not proficient and that subgroup made progress on the other state-designated academic indicator. For example, if the percentage of disadvantaged students not proficient in reading decreases from 70 percent to 63 percent the following year, that group has made sufficient progress.

The Department will issue proposed regulations that address in detail the requirements for State accountability systems. The purpose of this letter is to clarify the process for reviewing and approving State definitions of AYP and to provide you with additional guidance by highlighting criteria that will be used in this process.

GUIDANCE ON AYP CRITERIA AND THE PEER REVIEW PROCESS

States will be required to submit their definitions of AYP for review at the beginning of 2003, although those States applying for State Flex will have to submit definitions for approval this fall. In order to ensure that States can move expeditiously to implement their new definitions of AYP, States can submit the plans for review this fall even if they are not applying for State Flex. The Department will provide additional AYP guidance and more details about the requirements of the review process. All definitions will be peer reviewed, as required by the statute, by a panel that includes representatives of parents, teachers, State educational agencies and local educational agencies. Peer review panelists will make recommendations as to how well each proposed definition meets the requirements of the statute. Approaches to meeting the statutory requirements that are at least as rigorous as the requirements of the statute and the regulations will be considered, provided that a State demonstrates that its system meets the following criteria:

1. **A single statewide accountability system applied to** *all* public schools and LEAs.

o "All schools and LEAs" includes Title I and non-Title I schools and LEAs.

o Student assessments are administered and the accountability system is applied in the same manner for all schools, regardless of receipt of Title I funds.

2. *All* **public school students are included in the State accountability system.**

o A student attending the same school for a "full academic year" must be included when determining if a school has made AYP.

o A student that attends more than one school in a **district** during the school year is only included in determining if a district has made AYP.

o All student results are included in the school level report card.

3. **A State's definition of AYP is based on expectations for growth in student achievement that is continuous and substantial, such that all students are proficient in reading and math no later than 2013–2014.**

o Accountability systems must establish proficiency goals statewide, based on assessment data from the 2001–02 school year, that progressively increase to reflect 100 percent proficiency for all students by 2013–14.

o These goals must increase at steady and consistent increments during the 12-year timeline, although not necessarily annually throughout the 12 years (i.e., States cannot establish goals that will require the most substantial progress toward the end of the 12-year timeline).

o Increases in proficiency rates **must** occur for a school to make AYP. Progress in student achievement from the "below basic" to the "basic level" is not in and of itself sufficient to meet AYP requirements. However, States and LEAs are strongly encouraged to develop systems to recognize very low-performing schools that are making such improvement.

4. **A State makes annual decisions about the achievement of all public schools and LEAs.**

o States may calculate AYP for a school using up to three consecutive years of data.

o If a State chooses to average data over two or three years, it must still determine whether a school or district made AYP on an annual basis.

5. **All public schools and LEAs are held accountable for the achievement of individual subgroups.**

o Accountability decisions must be based on the achievement of each subgroup in the law, as well as overall achievement.

o States must set separate, measurable annual objectives for each of these subgroups that ensure they meet the deadline to reach proficiency within 12 years.

o Subgroups for accountability are major ethnic/racial groups, economically disadvantaged students, limited English proficient (LEP) students, and students with disabilities. The goals for each subgroup may be the same as long as each subgroup reaches 100 percent proficiency in 12 years.

6. **A State's definition of AYP is based primarily on the State's academic assessments.**

o Decisions about school and LEA progress must be primarily determined by achievement on academic assessments.

7. **A State's definition of AYP includes graduation rates for high schools and an additional indicator selected by the State for middle and elementary schools (such as attendance rates).**

o Other academic indicators may be included in addition to these required indicators.

o These indicators may only have the effect of indicating a school did not make AYP. In other words, a State may use these indicators to identify a school for improvement, but they may not be used to prevent a school from being identified for improvement.

8. **A YP is based on separate reading/language arts and math achievement objectives.**

o Each subgroup of students enrolled in schools and LEAs must meet annual objectives in reading and math for the school or LEA to make AYP.

9. **A State's accountability system is statistically valid and reliable.**

o In determining AYP, a State is not required to use disaggregated data when the number of students in a subgroup is (a) too small to yield statistically reliable information or (b) the results would reveal personally identifiable information.

o Each State determines a minimum size of a group, below which the results would not be statistically reliable for use in determining AYP. States make a reasonable determination of that number based on the technical specifications of their assessments.

10. **In order for a school to make AYP, a State ensures that it assessed at least 95% of students in each subgroup enrolled.**

o Schools must report all student results by subgroup. The number of students in a subgroup must be of sufficient size to produce statistically reliable results for the 95% requirement to affect AYP. In other words, if the number of students in a subgroup is too small to produce statistically reliable results, the State need not, on the basis of the 95% requirement, identify the school as not making AYP, even if fewer than 95% of the students in that subgroup take the State's assessment.

In general, the NCLBA sets the *minimum* requirements for statewide accountability systems. States should use these requirements to enhance their current systems. This letter is intended to amplify our proposed regulations and provide States with information necessary to be successful in the upcoming State accountability system peer review process. I encourage you to review and comment on our proposed regulations. Please know that my staff and I are available to work with you as we move forward. I look forward to our collaboration on implementing this most fundamental aspect of the NCLBA.

Sincerely,
Rod Paige

SCHOOL IMPROVEMENT OPTIONS

A school is identified for school improvement after it has not made AYP for two consecutive school years. A school moves to the next "step" or "year" in this chart if it continues to not make AYP.

SCHOOL IMPROVEMENT (YEAR ONE)

In general, schools identified for improvement must receive technical assistance that enables them to specifically address the academic achievement problem that caused the school to be identified for improvement. The LEA is required to provide technical assistance as the school develops and implements the plan, including specific assistance in analyzing assessment data, improving professional development, and improving resource allocation. In addition, the following must take place:

1. All students are offered public school choice.
2. Each school identified for improvement must develop or revise a two-year school improvement plan, in consultation with parents, school staff, the local educational agency, and other experts, for approval by the LEA. The plan must incorporate research-based strategies, a 10 percent set-aside of Title I funds for professional development, extended learning time as appropriate (including school day or year), strategies to promote effective parental involvement and mentoring for new teachers.

SCHOOL IMPROVEMENT (YEAR TWO)

1. Make available supplemental educational services to students from low-income families.

In addition, the LEA continues to offer technical assistance to implement the new plan, and offer public school choice.

CORRECTIVE ACTION (YEAR THREE)

Corrective Action requires an LEA to take actions likely to bring about meaningful change at the school. To accomplish this goal, LEAs are required to take at least one of the following corrective actions, depending on the needs of the individual school:

1. Replace school staff responsible for the continued failure to make AYP;
2. Implement a new curriculum based on scientifically based research (including professional development);
3. Significantly decrease management authority at the school level;
4. Extend the school day or school year;
5. Appoint an outside expert to advise the school on its progress toward making AYP in accordance with its school plan; OR
6. Reorganize the school internally.

In addition, the LEA continues to offer technical assistance, public school choice and supplemental educational services.

RESTRUCTURING (YEAR FOUR)

During the first year of restructuring, the LEA is required to prepare a plan and make necessary arrangements to carry out one of the following options:

1. Reopen school as charter school.
2. Replace principal and staff.
3. Contract for private management company of demonstrated effectiveness.
4. State takeover.
5. Any other major restructuring of school governance.

In addition, the LEA continues to offer public school choice and supplemental educational services.

Appendix F

Implementation of Restructuring (Year Five)

Implement alternative governance plan no later than first day of school year following year four described above.

Source: U.S. Department of Education. Available online. URL: http://www2.ed.gov/policy/elsec/guid/secletter/020724.html. Last updated September 11, 2003.

APPENDIX G

STATISTICS ON STATE CHARTER SCHOOL ENROLLMENT AND OPERATION

The dynamic and continuing growth of the charter school movement is evident in the following charts, which note the yearly growth of charter schools from 1999 to 2010, the year state charter laws were passed in each of the 39 states (and the District of Columbia) that permit them, the number of charter schools in operation and their total enrollment in 2009, and the approved increase of charter schools in 2010.

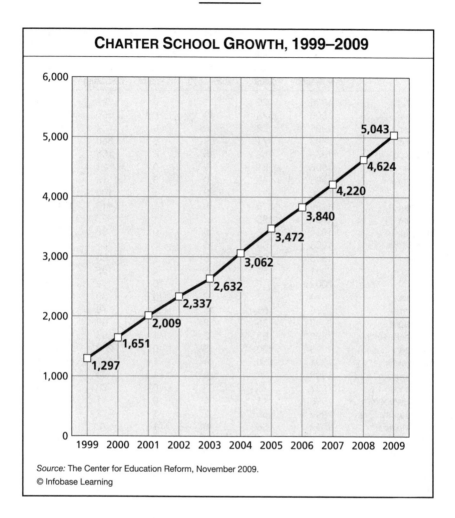

CHARTER SCHOOL GROWTH, 1999–2009

Source: The Center for Education Reform, November 2009.

© Infobase Learning

Education Reform

NATIONAL CHARTER SCHOOL AND ENROLLMENT STATISTICS, 2009

State	Year Charter Law Passed	Operating in 2008–2009	Open In 2009–2010	Approved to Open in Future	Total Operating	Total Enrollment
Alaska	1995	26	1	0	27	5,489
Arizona	1994	523	43	0	566	132,229
Arkansas	1995	28	6	0	34	7,812
California	1992	771	89	6	860	299,742
Colorado	1993	151	15	8	166	63,799
Connecticut	1996	21	0	0	21	4,298
Delaware	1995	19	0	3	19	8,990
DC	1996	91	9	1	100	30,026
Florida	1996	375	38	12	413	131,183
Georgia	1993	85	12	1	97	47,697
Hawaii	1994	32	0	0	32	7,878
Idaho	1998	30	5	0	35	10,936
Illinois	1996	80	8	1	88	33,400
Indiana	2001	50	5	4	55	17,521
Iowa	2002	9	0	0	9	1,462
Kansas	1994	37	2	0	39	5,001
Louisiana	1995	65	13	2	78	29,078
Maryland	2003	35	3	1	38	9,213
Massachusetts	1993	63	2	1	65	25,579
Michigan	1993	270	13	0	283	99,660
Minnesota	1991	158	4	1	162	28,371
Missouri	1998	38	6	1	44	18,880
Nevada	1997	25	3	0	28	8,559
New Hampshire	1995	11	0	0	11	2,055
New Jersey	1996	65	7	1	72	20,496
New Mexico	1993	66	6	1	72	13,117
New York	1998	125	29	19	154	44,000
North Carolina	1996	102*	0	0	102	34,845
Ohio	1997	323	15	0	338	94,171
Oklahoma	1999	15	2	0	17	5,706
Oregon	1999	92	16	0	108	16,809
Pennsylvania	1997	134	10	0	144	61,823
Rhode Island	1995	11	2	0	13	3,106
South Carolina	1996	34	4	4	38	10,815
Tennessee	2002	16	5	1	21	4,301
Texas	1995	354	33	14	387	129,853
Utah	1998	68	8	6	76	30,183
Virginia	1998	4	0	1	4	290
Wisconsin	1993	219	4	0	223	37,432
Wyoming	1995	3	1	0	4	294
TOTAL		4,624	419	89	5,043	1,536,099

*Total charters are capped at 100; some operate multiple campuses
Note: States that do not have a charter school law: Alabama, Kentucky, Maine, Mississippi, Montana, Nebraska, North Dakota, South Dakota, Vermont, Washington, West Virginia.

Source: The Center for Education Reform, November 2009.

INDEX

Locators in **boldface** indicate major treatment of topics. Locators followed by *c* indicate chronology entries. Locators followed by *b* indicate biographical entries. Locators followed by *g* indicate glossary entries.

Index

Index

Index

Index

Index